"Kevin Adams gently points us to tl
gers new life in our baptism. Weav
historical church all the way to The C      ‚.... ...... us to re-
signify and reimagine our lives by our identities as baptized siblings
of Christ. *Living under Water* grounds this sort of life as tangible,
real, and complex. This book is a warm invitation with a high challenge to put on our baptism and live out our baptism."

— **Angie Hong**
cofounder of Kinship Commons

"Kevin Adams's wise and winsome book is drenched in real-life
stories, dripping with theological insight, and soaked in gospel
hope. I couldn't put it down."

— **Melanie C. Ross**
associate professor of liturgical studies at Yale Divinity School

"*Living under Water* is a book of depth and range. It will take you
to turns in history and provide revelations on recent discussions of
race and politics. Through the prism of multiple stories, it shines
the light of pastoral wisdom and God's continued grace into the
lives of people who may not even know that they are longing for
baptismal identity. With a gift of words, an ear for cadences, and
the sight to see God's ongoing outpouring of grace, *Living under
Water* nourishes the garden of our hearts where 'hearts are still
restless until they find their rest in Thee.'"

— **Jul Medenblik**
president of Calvin Theological Seminary

"I've read many books about the biblical background and theological meaning of baptism, but here is a book about baptism that
is immersed in real life. Fueled by years of pastoral experience
and grounded in deep theological understanding, Kevin Adams
illustrates the meaning of baptismal identity with stories of gut-
wrenching, heart-warming power."

— **Leonard J. Vander Zee**
author of *Christ, Baptism, and the Lord's Supper*

The CALVIN INSTITUTE OF CHRISTIAN WORSHIP LITURGICAL STUDIES Series, edited by John D. Witvliet, is designed to promote reflection on the history, theology, and practice of Christian worship and to stimulate worship renewal in Christian congregations. Contributions include writings by pastoral worship leaders from a wide range of communities and scholars from a wide range of disciplines. The ultimate goal of these contributions is to nurture worship practices that are spiritually vital and theologically rooted.

### RECENTLY PUBLISHED

For complete list of published volumes, see the back of the book.

# Living under Water

*Baptism as a Way of Life*

Kevin J. Adams

WILLIAM B. EERDMANS PUBLISHING COMPANY

GRAND RAPIDS, MICHIGAN

Wm. B. Eerdmans Publishing Co.
4035 Park East Court SE, Grand Rapids, Michigan 49546
www.eerdmans.com

28  27  26  25  24  23  22      1  2  3  4  5  6  7

ISBN 978-0-8028-7963-9

**Library of Congress Cataloging-in-Publication Data**

Names: Adams, Kevin J., 1960– author.
Title: Living under water : baptism as a way of life / Kevin J.
   Adams.
Description: Grand Rapids, Michigan : William B. Eerdmans
   Publishing Company, 2022. | Series: The Calvin Institute of
   Christian Worship liturgical studies | Includes bibliographical
   references and index. | Summary: "A book from an experienced
   pastor about what baptism means and how it can become a way
   of life in church communities"—Provided by publisher.
Identifiers: LCCN 2021031622 | ISBN 9780802879639 (paperback)
Subjects: LCSH: Baptism. | Christian life. | BISAC: RELIGION
   / Christian Rituals & Practice / Sacraments | RELIGION /
   Christian Rituals & Practice / Worship & Liturgy
Classification: LCC BV811.3 .A33 2022 | DDC 234/.161—dc23
LC record available at https://lccn.loc.gov/2021031622

To Gerry Ann,
who lives baptism grace every day

*As baptized people, we are in the business of building bridges.*
*—Rowan Williams*

The church must recover the generative power
   of baptism.
                         —Walter Brueggemann


I'm a little concerned right now. About your salvation
   and stuff.
   How come you have not been baptized?
                         —Ignacio, *Nacho Libre*


[Baptism is] so great, gracious, and full of comfort,
   we should
   diligently see to it that we ceaselessly, joyfully,
   and from the heart, thank, praise, and honor God
      for it.
                         —Martin Luther

# Contents

# Foreword

I first knew Kevin Adams as my theology student at Calvin Seminary in the mid-1980s. He had four courses with me and, in them, proved himself to be not only a fine student but also a fine person. In the years following, as Kevin became my friend, I followed his career in ministry. Many hundreds of my former seminary students are ministers. Few have been as interesting as Kevin. He has established and grown a church in an unpromising California environment. At the outset, observers in the area advised him not to try. "People around here don't do church," they said. Kevin was undeterred. He had a call from God and so he pursued it. In so doing, his ministry has exhibited intelligence, imagination, flexibility, and ecumenical sensitivity.

*Living under Water* displays these traits in abundance. It's a book about baptism, and that makes it sound dubious. After all, people in the church tend to think of baptism in either of two ways: it's a contentious practice that starts arguments or else it's a small, boring ritual. Contentious? Sure. Does baptism regenerate a person? Should infants get baptized as well as adults? Should we sprinkle subjects or immerse them? Churches have split over these questions. Or else they have formed from them. It's significant that a sizeable number of Protestant churches are named *Baptist* churches and are known for practicing immersion and practicing it with adults only.

On the other hand, a fair number of Christians think of baptism as no more than a little church ritual in front of friends and relatives. The minister completes it in minutes. A few words are said. The subject's name is spoken. The Holy Trinity is invoked. A small amount of water is applied. Then it's over.

In this wonderful book Kevin shows his deep understanding of these and many more issues centering on baptism. You wouldn't necessarily think of a book on baptism as interesting—let alone fascinating. To me, this one is.

First, this book is full of stories. Kevin has had an adventurous ministry with a widely diverse number of people, each with their own history. In his stories, Kevin tells their stories. And their stories are absorbing, unexpected, surprising. Each story pulls at our imagination and expands it. Each suggests that life in the church is far more various and mysterious than we typically assume.

Second, Kevin is a Christian minister, not just a denominational one, and so he thinks of baptism as a *Christian* sacrament. You are not baptized as a Methodist or Lutheran or Presbyterian. You are baptized as a Christian. That's why, over the years, Catholics and Protestants, who differ on quite a few things, nonetheless accept each other's baptisms. If you are sprinkled or immersed in the name of the Father, and of the Son, and of the Holy Spirit by a person authorized to do it, you are a baptized Christian. Accordingly, Kevin's book reveals so many of the conversations he has had with a wide array of Christian ministers and priests who accept each other's baptisms. These are fascinating conversations, and they give Kevin's book real ecumenical heft.

Third, Kevin has done his historical research, and so we get abundant anecdotes from the history of Christian baptism—including that at many times and places it included a kind of exorcism. In some parts of the Christian world today, it still does. In this form of exorcism, to get baptized, or to present your infant for baptism, you renounce the devil. You say something like, "I renounce the devil and all his works, the pomp and vanity of this wicked world, and all the sinful lusts of the flesh." Kevin makes a strong case for this practice. It's a way to separate yourself from your old life, with its devilish influences and practices, and to align yourself with your new life and its redeemed set of influences and practices.

Finally, baptism is predominantly a way of establishing our identity as Christians. When a person is baptized, the church proclaims that this is not just an American person, or a brown or black or white person, or a Republican or Democrat person, or an Anglican or Catholic or Greek Orthodox person. No, this is a *Christ* person. This is a person we now identify as belonging to the dying and rising events of Jesus Christ and of all that they mean. These events are this person's events. This is a person living inside the shadow of Christ, and the reach of Christ, and the sovereign influence of Christ. All because this is a person who belongs to the people formed by the *events* of Christ. Baptism recognizes and proclaims our identity in this way, and so Kevin celebrates it.

*Living under Water* is a stellar treatment of baptism. That you will learn from it is inevitable. That you will treasure it is entirely predictable.

*Cornelius Plantinga*

# Acknowledgments

When I hear the word "baptism," a hundred memories flood my mind. Each a singular gift. Each a particular joy. Each a distinct honor. Each a special grace. Images of radiant people emerging from their immersion, or the toddler who after his baptism tenderly tucked his head into my chest, or the teenagers who emerged from a swimming-pool dunking with fists raised in exuberance, or the quiet reflection of an eighty-six-year-old grandmother. They were friends and neighbors, many astonished to be in a church setting.

At the beginning of my pastoral ministry, the word "baptism" made me think of theological categories and denominational distinctives. Thirty years later, the word brings to mind an astonishing array of people, each with a unique faith journey, often one just beginning. I had no idea baptism would bring such joy.

In writing this book, I see again the debt of gratitude I owe so many: people who trusted me with their doubts, their faith, their baptism, and their personal and family stories. Each is a unique working of divine providence. Each is a baptism tale worth telling. I did my best to honor each. I hope these stories will be a gift to anyone being baptized, doing a baptism, or witnessing a baptism. If in any place my memory is off, I ask your forgiveness and grace.

My debt of thanks cannot be expressed in a few lines, but let me at least direct gratitude to a few key contributors:

To John Witvliet, collaborator, visionary, and kingdom-minded tactician, who first applauded the idea for this book and took the first steps to help find a publisher.

To the Louisville Institute and the Lilly Endowment, who funded sabbatical space to write and to travel to New York, Montreal, New Mexico, Arizona, and Los Angeles to hear about baptism.

To interviewees—monks, fellow pastors, seminary students: you know who you are. Thanks for trusting me with your stories.

To faithful friends and readers of an early version of this manuscript who offered strategic, generous, and gracious advice that enhanced the book in countless ways and kept me writing: Tim Blackmon, Melanie Ross, Neal Plantinga, and David Rylaarsdam.

To my editor, Karen DeVries, who improved this project with countless helpful and graceful suggestions.

To David Bratt and the other good people at Eerdmans Publishing.

To the people of Granite Springs Church: I am grateful to belong to a congregation that loves and lives baptismal grace. Every Sunday you invite people to bring their faith and doubt and to deepen their belief. You courageously spent a year exploring baptism together, a cause of division in many congregations but one of joyful unity in ours.

To my fellow members of "Thursday Pastors' Group": we have learned so much from each other, sharing such grief, pain, and joy over the years. This is a small way to say thank you.

To everyone I have had the honor of baptizing: seniors and infants, spiritual veterans and covenant newbies, in church settings and in backyard pools.

To the staff of the Calvin Institute of Christian Worship: these words are the fruit of your stellar work and deep love for congregations.

To Dad and Mom, Sherm and Em Adams, who brought me to baptism in the first place.

To those who have written about baptism: I have done my best to give you the credit you deserve. I am grateful to wonder at the mystery of baptism together.

To the elders and staff of Granite Springs Church: Thanks for being fellow pilgrims on the walk of faith. It is a gift to work with you, shoulder to shoulder, spreading grace. Thanks for honoring me with the time and space to complete this project.

To my adult children: Luke, Rachel, and JJ. The world is a much better place because of your presence in it. Thanks for your patience and kindness as I slipped away repeatedly to work on this project.

A special thanks to my wife, Gerry, who lives her baptism every day, a remarkable example of someone who bears the image of God.

# *Baptismal Confidence*

[Christians] are a third race.

—Epistle to Diognetus

You are no longer foreigners and strangers, but fellow citizens with God's people and also members of his household, built on the foundation of the apostles and prophets, with Christ Jesus himself as the chief cornerstone. In him the whole building is joined together and rises to become a holy temple in the Lord. And in him you too are being built together to become a dwelling in which God lives by his Spirit.

—Ephesians 2:19–22

Baptism is the ground on which we stand linked to Jesus. His dying and rising and the power of his victory are ours because we are his. But if you imagine that you can get that power without that identity, well, good luck!

—N. T. Wright

S eated in my office, they argue as if I am not present. Their dialogue sounds as if they're on an episode of *Oprah*. When scheduling the meeting, they said, "We need premarital counseling." They want to know, "Are we compatible? Are we a spiritual match?" Or should they quit seeing each other, as her hyper-Christian neighbor demands? So there they sit, talking as if I'm invisible, quarreling about money, about their evening menu selections, and about jobs—especially her lack of interest in obtaining one.

Abruptly the conversation turns to their sex life and its frequency. "Since she's started attending your church"—he glares at me—"she wants to stop having sex." I sit silently, too whiplashed by the sudden change of topic to intervene, so he continues, unashamed. "But she can't"—he smirks—"because she has no self-control." In case I missed the implication, he adds, "She starts it. Not me."

She offers her defense: "When we started dating, I was far from God. Now I'm getting close again." She glows with self-satisfaction. "Now I'm getting myself 'right' with God, and God wants me to be pure. And sex is only for married people." She speaks it with a hint of spiritual superiority, placing herself on moral high ground.

"What does God have against sex?" he wonders aloud, looking in my direction. "And what does going to church have to do with it?"

Now she's clearly exasperated at his apparent lack of biblical savvy. "God wants us to save ourselves for marriage," she informs him, as if scolding a child. "I know—I've been married three times."

"How can you be so sure?" he asks, turning my way for support. Previously invisible, I'm now a potential ally.

Then it comes: a defining moment. She makes a sudden verbal lunge, like a fencer attacking an opponent with surprising speed and fury that come only from years of training. Thrusting a verbal blade, she jabs him with what she intends as a terrible truth: "Sometimes I'm not even sure you're a Christian."

Stunned by her riposte, he's beyond speech. Almost. "Not a Christian!" he parries. "Of course I'm a Christian. I've been *baptized*!" He states it emphatically, as if it defines him.

\* \* \*

Though he hasn't attended church for three decades, his baptism describes him, delineates his spiritual status. He knows who he is. And he knows *whose* he is. He is baptized!

What is it about baptism that gives such confidence?

In the sixteenth century the colorful church reformer Martin Luther advised his followers to wake every morning and say to the world, themselves, and the devil, "I am baptized!" Known for his courage and defiance, Luther recommended the proclamation as a ready response to trouble or discouragement. He would repeat it as a chorus: "I am baptized. I am baptized. I am baptized!" We fight, he says in his hymn "A Mighty Fortress Is Our God," the "prince of darkness grim." But, he continues, "One little word shall fell him." That "one little word" many read as a Latin word meaning "I am baptized."

Catholic priest and professor Henri Nouwen wrote *Life of the Beloved* for a friend struggling to define the Christian life: "All I want to say to you is you are the Beloved, and all I hope is that you can hear these words as spoken to you with all the tenderness and force that love can hold. My only desire is to make these words reverberate in every corner of your being, 'You are the Beloved.'"[1]

Baptism tells us we are beloved. It invites us to hear the affirming voice of God as he whispers his ongoing love for us. But a quick

1. Henri J. M. Nouwen, *Life of the Beloved: Spiritual Living in a Secular World* (New York: Crossroad, 1992), 30.

look at congregations shows we hear that baptismal affirmation in a hundred different ways. Few subjects are as emotionally charged for those inside the church or as off-putting for and misunderstood by those outside. Baptism has been used to show fraudulent piety and withheld to threaten with hell. It's been reduced to a polite naming ceremony and abused to split congregations. It's been postponed for fear of a damning sin still lying ahead. It's been dismissed as antiquated. It's been dodged and shrunk, debated and argued, and, maybe mostly, misunderstood and unapplied.

Raise the subject in a group of polite Christians from diverse backgrounds, and you'll feel the tension rise as the room divides into old alliances. One website warns, "96% of the church has a false baptism." Baptism has become such a topic of intramural skirmishes that, in all the confusion, some believers, trying to get it right, are baptized repeatedly; others engage it ritually, then seldom give it another thought; and still others shake their heads, refusing to participate and walking away.

When I raised with our church staff the possibility of a year-long reflection on the practice of baptism, they quickly tapped the brakes. I sensed the tide of my pastoral clout was in full ebb. What could it mean? What would it cost us? Whom would we lose? they wondered. In a congregation like ours, represented by every baptismal practice and accompanying emotion, how much damage would happen if we immersed ourselves in a year of exploring such a charged subject?

The staff had good reason to worry. Baptism has been a lightning rod for generations. Many pastors, parents, and participants have been electrocuted in highly charged debates about baptism: Sprinkling or immersion? Adults or infants? Spontaneous or after a season of preparation? Personal testimony or covenant promise? What is the role of the Holy Spirit? How does it relate to the Eucharist? Many congregations and entire denominations have split over disputes about baptism.

Our church is an eclectic mix of people from dozens of denominational backgrounds and countries of origin. Many regular attendees still carry high-voltage suspicions about anything that feels like "organized religion." And our baptismal practices and experiences have varied widely. We've immersed people in swimming pools and sprinkled them from crystal bowls. We've baptized people as old as eighty-six and as young as a month. One day we baptized three generations of the same family—a grandfather, a father, and a young son. I've baptized a deacon who had assumed he'd already been baptized, an ex-con who wanted as much cleansing water as possible, and those formerly baptized as Mormons and Jehovah's Witnesses. Currently our preferred baptismal font is a converted horse-feeding trough we bring into our facility for baptism Sundays. One day we immersed in it an elegant early retiree; on another day six boisterous siblings. We've baptized those with Ivy League degrees and those living in a transitional home for former prisoners. And that's just the beginning.

We did, as you might guess from this book in your hands, engage in a year of exploring baptism, a practice that still continues. Our services borrowed from and were informed by rituals and stories from the global and historic Christian church. Leaders from other traditions—Anglican, Baptist, Vineyard, Roman Catholic, and Greek Orthodox—led us in conversations about the similarities and differences between their practices and our own. We learned that baptism doesn't need to divide. It can instead unite, enabling us to sing the song of the gospel in a way spiritually illiterate and fragile people can optimally hear and in a way that invites everyone deeper inside the life of faith. Most of all we learned that baptism was not a onetime event but a *life*.

Mostly it was the stories that shaped us. Baptism stories helped us see and participate in the story of the gospel and of the church of all times and places.

It's helpful, of course, to think about baptism through the lens of systematic theology, exploring the contours of New Testament images of dying and rising with Christ. It's also helpful to consider baptism through historical theology, comparing and contrasting various understandings of first-century Christians, early church leaders, and Reformers. Many wise people have also pondered baptism through ecclesiology, focusing on adult or child participation, practices of immersion or sprinkling, and ancient or innovative liturgy. Many books have been written on each of these topics. But especially in a world of a thousand swirling story lines, some clamoring loudly for a return to what they title "traditional values" and others pointing to the poverty of such classic story lines, some clinging to formative tales of immigrant ancestors and others carrying a deep suspicion of any story line that aims to be more than strictly personal or entertaining, what we found to be most needed and helpful was a *narrative* approach to baptism. Church insiders and outsiders alike think and feel and decide through *story*.

Some are skeptical of stories. They mistrust stories' intent or doubt their ability to carry home a truth or shape us into new people. A CEO may put more trust in a snazzy PowerPoint presentation. A parent may trust more in the power of a moralistic lesson. A theologian may refer to dogma. But daily we live, even if unaware, by the shaping influence of stories. Shared stories transform two people into a married couple, make five freshmen into a championship sports team, or forge a variety of ethnic groups into a nation. It's no wonder that author Salman Rushdie claims, "The human being . . . is the only creature on Earth that tells itself stories in order to understand what sort of creature it is."[2] That includes our baptism stories.

It's one thing to believe a person should be baptized only once; it's another to stand on the shores of the Jordan River or a nearby lake when dozens of your beloved fellow churchgoers are getting immersed—again. It's one thing to believe that a child should (or should not) be baptized, and another to desire to have your infant immersed enthusiastically by an Orthodox priest or mechanically sprinkled by a drab, drowsy minister who looks like she'd rather be taking a siesta. It's one thing to hold on to a theological principle, and another to experience that principle as part of your life of faith.

We discovered in our diverse congregation that our widely varying baptism stories united us. Our array of experiences didn't diminish our faith convictions; they grew them. We found our-

---

2. Salman Rushdie, introduction to *Best American Short Stories 2008*, ed. Heidi Pitlor and Salman Rushdie (Boston: Houghton Mifflin, 2008), xvi.

selves drawn more deeply together, to each other and to those baptized before us—not just to those in our congregation but to the global church of today, to the forgiven saints and sinners of yesterday, and to those whose baptism stories are recorded in the Bible.

So much of the biblical conversation about baptism is story. The book of Acts overflows with stories: Three thousand converts baptized at Pentecost. A church-hater-turned-missionary named Paul. An Ethiopian eunuch, the ultimate racial and sexual outsider. A Philippian jailer contemplating suicide. A businesswoman named Lydia. Their families, and so many more. Even the Old Testament, as seen through the eyes of the early church, had baptism stories everywhere. Familiar stories like the creation, Noah and the flood, and Moses and the Red Sea were interpreted as baptism stories.

When we approach baptism through story, we find, to our great relief and delight, that our truest identity isn't dependent on our mode of baptism. Neither is it something we create or build ourselves. It is a gift we receive. We live under water. Baptism enters us into an alternate story line, one told since the dawn of creation, through which we understand our truest selves with all our joy and trauma and by which we are united with a group of people unbound by race or language, continent or generation. Baptism affects our devotion: our praying and doubting and Sabbath keeping and serving. But it also has everything to do with our everyday lives of marriage and work and decision making and worry.

During a forty-eight-hour period while writing this book, I heard profound and personal baptism reflections from Greek Orthodox monks in their isolated and beautiful monastery, from veteran Navajo pastors in a roadside café along Route 66, from a Southern California friend who is the pastor of an Assembly of God megachurch, and from a Venezuelan woman who revived a long-standing Latino congregation. All I consider friends. After learning about their baptism practices, all dramatically different, I had a case of "baptism whiplash." I wondered, "How can anyone talk or write about baptism in such a way that varied folks can come together to celebrate baptism?

This book is about baptism. Specifically, it's about a particular kind of identity and life that can flow out of the reality of being baptized. Underneath the debates about how much water to use, who should officiate, and what age participants should optimally be is a grace that every follower of Jesus can affirm, celebrate, and—wonder of wonders—*live*.

The collection of baptism stories comes in four parts, each wrestling with baptism questions. The first is focused on baptismal identity and asks: What is baptism? How do we really understand it? Why does it matter? Why is it so emotionally charged? And how can it guide our lives?

The second section follows the heart of an ancient baptismal liturgy: renouncing evil, living as anointed people, and putting on baptismal clothes. Stories there focus on questions such as: How does baptism threaten our status quo? How does it turn an ordinary person into a kind of exorcist? What is the link between baptism and personal identity? And what is the connection between baptism and following Jesus?

A third section reviews baptismal abuses. Like any good gift, baptism can be corrupted. And it has been—powerfully so. Questions there include: What is genuine baptism and what is hollow? Why is baptism so often divisive? How does baptism succumb to or combat the idol of nationalism and cultivate healthy patriotism? And how does baptism shape our views and experience of race and racism?

The fourth and final section is about the particular kind of hope that baptism cultivates. Questions here ask: Does baptism offer healing? Can baptism offer unity in a divided world? And why would anyone join organized religion?

I can't promise that all our baptism questions will be fully answered. While stories have remarkable power to shape and heal and stir hope, they seldom leave us fully satisfied. Author Flannery O'Connor was once asked to put the meaning of one of her stories in a nutshell. She replied that if she could have done that, she would not have had to write the story. She wrote about this reality, saying, "You tell a story because a statement would be inadequate, when anybody asks what a story is about, the only proper thing is to tell him to read the story."[3]

By nature stories—even God's own stories—cannot be told in a nutshell. They need to be fully told. We'll see again that that's true. But we'll also deepen our trust in the God of story and his grace of baptism.

On to the stories.

3. Flannery O'Connor, "Writing Short Stories," in *Mystery and Manners*, ed. Sally Fitzgerald and Robert Fitzgerald (New York: Farrar, Straus & Giroux, 1957, 1969), 96.

*one*

# Baptismal Identity

# The Script

## For Our Truest Selves

---

"Look, here is water. Why shouldn't I be baptized?"

—Acts 8:36 NIV (1984)

Every time that water is named by itself in the Holy Scriptures, there is a prophetic allusion to baptism.

—Cyprian

In baptism, therefore, every Christian has enough to study and practice all his or her life. Christians always have enough to do to firmly believe what baptism promises and brings: victory over death and the devil, the forgiveness of sin, God's grace, the entire Christ, and the Holy Spirit with his gifts.

—Martin Luther

---

It was the Age of Aquarius. Everyone did whatever they wanted. They made their own rules. They found their own way. A new generation of twentysomethings challenged convention, chucking the stories and values of their parents and what felt like parochial upbringings. Instead, in those days heady with creative music and new relational boundaries, they wrote a new script for themselves, a script that challenged the establishment.

At least it seemed that way. It was the 1960s. It was California. And Bob, then in his early twenties, became part of what he remembers as the whole hippie scene. "It was," he remembers, "the height of the Haight-Ashbury days." Popular slogans ranged from "Make Love, Not War" to "To fathom Hell or soar angelic, take a pinch of psychedelic." Bob says simply, "We did a lot of stuff." And what they did lasted. Bob and his friends created a counterculture, a bohemian presence in the San Francisco neighborhood that still exists today.

During the 1967 "Summer of Love," Bob moved a few miles south to live near Big Sur in a huge stone house on the side of a mountain with fifteen others. They did whatever felt good. Sometimes they took acid trips. Sometimes they took road trips, north to Mount Shasta or south to what is now Joshua Tree National Park, followed always by more acid trips. "Those were crazy days," Bob says. "It was a Charlie Manson–like, heavy, demonic scene with witches and sorcerers and UFO fanatics. We dropped a lot of rock."

He remembers the day an eye-catching young woman named Connie walked up to their particular slice of the Big Sur hillside. She had taken trips with their community and lived with them for a while. Now she entered their front yard from the shrub-lined hillside and declared, "I met this guy named Lonnie who told me about Jesus." As she and two friends walked inside the familiar house, she announced with clarity, "If you want to meet Jesus, go outside and pray with one of us." Bob remembered being in a unique state of spiritual openness at that moment. Eight months before, he'd had an especially bad acid trip that was still freaking him out. So, while most people stayed inside the house, Bob went outside and prayed with Connie to receive Jesus.

Once they finished praying, Connie announced, "We need to go to Tahquitz Falls to get you baptized." So off they went, on yet another trip, toward the mountains near Palm Springs. As Connie planned, at Tahquitz they met Lonnie Frisbee, the self-proclaimed "nudist-vegetarian-hippie" who had told her about Jesus. Lonnie had been using LSD to fuel his regular soul-searching, often reading the Bible while tripping. On one pilgrimage with friends he read the Gospel of John to the group. That was the first day Lonnie took a group to Tahquitz Falls, where he baptized them. He painted a beautiful mural of Jesus on the rocks around the pool. It was there that he had baptized Connie. And it was there, Bob remembers, in front of Lonnie's beautiful murals of Jesus, that Bob and his friends were baptized by a topless Connie.[1]

My own baptism seems tame by contrast. Ten days old, wholly oblivious to any brewing social change around me, I was carried

1. Author interview with Bob, July 2014. During a later acid trip Lonnie saw "a vision of a vast sea of people crying out to the Lord for salvation, with Frisbee in front preaching the gospel." This, many think, was later fulfilled by Frisbee's key role in launching both the Calvary Chapel and Vineyard Church movements. See also David W. Stowe, *No Sympathy for the Devil: Christian Pop Music and the Transformation of American Evangelicalism* (Chapel Hill: University of North Carolina Press, 2011), and Warren Cole Smith, "Lonnie Frisbee: The Sad Story of a Hippie Preacher," *BreakPoint*, March 10, 2017, https://www.breakpoint.org/lonnie-frisbee-sad-story-hippie-preacher/.

in my father's arms to a silver font. There my parents stood to-gether on mud-colored carpet. In front of us were rows of formal oak pews filled with family and church members in 1960s Sunday suits and dresses. There, Reverend Simon—graduate of a 150-year-old seminary, formally examined, ordained, and credentialed by the oldest denomination in North America—stood holding a red hymnal. With the congregation listening silently, he read word for word from the well-worn book's back pages a form of liturgy dating back 450 years. It recalled the story of God's salvation, reaching back to stories of Noah's ark and Moses parting the Red Sea before speeding forward to the apostle Peter's Pentecost ser-mon in the book of Acts. After rehearsing the drama of salvation, and following the prescribed formula, he asked my parents three oft-repeated questions:

> *First.* Do you acknowledge that although our children are con-ceived and born in sin, and therefore are subject to all miser-ies, yea, to condemnation itself; yet that they are sanctified in Christ, and therefore, as members of his Church, ought to be baptized?
>
> *Secondly.* Do you acknowledge the doctrine which is con-tained in the Old and New Testaments, and in the Articles of the Christian Faith, and which is taught here in this Christian Church, to be the true and perfect doctrine of salvation?
>
> *Thirdly.* Do you promise and intend to see these children, when they come to the years of discretion, instructed and brought up in the aforesaid doctrine, or to help or cause them to be instructed therein, to the utmost of your power?[2]

After my shy, shaking parents, eager to return to the semi-obscurity of a middle pew, answered in the affirmative, the min-ister baptized me in the name of the Father, Son, and Holy Spirit, then read a prayer from this same hymnal that said in part, "We

---

2. From a "Form for Administration of Baptism" commonly used for centuries by churches in the Reformed tradition, first published in an edi-tion of the Dutch Psalter in 1566.

beseech thee, through the same Son of thy love, that thou wilt be pleased always to govern these baptized children by thy Holy Spirit; that they may be piously and religiously educated, increase and grow up in the Lord Jesus Christ."

And so I was baptized, like my parents before me, and their parents and grandparents, going back at least the two hundred years of our family's known genealogical records to a town in the eastern Netherlands too tiny to register on maps. I entered a story with a prayer that I be "piously and religiously educated."

William Willimon, former chaplain of Duke University and now a United Methodist bishop, remembers assisting with two baptisms one Sunday morning. The first was a three-month-old baby girl whose parents were active in that Methodist congregation. The pastor read the prescribed forms, asked the parents baptismal vows, and baptized her. Then he took the child in his arms and said, "Mary, we have baptized you and have received you into the church. God loves you and has great plans for your life. But you will need the rest of us to tell you The Story and, from time to time, to remind you who you are and to keep you in God's family. We are especially going to appoint some members to guide you and watch over you as you grow in faith. And all of us promise to adopt you as a sister in Christ."

Next, the minister baptized a thirty-year-old man who had recently converted to Christianity. After the man made promises and received his baptism, he stood before the congregation alongside the minister, who said, "Tom, we have baptized you and have received you into the church. God loves you and has great plans for your life. But you will need the rest of us to tell you The Story and, from time to time, to remind you who you are and to keep you in God's family. We are especially going to appoint some members to guide you and watch over you as you grow in faith. And all of us promise to adopt you as a brother in Christ."[3]

To be baptized, either by topless Connie or by a formally trained pastor, by an Eastern Orthodox bishop or by a Method-

3. William H. Willimon, *Remember Who You Are: Baptism, a Model for Christian Life* (Nashville: The Upper Room, 1980), 71–72.

ist minister, is to enter a particular, life-giving, and life-altering script (Lonnie and Bob might call it "mind altering"). Whether baptized before church pews and organ, a mural created through an LSD trip, or a baptismal font dating back to the fourth century, baptism brings us into a certain story and invites us to live its script.

Everyone has a script. And everyone lives by one—even those expressly trying to avoid one. Some scripts are announced and obvious: "I'm going to get married, have 2.3 kids, and live in the suburbs" or "I'm going to make as much money as I possibly can by the time I'm forty." Some people inherit their scripts. I have a friend whose parents are medical doctors, whose grandparents are medical doctors, and whose siblings are medical doctors. Guess what profession she chose? That's right, a missionary! (But only after first becoming a medical doctor.) Others have scripts chosen by birth or circumstances. They are born into the Mumbai under-city, sorting through trash to feed their family without any real hope of change. Or they are born with fetal alcohol syndrome and can't concentrate enough to do a math problem or write a paragraph, let alone fill out a job application. Or they have parents or siblings or neighbors who are addicted to methamphetamine. Some others determinedly make choice after choice to claw and drag and pull their way to a new script. Others spend a lifetime living versions of the repeated mantra "I will not be like my parents . . . I will not be like my parents," and in so doing live a script profoundly shaped by, yes, their parents.

Baptism brings us into the biblical script, a particular story by which we make sense of our lives and find meaning and joy for them, whether someone prays that we become "piously and religiously educated" or someone douses us before murals. Anglican bishop N. T. Wright says about this script, "The point of the Scripture narrative is to say that baptism draws together all those stories about creation and Exodus, about Jesus, but also about the life of the church in the world. When we baptize someone, we are participating in that same narrative. We are saying, 'We are on this journey, this is our story, and it is now your story as well. And if you stick with us, we will help you live that story with us.' That's what baptism is all about."[4]

Wright summarizes what Christians for centuries have understood: that baptism encapsulates the entire Bible, starting in Genesis with creation, when God's spirit "moves upon the waters," and ending with Revelation's closing image of the river of life flowing through the eternal and electric city of God. In between is a life-shaping thread of baptism stories: Noah and the ark (Gen. 6), Moses and the Israelites' escape through the Red Sea (Exod. 14), Joshua and the crossing of the Jordan River (Josh. 3), Jonah swallowed by a huge fish (Jon. 1–2), and the prophet Ezekiel sprinkling the people as they receive new hearts (Ezek. 36), to name a few. Jesus tells a religious outsider, a Samaritan woman, he can give her living water (John 4), and later promises that those who believe in him will have "rivers of living water . . . flow from within them" (John 7).[5] The early church believed the saliva Jesus used to heal a blind man was a reference to baptism (John 9).

Sometimes the connections between baptism and the biblical story line are obvious. Acts tells us about a converted jailer and a businesswoman named Lydia, both baptized and dramatically switching scripts. But if you were to read through the Old Testament with early Christians, you'd see baptism stories everywhere. Take, for instance, the Old Testament story of Naaman (2 Kings 5).

Naaman was a man of profound influence, a five-star general in a powerful army. He knew all the top people. He dined in all the right places. He had more money than anyone could know what to do with. He had servants at his beck and call. He had an entourage that went with him wherever he went. He had the king on speed dial and could reach him any hour of any day. He had a house in

---

4. N. T. Wright, "Space, Time, and Sacraments," lecture at Calvin College, January 6, 2007, in "N. T. Wright on Word and Sacraments: Baptism (Part 2 of 3)," *Reformed Worship* 90 (December 2008), https://www.reformedworship.org/issue/december-2008.

5. Unless otherwise indicated, all scriptural quotations come from the New International Version (2011).

a high-end neighborhood and vacationed at a seaside villa. And, the Bible adds in one of its most beautifully disarming phrases, he was a leper. It's his leprosy that sets the stage for intrigue and an unexpected change of heart.

When my wife and I moved to our adopted hometown to plant a new congregation, we met hundreds of Naamans. During our first month there, a city official told us that new churches didn't last in that neighborhood. People in our area weren't really "into" church, he said. They'd rather go golfing or watch soccer or televised football. They live well, eat well, and do well. Over and over, in a hundred ways, locals told us that no one here is really seeking God. "Move to a 'rough' neighborhood," they recommended. "People need God there. Look around. See all these new houses and new roads and new schools and new marriages? What do we need religion for?"

A philosopher might say these folks are living the script of the Enlightenment: they find a solution for every problem and a pill for every illness. A Bible reader might say, "There are Naamans as far as the eye can see." But despite the warning from that dour city employee, we soon learned from conversations and backyard neighborhood barbecues that it doesn't really matter what kind of designer life people put together for themselves or their family. Something always ruins it. And then they look for a new script.

Robert Allen Dickey can relate to Naaman and the people in my neighborhood. His script, like theirs, seemed to be working just fine. He chose it, and he lived it with vigor. Dickey, a baseball pitcher, won two games for the 1996 US Olympic bronze-medal-winning team. A first-round draft pick out of the University of Tennessee, he once threw 183 pitches in an eleven-inning, complete-game victory, defiantly refusing to be taken out by his college coach. All who knew him had high hopes for his professional career. But then his script shattered. The Texas Rangers reduced their signing bonus from $810,000 to $75,000 after a routine physical showed his throwing elbow lacked an ulnar collateral ligament. That's like an aspiring singer learning she has no vocal cords or a biochemist learning she has Alzheimer's. Upon learning the Rangers had rescinded their offer, family members pronounced his script bankrupt and criticized him for not finding a real job.

But Dickey couldn't help himself. In a last-ditch effort to live his dream and salvage his preferred script of making the major leagues, Dickey switched from conventional pitching to become a full-time knuckleballer. He spent parts of fourteen seasons in the minor leagues learning to master the floating, darting pitch. It wasn't until he was thirty-seven years old that he became almost unhittable and was selected for the major league All-Star Game.

Dickey was plodding through an underwhelming season with the Triple-A Nashville Sounds, his eleventh in the minor leagues, when on a dare he decided to swim 250 yards across the Missouri River. It began, a writer for NPR notes, as an adventure that could have been a deleted scene from *Bull Durham*.

His teammates came down to watch, assuming he'd be fine. Dickey remembers thinking, "Maybe if I can get across the Missouri it will say something about me and my courage. Maybe it will prove my worth somehow—be a metaphorical baptism, a renewal, a chance to start fresh. Maybe if I somehow get across, swim like a madman through the turbidity, God will help me close the prodigious gap between the man I am and the man I want to be."

That's when he almost drowned. "When I was sinking I had resigned myself to death," Dickey recalled. "I really did have the feeling of weeping underwater," he said. "I didn't expect to survive." But when his feet touched the bottom, an adrenaline rush launched one last push toward the bank. Dickey crawled up, with a teammate's help, because he had nothing left. He came to see that day as a baptism of sorts.[6]

"I went into the Missouri River, I was hanging on by a thread professionally. . . . When I came out of the river I was so consumed with wanting to live in the present well—wanting to enjoy every second—that I think that carried over directly into my pitching." His harrowing experience led him to seek therapy, find comfort in his faith, and work on his marriage. He would also be named

6. Dave Davies, "'Winding Up' as the Mets' Knuckleball Pitcher," NPR, *Fresh Air*, April 10, 2012, http://www.npr.org/2012/04/10/150283169/winding-up-as-the-mets-knuckleball-pitcher.

the Pacific Coast League's Pitcher of the Year.[7] That day, on the muddy bottom of the Missouri River, Dickey switched scripts. "When you go through something like that, you certainly look at life through a different lens," he said. "So much of my identity was wrapped up in baseball, and when I got out of that river, I vowed that I wasn't going to do that anymore."[8]

Like Dickey, most of us, especially in North America, live by a script that promises to make us safe and happy. We play or research or purchase or collect experiences until we're satisfied. To such a life, baptism can function merely as a custom, a formality, a tacit approval of the status quo, an endorsement of the majority lifestyle. But the Bible, as in the story of Naaman, teaches that every other script is bankrupt. To be baptized is to renounce even the most comfortable alternative scripts of our culture and to enter fully into the story of grace.

Swiss theologian Karl Barth called this script "the strange new world within the Bible." He saw that often we cannot find in the Bible "many of the things for which we look." Instead we find "an alternative message" that disrupts well-loved scripts of every culture with the Bible's own kind of newness.[9] We find a God we would never guess or predict, a God whose name we know and whose story we tell. God summons Abraham and Sarah suddenly. Through a burning bush he calls Moses, a most reluctant leader, to an almost unbearable assignment. He speaks through donkeys and through fish that swallow prophets (Jonah). He turns seawater into walls and marches his people through (Exodus). All of us are uncomfortable with this. We are desperate not to sound silly. But at the heart of our ageless script is a God so elusive and free and

7. John Baldoni, "Knuckle Down: Leadership Lessons from R. A. Dickey," CBS News, *MoneyWatch*, April 16, 2012, http://www.cbsnews .com/news/knuckle-down-leadership-lessons-from-ra-dickey/.

8. Mark Emmons, "New York Mets Ace R. A. Dickey Says Oakland A's Reliever Grant Balfour Kept Him from Drowning in 2007," *San Jose Mercury News*, July 29, 2012, http://www.mercurynews.com/ci_21188127/new -york-mets-ace-r-dickey-says-oakland.

9. Walter Brueggemann, "Counterscript: Living with the Elusive God," *Christian Century*, November 29, 2005, 22–28.

hidden and unpredictable and even at times violent that he does not conform to our tidy expectations. "This God," Barth said, "is the one who keeps life ragged and open, who refuses domestication but who will not let our lives be domesticated either."[10]

When Christians think about baptism, it's often to debate the amount of water used or the proper age or place to be baptized. But what if such conversations miss the main point? What if baptism is designed to be not an event but the deepest part of our identity, the central, guiding reality that defines our lives? In a wise reflection on baptism, veteran pastor John Timmer wrote, "Our problem, then, is this: We don't understand baptism very well. We have an underdeveloped understanding of baptism. I can tell from my annual interviews with eleventh and twelfth graders. I always ask them, What does your baptism mean to you? What if you had *not* been baptized? What difference would that make? Then I sit back and watch them agonize over an answer. They agonize over it because they never gave it much thought. . . . Baptism just isn't part of their living experience."[11]

These young adults spent nearly two decades in the church without coming to understand their baptism and its countercultural way of viewing race, sex, money, and everything we see. But in a world with a hundred groups to join, a thousand songs to sing, and countless tantalizing stories promising the good life, baptism initiates Christians into an alternate story offering an inherited identity, a sense of belonging, and a set of lenses through which to see God at work in our sin-damaged world.

That's true for aspiring professional athletes, theologically puzzled teenagers, and Orthodox monks. A few summers ago I visited the Monastery of the Holy Archangel Michael in a quiet, secluded valley of New Mexico. Five monks and their abbot live on fifteen beautiful, arid acres, eking out a living by selling candles, growing a lot of beans, and brewing their own beer. The first

10. Brueggemann, "Counterscript."

11. John Timmer, "Owning Up to Baptism," in *A Chorus of Witnesses: Model Sermons for Today's Preacher*, ed. Thomas G. Long and Cornelius Plantinga Jr. (Grand Rapids: Eerdmans, 1994), 282–83.

night of my stay, Father Silouan, the abbot, invited me to join him and his dog, Penguin, for their nightly walk. "So you want to talk about baptism?" he asked, arrayed in monastery finery: Birkenstock sandals, tattered clothes, and a cheerful demeanor. "Let's go for a walk."

Walking along, each footfall raising red clouds of dust, he told me his story. He grew up Roman Catholic, rebelled against everything he learned at home, and then became a Hindu monk. One day, as he walked in Manhattan's Lower East Side, he picked a flyer off the ground inviting people to believe in the Virgin of Guadalupe. Somehow, in reading this simple tract, his heart turned a corner. It didn't just encourage him to faith; it started his life in a whole new direction. To him it signaled far more than a heartfelt love for the Virgin Mary and her divine son. In his deepest self, he sensed, "This is it." So he became a Roman Catholic parishioner, then an Orthodox monk, and eventually an abbot. He knows something about scripts.

As we walked, he first informed me, "Baptism is about ontology. It's a state of being. You Protestants don't understand it, but baptism is about our identity." He said all this as a gentle but clear admonishment, frequently turning to look at me, his eyes flashing for my acknowledgment. "We tend to go from one politically correct thing to the next. We are gay or straight, young or elderly, Caucasian or Navajo. But to an Orthodox Christian, these are only 'screens' people use. We start by saying 'God is a person.' The three persons of the Trinity share the same essence. And we, via the healing of baptism and the Trinity's divine hospitality, can participate with them on some level, because we too, like them, are persons."

He was warmed up now, eager to think aloud about a subject he loved. "If people in the early church talked about their identity, if they asked, 'Who am I?,' they would answer, 'I am a person who has died and risen with Christ.' That is the seedbed of Orthodoxy. To answer questions of identity with 'I am baptized' is a summary of that reality. Life, then, is about knowing who we are." He quoted an early church father who said, "When we find out who we truly are, we find out who God truly is."

We had paused on a bridge overlooking a bubbling stream. The sun was setting on red ridges above our heads, and suddenly Father Silouan seemed overcome by the reality of what he had just said. He started swaying, moved into a dance of sorts, and started fervently singing a kind of liturgy: "You made yourself known to us as three in one . . ."

After a moment or two, he turned back to conversation. "When we are baptized into the church, we become part of it, a part of something bigger than us as individuals. In a sense, we don't exist on our own anymore. We are dead and have been raised with Christ." Right then I knew why he answers each phone call, "Christ is risen!" Riding a tidal wave of verbal momentum, he continued. "People tend to live in fear. We are afraid of losing our self, but we will all die, and we have already died in Christ, so we can let that fear go." Because of baptism, we can live in the *kairos*, in the eschaton, and not just in the present moment.[12]

Ask Father Silouan, "Who are we?" and the good abbot will say we are not suburban Christians or rural Christians, gay Christians or Mexican Christians, nor are we "baptized rural farmers" or "baptized millennials." All such division shrinks baptism to a secondary place. We are the baptized, *first*.

How does this work practically? How can a Christian person or congregation accept and live their baptism in a way that frees them from a thousand implicit and explicit habits and the loves of our particular subculture to join the story of the church of all times and places? How can we see baptism as a lifelong invitation to "switch stories" and to winsomely follow the Westminster Confession's encouragement to be people who are "improving our baptism"?[13]

---

12. Father Silouan is a theologian who uses theological parlance freely, much like a medical doctor who uses terms obvious to her because of her medical training. *Kairos* is a Greek word that means "the right time" or an "opportune or decisive moment" (Merriam-Webster.com). *Escaton* means "the final event in the divine plan, the end of the world" (lexico.com).

13. The Westminster Longer Catechism asks in question 167, "How is our Baptism to be improved by us?" The answer: "The needful but much neglected duty of improving our Baptism, is to be performed by us all our

For help, we can go back to our Old Testament baptism story. Part of what Naaman needed to have cured was his reliance on a false script. He needed to identify, and then renounce, the only script he had known all his life, one he had adopted to good effect. Early church baptismal liturgies (and some still today) call those about to be baptized to "renounce Satan and all his ways." My friend Chris, an Orthodox priest, tells me people occasionally giggle when they do this. It feels silly to spit in a church ceremony as you renounce the devil. But he takes this ancient rite with utter seriousness. So should we.[14]

Chris, and all of us, might get inspiration from the prophet Elisha. Elisha is an Old Testament miracle worker and spiritual guide. He may lack Naaman's prestige and military muscle, but he knows a false script when he sees one. Naaman is sophisticated and well read, a cultural mover and shaker. He isn't looking for a spiritual remedy. He is sure his only problem is leprosy, and he's come for a quick fix. But Elisha knows that a false script blocks Naaman's relationship with God—Naaman's living a story line of self-sufficiency. The rising star, accustomed to performing and succeeding, expects the prophet to do some conjuring, or make a spectacle. But the prophet offers a surprising cure. Elisha does not want anyone to think it's his own power that heals Naaman, so he tells Naaman to dip himself seven times in the muddy Jordan River.

That's changing scripts. It seems too easy. There's nothing for Naaman to do? Or pay? No specific words to say? No. That's it. Just receive. Dunk in the Jordan seven times? There were rivers back in Syria that made the Jordan look like the spill of a leaky faucet. Yet eventually Naaman did what he was told. When he came out of the water, his complexion was radiant. Naaman was so grateful that

---

life long, especially in the time of temptation, and when we are present at the administration of it to others; by serious and thankful consideration of the nature of it, and of the ends for which Christ instituted it, the privileges and benefits conferred and sealed thereby" (http://thewestminsterstan dards.com/wlc-167-how-is-our-baptism-to-be-improved-by-us/).

14. We will more fully explore this vintage baptismal idea of "renouncing" in chapter 4.

he converted on the spot and reached into his luggage for a wad of cash, but Elisha pointed to God and refused to take a cent.

Every Bible story, said Martin Luther, reminds us of baptism's gospel reality. Early church fathers like Origen found this story of Naaman especially applicable. He first resisted baptism because he "did not understand that our Jordan washes away the impurity of those with leprosy and heals them." Origen explains further in a sermon on Luke: "Men covered with the filth of leprosy are cleansed in the mystery of baptism by the spiritual Elisha, our Lord and Savior. To you he says, 'Get up and go into the Jordan and wash and your flesh will be restored to you' (2 Kings 5:10). . . . When [Naaman] washed, he fulfilled the mystery of baptism, and 'his flesh became like the flesh of a child.' Which child? The one that is born 'in the washing of rebirth' [regeneration—Titus 3:5] in Christ Jesus."[15]

We've been using the idea of "script," but we might better say baptism joins us (and Naaman) with those who live what Walter Brueggemann calls a "counterscript," an alternate reality as part of an alternate community that goes against the grain.[16] Each generation tells the next, from the 1967 Summer of Love to today's emerging adults, to "find themselves," to create their own identities. But the Bible invites us to *live* one.

Dhini was three years old when she came to her new home. Her pastor, Craig Barnes, describes her as having "milk chocolate skin, jet-black hair and brown eyes the size of saucers. She didn't speak more than a few words of English." Her new mom and dad "brought her home from India after spending well over a year struggling to arrange her adoption."

"Dhini has had a number of issues," Barnes writes. "She was born with a large mole on her shoulder that could become cancerous if it's not removed; a series of complicated surgeries and skin

15. *Origen: Homilies on Luke, Fragments on Luke*, Fathers of the Church, trans. Joseph T. Lienhard (Washington, DC: Catholic University of America Press, 1996), 136, in Everett Ferguson, *Baptism in the Early Church: History, Liturgy, and Theology in the First Five Centuries* (Grand Rapids: Eerdmans, 2009), 404.

16. Brueggemann, "Counterscript."

grafts will take years to complete. Also, since she spent her first three years of life in an orphanage where she was left alone most of the day, her motor skills were not so good. And who knows the primal abandonment issues such a little girl may face?"

But Dhini also had two adoptive parents madly in love with her and a congregation that "had been praying for her a year before [they] knew her name." Most of all, she has God placing her into his script, symbolized in her baptism.

"I got through most of the baptismal liturgy pretty well," Barnes remembers. "But when I saw her in the arms of her father, arms around his neck, and I came to the words about being adopted into the family of God—I was done with words. No one offered to take over for me, so the congregation just worshiped a while with tears as our silent prayers of gratitude. Eventually, her new father poured the water of a holy covenant over the head of his new daughter. We were all a mess."[17]

Why were they so overwhelmed? Dhini didn't know about false scripts. She couldn't even read. But she inherited a grace that changed everything about her life. She was given a script.

Over the centuries people have feared the script, with some good reason. Many have postponed baptism or dodged it altogether, believing it a sort of final cleansing that can't handle all our future sins (more on that later). At times we confuse the script, thinking it's a memoir all about us (more on that later too). But as with Dhini, God directs, acts, and produces this story. We simply receive it as a kind of identity—a baptismal identity.

God's counterscript often surprises us with its beauty. At other times it surprises us with its ragged and disjointed ways. Whenever we get too organized or too tidy, whenever we consolidate all of God's baptismal goodness in the back of a red hymnal, whenever we make God predictable or domesticated, he surprises us by telling us to wash in a dirty river or to adopt a child from another continent or to make our lifelong love for baseball secondary or to send us to a hippie to turn the first page of the counterscript.

17. M. Craig Barnes, "After Adoption," *Christian Century*, July 13, 2012, https://www.christiancentury.org/archive/74902/201207.

After Bob's experience at Tahquiz Falls, he felt spiritually un-settled. Though Connie and his friends considered that event a baptism, he didn't. Ask him and he'll tell you: "I wasn't really baptized as a Christian that day in the pool." Maybe that's because he kept using LSD for a long while afterward, or because he wasn't sure that topless baptisms count. So he was baptized a second time, in a small church in Chico, California. The circumstances were much less dramatic, but today, fifty years later, he considers Tahquiz Falls the start of his Christian life. It was the day he started living the script.

You've likely noticed that generations of Christians can't agree on the way baptism is supposed to happen. Maybe that's because we have clues about how God works. But in the long run, God and his script are too unpredictable. Just when we have a plan, he'll send us an Ethiopian official or a ragged jailer with family in tow. If we crave spontaneity, he'll work for hundreds of years through church order and wise practices. We are all tempted to choose the parts of his story we like best and ignore the others.

But Christians of all times and places agree on this: the entry point into God's script is baptism. So it follows that "the church must recover the generative power of baptism."[18]

18. Brueggemann, "Counterscript."

# TWO

# Kiddie-Pool Piety

## The Birth of a Life

---

"Very truly I tell you, no one can enter the kingdom
of God unless they are born of water and the Spirit."

—John 3:5

In the single act of baptism the Christian finds a call to
Christian service, a clue to the meaning of human suffering, a basis or "fountain" from which the Christian
can grow in the spiritual life, and a sign of assurance
for an unsteady faith or a wounded conscience.

—John Witvliet

It is a sign under which the whole of life is to be lived.
Our baptism is always with us, constantly unfolding
through the whole of life.

—Hughes Oliphant Old

---

The inflatable kiddie pool caught my eye. Three feet high, deep-sea blue with faint outlines of yellow fish, and empty. After five semesters, walking through the college courtyard to the classroom where I teach is now routine. Students don't throng campus walkways before 8 a.m. classes. Only the unusual snatches attention: boundaries for the annual zombie-human war, or a ten-foot Jenga tower erected by an enterprising nonprofit to recruit students. But a kiddie pool?

When I stepped from my classroom an hour later after a brilliant lecture on pop culture, the courtyard had been transformed. Hundreds of chairs stood at attention in neat rows. An outdoor public address system squawked its final warm-up. A crowd mingled, their anticipation palpable. Several students had already snagged front-row seats. The focal point of the chairs, the sound system, and the crowd was the kiddie pool—now full.

I asked the student I was walking with a question I often find myself asking: "What is happening?"

"Chapel is outside today," he informed me. "It's the annual baptism service." I didn't know if I should grab a good seat or run away.

Minutes later every chair was full. Some, like me, stood in back. Others perched on nearby stairs or lazed over a second-floor balcony rail. Several students stood in a line wearing shorts and holding towels.

After a quick test of the sound system, the college president, also sporting shorts as well as a jersey from the university baseball team, began to speak. "Today's chapel is about baptism, and it's going to be a great day—unforgettable for some of you." He went on to explain several biblical metaphors about baptism and then ended with a persuasive invitation. "Some of you came here today because you're planning on getting baptized. But I especially want to challenge those of you who haven't planned on getting baptized. Listen to the Spirit speak. Listen for his call to come forward and profess your faith."

Sarah went first.

As if on cue, the president stepped to the pool's back rim as the campus chapel director and Sarah stepped forward. As they did, a student in the seats shouted, "Yeah, Sarah!" Another added, "Come *on*, Sarah!"

"Sarah," asked the chapel director with a wry grin, "tell us your name." A roar of approval rose from the crowd of students.

"My name is Sarah," she deadpanned to enthusiastic laughter. I've attended enough morning chapels to know this high-octane zeal wasn't typical midmorning.

Then the chapel director established the liturgy that for the next hour would guide the baptisms: "We want to give everyone a chance to share how the Lord has brought them to this place of wanting to publicly declare their faith. As the president said, 'This is big in the kingdom of God.' There is nothing magical about being dunked under water, but this is big in terms of Sarah and these others *declaring*"—he emphasized the word—"that God has cleansed them, that they have been buried with Christ. So"—and here he turned back to Sarah—"would you just share with us a little of why you want to be baptized?"

Composed and confident, eager to address her peers, Sarah articulated her faith. "I was actually baptized when I was younger, so I'm a double dipper; I'm doing it twice." At this the students burst into eager laughter. Pausing to let the amusement fade some, she began again earnestly. "But all I really remember from back then is trying not to trip on the stairs or swallow the water. That was how I lived my life too. I didn't really know what I was doing. I knew there was a deeper meaning to things, but I didn't really know God then.

"I'm not really the same person that I was when I was a kid. And I'm not the same person I was a few months ago," Sarah continued. "So the reason I want to get baptized today is that I *know* I am a new creation in Christ, and I *know* he has set me free from so many things." At this the students began to whoop and cheer with delight, encouraging her, encouraging each other. She finished, "I am getting baptized today because I want to declare that I am a follower of Jesus Christ, and I'm not going back."

Then several friends, fellow students who played key roles in her spiritual renewal, stepped into the kiddie pool with her. Before her coming immersion, the campus chapel coordinator prayed for her:

> God, what a privilege. It's so amazing to be out here and to celebrate your life in us. Thank you for Sarah. Thank you for her transformation. Thank you for how you've been working in her, for all the ways you're revealing yourself to her, for the way you have solidified your love and communicated your unconditional acceptance to her, and most of all for her heart that wants to declare you Lord over her life. Help her move on from this moment—what an amazing step! Father, would you bless her now? Please let this day always burn in her as a memory that she is yours, that she is all in, and that she is going to go and serve you in this world. Father, we thank you in Jesus' name!

His "Amen" launched another round of whistles and shouts, the prayer of blessing ending with rising cheers. Then they dunked Sarah between the outlined yellow fish. Soaked and jubilant, she rose from the deep blue pool to the ardent cheers more often heard at fraternity parties or sporting events. Here it was for a baptism. What a wonder! What wasn't to admire and applaud?

I'm struck as I teach on that campus by the piety of the students. I teach a senior core course the curriculum forces them to attend. Some do with enthusiasm; many find that the early morning hour cuts into their sleep allotment. The course, one of eight required Bible and theology courses needed to graduate, is called "Christian Perspective." We discuss economics and politics, science and pop culture, all through the lens of following Jesus. In their writing and speaking, the students' piety is clear. Even in a required early morning course, their earnest enthusiasm for Jesus is unmistakable. Anyone cynical or hopeless about the next generation's ability to love and serve God with abandon would find themselves transformed by spending a day on that campus or reading their assigned papers (ignoring the edits needed).

But that morning, watching the parade of baptisms, listening to the students relay their baptismal intentions and motivations, I was also struck by the astonishingly weak link between their baptisms and their life of faith. Biblical baptismal images are colossal. Each one invoked during this baptism chapel is a favorite of the church of all times and places: Baptism is washing. Baptism is dying and rising. Baptism is the start of a new life. Baptism is joining a community of fellow believers. Baptism, braced by these life-altering images, is designed to be the central pivot of life, the hub through which every spoke of piety—praying, giving, fasting, selfless serving, communal living, mission—links to and works with the others. It is the lens through which a believing person sees all the daily and weekly and lifelong rhythms of devotion more clearly.

Despite the heartfelt student piety, robust all-campus discipleship programs, mandatory biweekly chapel, and eight theology courses taught by insightful faculty, baptism that day was an undersized spiritual event. Even in the midst of robust campus cheer and enthusiasm. While publicly stating, "This is big!," my campus friends, all wonderful people of faith, behaved as if it were small. Instead of visualizing baptism as an anchor for a lifetime of faithful living, baptism was a spiritual sideshow, one more spiritual episode in a life of many. It had the same weight as a moving sunset or inspiring song, perhaps a powerful sermon or a captivating video clip. Nothing more.

To put it another way, amid all the devout intention and enthusiasm that sparkling April day in a Northern California college courtyard, baptism was mainly about those being baptized. It centered on their personal, individual experience. It focused on their current love for Jesus, their present feelings of faith. The kiddie pool was central, but the capacity to build a baptized *life* was not. To shrink baptism into travel-sized individual experience is to miss much of the sacrament's grace. Why not receive and practice baptism as a lifelong gift, the fulcrum of one's entire faith?

Theologically speaking, the baptisms that morning (or for some, like Sarah, the repeat baptisms) were "episodic"—that is, the participants, like those in many North American settings, conceived of their baptism as a special moment, as one more (though perhaps slightly more weighty) event in their life of faith. It was another photo in their lifelong spiritual montage, another You-Tube video clip in their lifelong spiritual documentary. To put it in terms of the college's required weekday campus chapel services: some services feature "episodes" of music. The campus favorite is high decibel and intense; others include inspirational speaking; others still offer moving videos or testimonies from overseas mission trips. That particular baptism chapel seemed to be another episode among the rest, all only loosely tied together.

This isn't surprising. Our culture insists, even demands, that we each create our own identity. Every one of us, consciously or not, is expected to be in the business of identity construction. We learn to be the architects of our own identities. From our earliest days, through adolescence, and all the way to retirement, we are expected to draft and then build our lives. It is up to us, we're told. It is our responsibility. And so we do the best we can. Some of us construct well-known successful identities. Others build a life that appears to be a collection of contradictory blueprints. Some feel as if construction never began or stalled because of insufficient emotional funds.

For all of us, episodes are the raw materials with which we build our identity: we attend a Beatles concert, we break our collarbone, we taste our first romantic kiss, we graduate from an Ivy League school, we marry, we surf in Hawaii, we get baptized in a backyard pool, we go on a mission trip to Haiti or Fresno. We assemble, arrange, and present the best of these collected episodes as our true selves, just as we'd assemble Lego blocks or post albums of photos on Facebook or Instagram. Here we are. Look at us. We are what we do and experience and feel. We are collections of life's episodes.

So we assemble these episodes and present ourselves to the world as teachers or professional basketball players, as mothers or scientists, as farmers or Ivy League graduates, as all or none of the above. We are competent and kind; we are intelligent and well read; we are careful with the environment. We design. We construct. We build our identities.

But the major biblical images of baptism conceive of identity as a gift. We don't *build* our own identity; we *accept* it. Early Christians—and many wise ones since—taught that to participate in baptism is to *receive* an identity. It was to enter a particular God-designed, God-engineered, God-built life. In such a view baptism isn't an episode but the font of life. After baptism, for the rest of our lives, our faith practices—daily prayer and Sabbath keeping, selfless service and Bible study—reinforce and develop this baptismal life of grace. They all enhance our life as "the baptized."

Maybe this all sounds grandiose and hopelessly theoretical. Maybe it sounds vain or patronizing to evaluate the actions of young students expressing such vibrant faith and the godly faculty encouraging them. "What?" I can hear someone saying. "Would you rather they whoop and whistle themselves to oblivion at a underaged drinking party?" No. Surely not. But imagine if they and all of us were to accept baptism for the inconceivable grace it is? Imagine them living with less performance anxiety, even "spiritual" performance anxiety, and less inner turmoil. What if baptism were the fountain of a Christian life of piety rather than one more spiritual episode among a thousand? What if baptism became not just an expression of faith but a source of deep reassurance in times of doubt or failure, a sign of God's abiding presence even when we stagger through the emotional chaos of grief or prayerlessness or overwhelming doubt? What would it look like, to quote the campus chapel director who was quoting the university president, if baptism "was *really big* in the life of faith," if we had a baptism-shaped identity as the centerpiece of our entire life of faith?

As a pastor, I've walked with people through the emotional crash that can come after an intense spiritual high. I've seen the spiritual self-doubt that happens after a particularly poignant spiritual episode, when a person looks back and tries to judge his or her own motives and intentions: "Was I sincere then?" or "Should I, like Sarah, be rebaptized because I'm *more* sincere now?" How many times should a person walk up the aisle to receive Jesus?

What I'm suggesting is what Christians of many centuries and traditions have taught and lived: that we receive our baptism as the core of a uniquely Christian identity, that we let it form and shape our deepest sense of self, an identity we can return to in whatever spiritual trough or doubt or neurosis comes our way. Instead of baptism being just another building block to use as we labor to construct our sense of self, baptism can be the spring of our life of faith. A lifetime of prayer and fasting and giving and storytelling and whooping and cheering can spring from and deepen and reinforce the identity we receive in our baptism.

Let's make this practical. Imagine that same college baptism chapel reframed from such a perspective. Suppose the college, whose campus is a former factory undergoing a profound and exciting transition, had, in the middle of adding dorms and athletic fields and chemistry labs, designed and built a baptismal font that evoked a womb. It is difficult, of course, for bricks and stones to precisely resemble a womb, but this was a popular model for early church baptismal fonts. Some were many-lobed or labial to suggest this central biblical image of baptism as a birth from the womb of the Holy Spirit or the church. The water of baptism, the young church taught, is the "amniotic fluid" of Christian life. Artwork on and near these early church fonts often made explicit references to these waters of birth. In baptism we are born. Again. We start over. Like Sarah, the college chapel's first to be baptized, who contrasted her past misunderstanding with her full confidence now: "I *know* I am a new creation."[1]

1. Some bishops thought that, given the womb image, a baptizand's first postbaptismal act should be to nurse at her mother's breast—in other words, to receive communion. See Samuel Torvend, *Flowing Water,*

Suppose, further, that on that sparkling California day the chapel coordinator paused to emphasize this provocative biblical image as a way to frame a *life* of baptism. Such a provocative image might in such a setting (or any contemporary venue) prompt snickers. But it might also deepen the assurance and conviction of those being baptized if in his prebaptismal encouragement he had said something like, "When you were conceived and before you were born, you swam in the waters of life in your mom. The waters in this font are like the amniotic fluid of our life before God. He is, by the Holy Spirit, birthing us. You are embarking on a baptismal *life*." In a world where many students delay adulthood precisely because of their uncertainty over life's biggest questions and the burden they feel to answer them for themselves, they would through baptism be entering an alternative reality, a counterculture where identity isn't a pressure-packed test of skill and savvy but a life to be received.

Now imagine the hypothetical college president quoting words inscribed on the campus's newly built baptistery, the same words written in the fifth century on the walls at the Basilica of St. John Lateran in Rome:

> The brood born here to live in heaven has life from water and the fructifying Spirit. Sinner, seek your cleansing in this stream that takes the old and gives a new person back. No barrier can divide where life unites: one faith, one fount, one Spirit make one people. . . . Washed in this bath the stains will float away that mark the guilt of Adam and your own. The stream that flows below sprang from the wounded Christ to wash the whole world clean and give it life. Children of water, think no more of earth; heaven will give you joy; in heaven hope. Think not your sins too many or too great: birth in this stream is birth to holiness.[2]

---

*Uncommon Birth: Christian Baptism in a Post-Christian Culture* (Minneapolis: Augsburg Fortress, 2011), 81.

2. Regina Kuehn, *A Place for Baptism* (Chicago: Liturgy Training Publications, 2007), 10.

We once surveyed the baptized attenders of our congregation, asking them to describe their baptisms. The diversity of baptismal place was astounding: a backyard river, the Pacific Ocean, a South American cathedral, a country church, a backyard Jacuzzi, the Jordan River, and yes, a college campus. None of them argued that their place was the most important part of their baptism. None mentioned womb-shaped fonts or kiddie pools lined with yellow fish. But the diversity can get a person thinking: How might a womb-shaped font communicate the sacramental grace? Being birthed is not about performing, or understanding, or deciding. We *receive* life. In the same way, baptism begins a life of faith. Every subsequent act of Christian obedience depends on and flows from this beginning.

To reinforce the grace of baptism as a received identity, let's imagine that chapel service reconstructed a second way. Suppose campus leaders framed baptism as dying and rising with Christ.[3] In this scenario, campus architects planned a baptismal font based on another of the early church's favorite baptismal images: a tomb.[4] In fact, they built the font to look like the famous one built in 374 in Milan, where Bishop Ambrose baptized Augustine. Its eight sides, dug into the cathedral floor, represent the eighth day of God's creative work: resurrection day. At their baptisms, candidates moved down its three steps, symbolizing the three days Jesus was in the tomb. They faced west, renouncing Satan, and then turned east toward Jerusalem and were plunged into the water, receiving resurrection life. The presiding pastor or bishop would read Romans 6 and talk of Jesus dying and rising, accenting how baptism symbolizes our own dying and rising.

Suppose further that wise campus administrators even added around their replica font this inscription that the wise Bishop Ambrose placed on the wall above the baptistery in Milan:

3. This is a favorite baptismal image from Rom. 6 that one campus leader alluded to that day. My suggestion here is to frame the entire life of discipleship and every chapel topic with this image.

4. More on this image in chapter 3, where I talk about suffering.

For all those who want to abandon the sins of a former
life,
let their hearts be washed here and find their minds
restored.
Let them come quickly and not hesitate for a moment:
those who approach and are washed leave whiter than
snow.
Let the saints come to the font and be washed in the
kingdom of God.[5]

Standing at the edge of this tomb-like font with an inscription summarizing God's grace working in our lives, we imagine a wise campus leader saying something like,

Baptism reminds us of the Red Sea. The people of Israel went into the sea and worried—and rightly so. Water, after all, can kill you. It can drown you. That sea was, the Bible says, the water of chaos (Exod. 15; Gen. 1; 1 Cor. 10). It's a frightening image, but helpful too. Baptism signals the person baptized is going through death and resurrection in this worship service. It is death to narcissism and conceit and vainglory and anxiety, and it is awakening to a new and resurrected life with new patterns of piety, such as love and service and compassion.[6]

This powerful, Pauline dying-and-rising metaphor was there that April day on campus. It was named in the introduction and reinforced by a young man who, when standing in the kiddie pool explaining his own desire to be baptized, said:

---

5. S. Anita Stauffer, *On Baptismal Fonts: Ancient and Modern* (London: Grove, 1994); Torvend, *Flowing Water, Uncommon Birth*, chapter 4.

6. Ambrose piled image after image into his inscription, as if to say baptism overflows with meanings, each image "illuminating the diverse power and presence of baptism in the *life* of the baptized" (Torvend, *Flowing Water, Uncommon Birth*), chapter 4.

When I went to high school I fell away from God. I felt like God didn't love me anymore and thought that God had abandoned me. Then Sidney gave a chapel talk about dying to self. And after that message I began to realize that God didn't give up on me; I was trying to force God to live in my life when I had other things in my life that were in his place. So I'm being baptized today because I'm dying to myself and want to live for God. Anything in my life that I need to give up, I'm willing to give up because I know God loves me and I want to be a part of this community.

Exactly. As he finished, students again clapped and whistled their affirmation. Now suppose that after his words he descended three steps into a tomb-shaped pool, renouncing his old way of life and receiving his new life. And suppose those presiding over his baptism used the common orthodox formulation, "You are baptized into the name of the Father, and the Son, and the Holy Spirit," emphasizing that resurrected life is something we receive, not something we determine.

Each of these reconstructions or reformulations of the original chapel service builds on themes that were present, but each reframes baptism to be less dependent on the individual's earnest intentions or faithful follow-through.

Consider one more reconstructed version of that day. One student, before his immersion, reflected, "Growing up, my parents were drug addicts. But I knew God would take care of them. And he did. He changed them—washed them. Today my mom is a pastor, and my dad is the sports leader at our church."

His words brought a fresh batch of student clapping and whooping. It's easy to see why he cited washing, another frequent biblical image that puts baptism at the center of a life of faith practices. Like the images of the womb and of dying and rising, this washing image can guide a lifetime of Christian piety. In his inscription, Ambrose envisions baptism as being "marked by the hand of the Good Shepherd, being washed in the wounds of Christ," and as a "life-giving washing of the whole world."

It's no surprise that many baptismal fonts are designed to look like washbasins. Looking like a kitchen or bathroom sink, these water repositories underscore baptism as a kind of cleansing of one's past. Ambrose points to Noah's story as an ancient testimony to this meaning of baptism.[7] No one, he says, could doubt its meaning: human depravity required salvific cleansing.

Ananias, who helped the apostle Paul understand God's call on his life, said, "And now what are you waiting for? Get up, be baptized and wash your sins away, calling on his name" (Acts 22:16).

One of our church elders befriended a man who lived at what the man called a "halfway house"—a transitional home between prison and his future life. Their first conversation led to many more. Soon several from the congregation were meeting regularly at the home, and several men living there became regular attendees. After months of friendship and listening, the man decided it was time to get baptized. It was the early days of our church, when in our warehouse facility we weren't equipped to dip. So we, like thousands of churches, brought in a basin of water to symbolize washing. Telling his story that day, the man said, "This bowl isn't big enough for me. I need to put my whole head and body in there because of everything I've done!" His instincts were exactly right. He had a powerful notion of the new life this washing symbolized. And he inspired us to get a much bigger baptismal font!

The point of this series of imaginary chapel alternatives is not to suggest the inadequacy of a kiddie pool. Rather, it's to emphasize how baptism functions as the central image of a person's journey of faith. Each biblical metaphor noted here—and there are many more besides—points participants and witnesses to a *life* of baptism. The metaphors, the fonts, and the words that surround them are a summons to orient our entire life around our identity of being baptized in Christ. Baptism is the fulcrum for an entire life, the hinge connecting every episode of life.[8]

A hot debate during the Protestant Reformation of the 1500s was what to do with the sacrament of penance. Everyone agreed

7. Ambrose, *De mysteriis* 3.10–11, in Robin M. Jensen, *Baptismal Imagery in Early Christianity: Ritual, Visual, and Theological Dimensions* (Grand Rapids: Baker, 2012), 18.

8. John Witvliet calls this "baptismal piety." John Witvliet, *Worship Seeking Understanding: Windows into Christian Practice* (Grand Rapids: Baker Academic, 2003), 151.

that even the most zealous Christians keep sinning after their baptism. That sparkling April day in the courtyard, it was a repeated refrain from the students. Over and over they said, "I want to start new." "My first baptism didn't mean much to me." "In so many ways, I'm a different person now." Underneath many of those comments was a big question about how we think about our postbaptismal sins and doubts and wanderings. The medieval answer was to regularly engage in the sacrament of penance. The remedy of the college students at that courtyard chapel was to get baptized again and "mean it" this time. But several reformers (Luther and Calvin among them) taught an alternate response, viewing baptism as the beginning of a lifelong practice of repentance, of dying and rising. They expected baptism in a spiritually alive person to lead to a lifetime of repenting.

In other words, baptism has repentance built into it. Continuous repentance is a part of what baptism makes alive in us. If or, more accurately, *when* we drift spiritually, or lose zeal for prayer, or dodge communal life in the church, or find solace in methamphetamines or alcohol or the arms of a series of lovers, and then return to a life of faith, that return doesn't require a new baptism. The way forward is to return to the root of baptism, to the images we highlighted: we are born again, and that begins a series of "rebirths"; we are "raised with Christ," and that begins a lifetime of "dying and rising"; we are washed, and that begins a series of cleansings. Repentance is in a deep sense the ongoing work of baptism, the font of a pious life.

What difference does this make? Think again of Sarah. Her prebaptismal testimony was clear, articulate, and compelling. Hearing a twenty-year-old profess such buoyant, contagious faith stirs one's own. (It's no wonder campus videographers were prepped and present at the service to record and then share the video of this event as a keepsake for the participants and to later distribute it to family, alumni, and those an advancement executive might call "friends of the college.") We want to affirm her faith and her forward steps on the path to Christian discipleship. It's more than a bit dangerous to analyze the heartfelt words of someone so earnest and devout. But imagine that she had a sense of the life-giving and lifelong nature of her baptism. Further, imagine that she had a robust picture of the way her baptism serves as the center of her lifelong *piety* (we might say *sanctification*). With such a baptismal understanding, no matter what her favorite metaphor is—washing, rebirth, dying and rising—she would develop a baptismal identity that would be a gift that would bring her deep and abiding assurance. It would birth and nurse her ongoing faith formation so, like Martin Luther before her, she could return to it again and again.

Knowing baptism is designed to "elevate, nourish, and confirm our faith,"[9] she could then view her recent spiritual growth on this college campus as the result of rather than the absence of her baptismal identity. Instead of making a quip that minimized her naive, youthful faith and becoming a self-proclaimed "double dipper," she could see her original baptism as the beginning, a root, a rudder, a fountain to return to again and again. Her "baptismal piety" could be the root of all her prayer and Sabbath keeping and selfless service as well as the source of this glowing and moving testimony. Her life (and her baptism) would not be a series of episodes but a unified whole, a complete grace.

Isn't it fascinating that the church of all times and places wrestles with similar issues? In the 1500s a wise pastor, with words that could have been repeated on that California college campus, said, "We must realize that at whatever time we are baptized we are once for all washed and purged for our whole life. Therefore as often as we fall away, we ought to recall the memory of our baptism and fortify our mind with it that we may always be sure and confident of the forgiveness of sins."[10]

Toward the end of the morning's baptismal parade, after repeated stories and images, mixed metaphors, and tears of joy and clapping and hollering and earnest piety, and even a young woman who was almost baptized with her dog, both known and loved on campus, one of the students from my 8 a.m. class stepped

9. John Calvin, *Institutes of the Christian Religion* 4.15.14, https://www .ccel.org/ccel/calvin/institutes.vi.xvi.html.

10. Calvin, *Institutes* 4.15.3.

forward. This strapping basketball player dwarfed the kiddie pool and those standing near him. He said:

> I'm Keith. I was sitting here today and wasn't expecting to do this. I've had other opportunities to be baptized before in the past, but I've actually never been baptized. But just sitting here, the Spirit was tugging on my heart and I feel like it's a really great way for me to express how I am in Christ and that God really does love me. And I'm moving on, I'm graduating this year, and this is my school, this is my community, and I love all you guys here, and moving forward, I want to do this in front of you guys. This is special, thank you very much.

A burst of applause followed. Of course it did. I wish you could have witnessed this 250-pound mass of muscle pour out such tender affection. He wanted everyone to know his heart. He belonged. This college was his spiritual family. My heart went out to him. How could it not? But his words accented yet another question behind the morning's events. While it's true that some biblical baptisms had a kind of unexpected spontaneity, an impulsive quality—the baptisms of the Ethiopian official by a river (Acts 8) and of a Philippian jailer and his family after an earthquake and suicidal thoughts (Acts 16) are two such examples—is it optimal to have baptism on campus at all? What about the rigorous baptismal preparation of the early church? Can any spontaneous baptism at a four-year educational institution be anything more than a spiritual episode? Doesn't baptism ideally need a church?

# THREE

# Drowning in a Coffin

## Joining the Suffering

---

"You don't know what you are asking," Jesus said.
"Can you drink the cup I drink or be baptized with
the baptism I am baptized with?"

—Mark 10:38

Don't you know that all of us who were baptized into
Christ Jesus were baptized into his death?

—Romans 6:3

Three times you were plunged in the water and came
forth, signifying Christ's burial for three days. By this
action you died and you were born, and for you the
saving water was at once a grave and the womb of
a mother.

—Cyril of Jerusalem

---

W hen Saint Patrick was planting the Christian faith in Ireland, Aengus, son of Natfraoch, was king of Munster. The day Patrick arrived in Munster to preach, Aengus welcomed him and led him to the royal residence of Cashel. There Aengus accepted the good news about Jesus, came to the faith, and asked to be baptized. Before a large gathering of Aengus's Celtic subjects, Patrick baptized the king. During the ceremony, Patrick drove the point of his crozier through Aengus's foot. It remained there until the floor was covered with the king's blood. All the while the king remained silent, assuming suffering was part of the baptism. I can tell you, it always is.

A friend told me about a baptism in his previous church. The congregation was to have a baptismal service in a local river. The night before, church deacons went into the river to establish a sure path for the pastor to go the next morning when he took his place in the river, ready to baptize new congregants. These loyal deacons put markers in the river, ensuring their beloved minister would get wet, but not inappropriately so. But several inventive high school students of that congregation knew of this activity, and they, too, went to the river that night to realign the deacon-placed ropes and markers to their own liking. The next morning, at the prescribed point in the baptism service, the buoyant pastor, trusting his deacons' judgment, strode confidently into the river toward the well-marked place. A few strides in, he plunged into deep water just as the enterprising students had hoped, and to their great delight he was quickly immersed, a kind of rebaptism the baptizer didn't intend.

The Irish king's instincts—and those of the enterprising students—were right. To be baptized is to enter into the suffering of Christ. This is no secret or surprise. The apostle Paul, forthright as always, informs his readers, "Now I rejoice in what I am suffering for you, and I fill up in my flesh what is still lacking in regard to Christ's afflictions, for the sake of his body, which is the church. I have become its servant by the commission God gave me to present to you the word of God in its fullness—the mystery that has been kept hidden for ages and generations but is now disclosed to the Lord's people[:] . . . Christ in you, the hope of glory" (Col. 1:24–27).

Reynolds Price taught English at Duke University. He wrote more than thirty books, among them poetry, memoirs, and a National Book Award winner. In 1984, at the age of fifty-one, a large, cancerous tumor was discovered entwined with his spinal cord. So began his arduous battle to withstand and recover from a devastating affliction. First came puzzling symptoms, such as difficulty walking; then came three surgeries, radiation, the occasionally comic trials of rehab, the steady rise of pain and reliance on drugs, his discovery of biofeedback and hypnosis, and a series of events that led to paralysis in his lower body.

After one surgery, he wrote a memoir reflecting on his experience. A young man himself dying from cancer wrote him to ask, "How can you still believe in God with all this suffering happening to us?" Price, bound to his wheelchair and dependent on the care of others, wrote back to this young man who had aspired to be a physician, "If you survive this ordeal in working condition, you're almost certain to be a far more valuable doctor and person than you'd otherwise have been."[1]

In an interview with Terry Gross on NPR's *Fresh Air*, Price said, "We have to learn what all the creeds of the world tell us, which is that life is enormously unpredictable. That catastrophe can hap-

1. Reynolds Price, *Letter to a Man in the Fire: Does God Exist and Does He Care?* (New York: Scribner, 2000), 64.

pen in any life, at any moment. A lot of American popular culture and society is dedicated to making us believe that everything is OK and that it is going to stay OK."

He continued, "I'm still a boy who grew up in the South in which all my white and black elder people would say to me, 'Don't say I'm going to see you tomorrow; say, "I'll see you tomorrow if the Lord be willing and I don't die."' And I literally am the sort of person who doesn't say anymore, 'I'm going to do something,' but 'I'm hoping to do something,' because I've learned that hopes are one thing and reality is another." Then Price added a statement, less brooding than reflective, one he'd obviously pondered repeatedly: "I think one of the things that is most mysterious of all to anyone who has religious convictions, of course, is finding out why God is so interested in pain."[2]

Might it be that baptism is designed to be part of the answer to why God is so interested in pain? Of every conceivable way to initiate a person into a faith, why are Christian believers initiated through baptism? Why begin the life of faith with a kind of drowning, a dying to our selves? Might baptism be framing the specific suffering each of us will experience, individually and collectively?

Originally the word "baptize" was used in recipes. Nicander, a second-century poet, recorded a pickle recipe that used the word. He said a pickle should first be "dipped (*bapto*) into boiling water, followed by a complete submersion (*baptizo*) in a vinegar solution."[3] Ancient clothiers used the word to describe the process of submerging cloth into a colored dye. A few pagan religions used the word to signify death. "To baptize literally meant to be drowned or, more freely, to be subjected to the waters of chaos."[4]

2. Terry Gross, "Price's 'Letter to a Godchild,'" NPR, *Fresh Air*, June 19, 2006, https://freshairarchive.org/index.php/segments/prices-letter-godchild.

3. "Baptism," OrthodoxWiki, last updated August 13, 2018, https://orthodoxwiki.org/Baptism.

4. John Witvliet, *Worship Seeking Understanding: Windows into Christian Practice* (Grand Rapids: Baker Academic, 2003), 156.

John Calvin, born and raised in the 1500s, suffered from a host of medical conditions, including lung trouble, gout, severe hemorrhoids, and excruciating pain in his kidneys and bladder. In 1558, he came down with quartan fever, a form of malaria. Theodore Beza, an admiring contemporary, described Calvin in 1563 as "exhausted by labor" and "broken down by suffering." When Calvin's end came, he was buried, by his own request, with "little ceremony" in an unmarked grave.[5]

Though none of Calvin's maladies were as immediately life-threatening as Price's, his personal experiences only deepened his understanding of baptism. In his writing and preaching, Calvin repeatedly underlines the tie between the biblical baptismal image of dying and rising and the biblical summons to self-denial. He wants readers and listeners to know how baptism frames a believer's and a community's inevitable life of suffering. "In the word baptism," he writes, "there is an apt metaphor. For we know that in baptism believers are initiated into self-denial, into crucifying the old man, and into bearing the cross. . . . Now, whenever there is mention of baptism, let us remember that we are baptized under this condition and for this end—to fix the cross to our shoulders."[6]

In a few turbulent decades during the 1500s, the worldwide, centuries-old church splintered from the twin trunks of Roman Catholicism and Eastern Orthodoxy into a cluster of new branches. In those chaotic days, church leaders hoped to steady the rising varieties of church types by suggesting a short list of "marks" or attributes by which a believer could discern a "true" church; these lists included proper preaching, church discipline (discipleship), and proper celebration of the sacraments. Martin Luther added something other branches did not:

5. Richard Cavendish, "John Calvin Dies in Geneva," *History Today* 64, no. 5 (May 2014), https://www.historytoday.com/archive/john-calvin-dies-geneva.

6. *Calvin's New Testament Commentaries: Harmonies of the Gospels Matthew, Mark, and Luke,* trans. A. W. Morrison (Grand Rapids: Eerdmans, 1972), 1:118, in Witvliet, *Worship Seeking Understanding,* 156.

These Christian, holy people are recognized by the holy possession of the sacred cross.

They must endure every misfortune and persecution, all kinds of trials and evil from the devil, the world, and the flesh (as the Lord's Prayer indicates) by inward sadness, timidity, fear, outward poverty, contempt, illness, and weakness, in order to become like their head, Christ.[7]

Like Calvin, Luther could not imagine a true (spiritually healthy) church that did not honor suffering. The path of faith is the way of the cross. "The true church suffers," Luther said. Baptism tells us this is always so. Is it a surprise, then, that churches in the early centuries of Christianity shaped their baptismal pools to evoke a tomb?

For its first twelve years, our congregation met in a dilapidated warehouse. Paint hung half-peeled from exterior walls. The heating unit could not work fast enough to warm us on cold winter mornings. One intern tallied the number of mice he captured by drawing stick-figure rodents in a neat row in his cubicle. Another suggested we get a cat to solve the problem. But no one had a solution to the bats that occasionally swooped over the congregation. One made its initial entrance during a communion service. After I said the words "The blood of Christ for you," it launched from its perch in the rafters thirty feet over my head and initiated a flight pattern of various loops and darts over congregants' heads. A local exterminator told us it would be illegal to remove them.

To say we were excited to begin plans to move from our rundown industrial setting to a more permanent facility in a growing neighborhood barely captures our elation. Those were heady days. The possibilities were endless. We felt giddy with ideas. In one dizzying conversation about our new facility, a few of us wondered aloud whether we should install a Jacuzzi in one of the patios. Think of the advantages! It could be a baptismal pool *and* a gath-

---

7. Martin Luther, "On the Councils and the Church (1539)," in Roy Long, *Martin Luther and His Legacy: A Perspective on 500 Years of Reformation* (Morrisville, NC: Lulu.com, 2017), 50.

ering spot for small groups and church leadership meetings. What inspiration could bubble up from such gatherings!

Most of our congregation's baptismal services to that point were for young people, held in suburban California backyards with pools. Teenagers stood in front surrounded by parents and friends, younger siblings, and biblical novices. Every gathering was unforgettable. Each described his or her faith. Each was immersed with me on one side and the youth pastor, who had helped many "cross the line of faith," on the other. After the baptisms everyone jumped in the water for a celebratory pool party. This was our baptism liturgy, and everyone approved. We repeated this scene regularly.

But the disadvantages became clear one Sunday afternoon. A family I met through coaching a recreational youth soccer league inched toward faith over many years, slowly moving from their Christian Scientist background to our eclectic Protestant congregation. Their journey with us included hundreds of conversations, dozens of meals, several panicky emergency conversations, and unexpected twists and turns. But finally they found themselves as faith "insiders," though still somewhat timid and cautious.

That memorable afternoon they were baptized together: mom and dad, teenage brother, and younger siblings. All were dunked, one after another, in the whirling, bubbly, comfortable water of a California Jacuzzi. The only thing we lacked that day was witnesses. It was just the baptized family, their Jacuzzi-owning host, and the pastor. It felt nothing like a church event. The rest of the church didn't know them well or at all. Their baptism, though announced to our entire congregation, felt more like a private family affair. In one sense we understood: there are a hundred things to do on a glorious Northern California Sunday afternoon. And every baptism has its own irrepressible joy no matter the number of attendees. But in another sense I was disillusioned. Where were the witnesses to joyfully affirm their entry into the eternal status of baptismal dying and rising? How were we as a church communicating—or not—their entrance into and our solidarity with the community of the suffering—becoming part of the "pickled"?

That got us rethinking. Over the years we had mused about the exact kind of baptismal font best suited for our new facility.

I was raised in a church with a basin up front symbolizing our baptismal washing in Jesus's work on the cross. But witnessing a decade of immersions and reading the Bible through the eyes of biblically illiterate teenagers and their spiritual-novice parents had shaped our collective imagination. Surely, we reasoned, we could find a biblical text to engrave on a Jacuzzi. But just as surely, that would overlook the ancient and biblical baptismal emphasis on dying to ourselves and entering the community of those who suffer for Christ.

As welcoming and multiuse as Jacuzzis seemed, they don't often appear on the church baptism scene for good reason. Historic baptismal fonts were designed to "make a permanent visual imprint on our memory."[8] The architectural idea was to remind candidates they were joining the ranks of those who die and rise with Christ. These fonts, and sometimes the buildings that housed them, emphasized baptism as a life-shaping identity rather than a onetime event. Even novice believers knew from their prebaptismal discipleship that in baptism they were stepping into an entirely new "baptismal way of life."[9]

It's no wonder the oldest baptismal font yet discovered is shaped like a coffin. It's in Syria's Dura Europos church, a private home converted to a church edifice between AD 233 and 256. The font—surrounded by frescoes of the Good Shepherd, Jesus healing the paralytic, Jesus and Peter walking on water, and a much larger one depicting the three Marys visiting Christ's tomb—has a rectangular tub large enough for a reclining adult.[10] A tomb font makes sense even for infant baptism once you understand that "infant baptism anticipates the total life span of the Christian and not only the washing away of original sin."[11] Regina Kuehn contrasts the baptism fonts of the early church—coffin, tomb, womb, cruciform—with what she calls the "'water theme-park' baptistries

8. Regina Kuehn, *A Place for Baptism* (Chicago: Liturgy Training Publications, 2007), vi.

9. Kuehn, *A Place for Baptism*, vi.

10. Robin M. Jensen, *Baptismal Imagery in Early Christianity: Ritual, Visual, and Theological Dimensions* (Grand Rapids: Baker, 2012), 162.

11. Kuehn, *A Place for Baptism*, 26–27.

with abundant greenery and blooming plants . . . (that) do not bear any sign of the numinous or carry the weight of the sacramental character, nor do they allow us to sense the radical nature of our baptismal promises."[12] For centuries Christians emphasized baptism as the entrance to a cruciform *life*, a life that would surely include dying and rising.

Peruse a recent church supply catalogue. It offers everything from candles to communion cups, from liturgical robes to chalices and wall hangings with embroidered Bible verses. You'll find all sorts of baptismal merchandise ready to be shipped overnight: booklets, key chains, jewelry, and other keepsakes that can all be customized to help baptismal parties and loved ones remember their baptisms. And you can buy a baptismal font: permanent or portable, custom-colored to match your sanctuary with inlaid stone or fiberglass. Would you like heated water? Shall the minister get wet or stay dry? How many people do you want your baptistery to hold? The possibilities seem endless, but you will be hard-pressed to find one shaped as a tomb.

Our congregation, like so many in North America, serves people enamored with every trend in fashion, décor, and experience. A philosopher might say we children of the Enlightenment try to go from strength to strength and success to success, avoiding darkness and disorientation. A thousand voices tell us we can educate and work and purchase our way to happiness. A hundred rituals—personal, long-practiced, and cultural liturgies—reinforce this identity. We believe, and are taught to believe, that there is a treatment for every trouble, a technological solution for every problem, and that if we want it, we need it.

This ever-present story line shapes the identity of both adults and children by promising us the good life, which we take to mean one mostly insulated from pain and suffering. We expect to be happy, and we will blame anyone or anything when we are not: politicians, pastors, principals, our children, even the cable guy. Our school system and city government are expected to perform. So is our church. We feel cheated and angry when we are not

12. Kuehn, *A Place for Baptism*, vi.

happy or healthy or safe. When this script seems to fail, we are disoriented. We work with greater resolve, banking on our consumer liturgy to restock our lost sense of security. We may even exchange our school or principal or church for another. Could it be that certain practices of baptism set people up for a spiritual life defined by their needs and wants, and lead to their drifting off once a congregation isn't "working for" them anymore? How might our understanding of baptism and the Christian life as a whole change if we were baptized in a coffin-shaped pool? How can being baptized define us and our suffering?

In the early 1990s, our denomination's main mission strategy was to parachute church leaders into growing cities throughout North America. Well trained theologically and practically, examined and affirmed in advance by church-planting peers, these people would, through personal conversations and publicity, prayer support and financial backing, grow a congregation of two hundred to three hundred Sunday worshipers within five years. At least that was the plan. This presumptive outcome was attractive to supporting benefactors and congregations who eagerly expected a good return on their financial and kingdom investment. That plan was designed by good people with a deep love for God and a desire to reach spiritually inquisitive people. It was also, unfortunately, naive. Twenty years into these efforts, fewer than 5 percent of church plants achieved that baseline goal. These well-intentioned but unrealistic expectations set up dozens of church planters and those who supported them for a sense of profound failure and grief.

During those start-up days, I attended a church-planting seminar for denominational and organizational leaders. (I still wonder how I received that invitation and why I accepted it.) I remember talking with a church-planting executive from another denomination, who told me, "The first thing I tell church planters is 'Get a core group of people together.' The second thing I tell planters is 'Get rid of your core group.'" Over ten years of starting a congregation with just such a "parachute drop," I had largely experienced what he was describing. The people drawn to the risky, high-octane, high-cost months around a church's birth often leave when things get a bit more stable. But I had never conceived of gathering and then jettisoning people as a *strategy*. He didn't mean to be harsh, just realistic. But in my heart I kept hoping (naively?) that people who began to follow Jesus and join the church would stay. I wanted it to be like our congregation in Minnesota: when you belonged, you attended every week—for life!

A while back a friend of mine, a wise veteran pastor and a prototypical people person, informed me, "I'm hoping our church will grow this year, and I know practically that we will need to blow through about three hundred people to increase in attendance by forty." He said it matter-of-factly after thirty years of (cutting-edge) ministry. But it struck me that it was—for him, for those who came and left, and even for those who remained in his congregation—a form of suffering. Could a robust, Luther-like view of baptism offer a way to redeem such suffering?

More and more people attend church as spiritual tourists. They stay as long as it's as interesting as their last vacation. Those who fancy themselves "spiritually mature" explore a buffet of congregations to find the optimal place to be "fed" in their effervescent faith. A friend of mine is a pastor near a large Christian university in Southern California. As his congregation grew, many faculty from that college began to attend. He was pleased, even flattered. For three or four years, things went splendidly. Then these spiritual veterans started leaving one by one. Some had lunch with him and offered reasons. Others quietly slipped out the back door. His self-satisfying pleasure turned to pain. Such attrition is costly for pastors, church leaders, and congregants of every kind.

In such a church world, baptism can be viewed as a kind of spiritual commodity the church should provide on request. Regularly our church gets calls from people who ask to have their child baptized there. (Some even go on to refine their request: ". . . and could it be this Sunday?") They have no connection with our church and little understanding of baptism or faith.

How might a congregation help such callers to see baptism as an invitation to die and rise with Christ, to enter his tomb and to rise in new life? Maybe we could direct them to a new and improved (and at this point, imaginary) section of our website that shows a tomb-shaped baptismal font. What if we conceived of all church activity—indeed, all of life—as flowing out of our baptismal identity, an identity begun in a tomb? Would such a framework provide participants and supporters with what a business executive might call "expectation management"?

Years ago, a cameraman was in India filming Mother Teresa's work for a documentary. All the while she was caring for particularly miserable and distressed people on the poorest streets of Calcutta. As she leaned forward to clean the sores of an especially filthy man, wiping up pus and bandaging his wounds, the cameraman blurted out, "I wouldn't do that if you gave me a million dollars!" Mother Teresa replied, "Neither would I."[13] She did such ministry because of a call to selfless service, begun in her baptism.

Decades before Mother Teresa, Dietrich Bonhoeffer's decision to study theology was greeted with a blend of polite curiosity and dismay by his overachieving family, especially his nationally known, academically gifted psychiatrist father. But Bonhoeffer was not easily deterred, and by the age of twenty-one he had a doctorate from the University of Berlin for a paper he titled "The Communion of Saints."

In a 1932 sermon on baptism (based on 1 John 4:16), Bonhoeffer declared that God gives the baptized "the real, indestructible foundation upon which his life is being built." Baptism means that "the beginning and end" of each baptized person is "in the hands of God."[14]

---

13. This story was told by Fr. Ray Williams at the Triumph of the Cross Conference in Asheville, North Carolina, in September 2008. See also ThoughtCo, "The Daily Prayer of Mother Teresa," *Learn Religions*, updated August 28, 2018, http://catholicism.about.com/od/dailyprayers/qt/Daily-Prayer-Of-Mother-Teresa.htm.

14. Glenn Borreson, "Bonhoeffer on Baptism: Discipline for the Sake of the Gospel," *Word & World* 1, no. 1 (1981), http://wordandworld.luthersem.edu/content/pdfs/1-1_Evangelism/1-1_Borreson.pdf, citing Dietrich Bonhoeffer, "Taufrede für einen Neffen, 12 Mai 1932" and "Ansprache zur Taufe eines Neffen, Oktober 1932," in *Auslegungen-Predigten 1931 bis 1944*, vol. 4 of *Gesammelte Schriften*, ed. Eberhard Bethge, 6 vols. (Munich: Chr. Kaiser Verlag, 1958–74), 147–53.

"Baptism is no mere human possibility," Lutheran pastor Glenn L. Borreson writes about this sermon. "It connects one with the destiny of Christ and his dying and rising." Baptism means God is *for* us; we have God's "promise of an eternal love."[15]

As his sermon progresses, Bonhoeffer outlines the promises of God he would later live personally with imprisonment and execution. Baptism, he said, means we are called to be "entirely in the world, rooted strong in the earth but now seeing this world in a light which shows to [us] its needs and its hope."[16] In baptism, Borreson explains, one "is not taken out of reality but awakened to it." In baptism God becomes "the creative power for the future, even to involving the baptized person in the sufferings and helplessness of the world."[17]

A few years later, in 1935, already in trouble with church officials cozy with Hitler, Bonhoeffer began teaching at a seminary in Finkenwalde, training pastors for the Confessing Church of Germany. His new ministry post was a response to Nazism's threat to Christianity and indicated his readiness to suffer for the sake of the gospel.[18] He called baptism a "breach" where "Christ invades the realm of Satan, lays hands on his own, and creates for himself his Church,"[19] adding that this "breach with the world" must "come out into the open through membership [in] the church and participation in its life and worship."[20]

Soon Bonhoeffer attacked the Nazis' revised church constitution, which excluded baptized Jews from church leadership positions. Churches, he argued, should choose leaders on spiritual grounds, unregulated by state authority. The new government policy, adopted by many German church leaders, displayed a racism contrary to the Bible. Since baptism is of God, "the baptized Jew cannot be excluded from the church on racial grounds

15. Borreson, "Bonhoeffer on Baptism," 23.
16. Bonhoeffer in Borreson, "Bonhoeffer on Baptism," 23.
17. Borreson, "Bonhoeffer on Baptism," 23.
18. Borreson, "Bonhoeffer on Baptism," 24.
19. Dietrich Bonhoeffer, *The Cost of Discipleship* (London: Touchstone, 1995), 231.
20. Bonhoeffer, *The Cost of Discipleship*, 234.

without degrading the sacrament to a 'purely formal rite to which the Christian communion that administers it is indifferent.'"[21] He urged German Christians to identify with baptized Jews, to be joined together in cross-shaped discipleship, even if it meant losing personal privileges.

Bonhoeffer continued to press the church to live the reality of baptism, even if it meant suffering. Only months before the gestapo arrested him, he penned the essay "On the Question of Baptism." It challenged the church to deeper baptismal discipleship that integrated worship and living courageously in the world. Believers are called to "share in God's sufferings through concrete involvement in the problems and possibilities of the human community."[22] Can baptism so conceived form an identity marked by suffering, a people willing to accept a life of "dying and rising" and courageously brace for trouble?

Jesus frequently pointed his disciples to the reality of suffering for his sake. They did their best to ignore him, fighting for first chair and competing for attention. In Jesus's hour of deepest need in Gethsemane's garden, faced with suffering, they ran, denied any association with him, and made awkward knife thrusts. Only after reflecting on Jesus's death and resurrection did they grasp the idea that suffering is a core part of faith.

Earlier I described an overly optimistic era in our denomination's church planting. As part of that effort, I vividly recall, there were assessment centers where the aptitude of potential church planters and their spouses was tested for this unique work. It was three intense days under the microscopic evaluation of veteran church planters. Only a quarter of the prospective couples were approved and sent on to plant churches. I remember our lead assessor saying wistfully after more than one event, "I'm almost sad when we identify a church-planting couple. It's as if we put a bull's-eye on their back and invite the enemy to have at them." But their baptisms already put this mark on them. The apostle Paul, a fellow church planter, wrote, "I want to know Christ . . . [and] his

---

21. Borreson, "Bonhoeffer on Baptism," 26.
22. Borreson, "Bonhoeffer on Baptism," 26–27, 30, 37.

suffering" (Phil. 3:10) and "I fill up in my flesh what is still lacking in regard to Christ's afflictions" (Col. 1:24).

We don't look for suffering. But it is there, for church planters and pastors, church members and Irish nobility. It is, as King Aengus suspected, always there, a built-in part of the Christian life, core to a baptism-shaped identity.

Still, it gives one pause.

One Sunday five people were baptized in our congregation. Following the imagery of Romans 6, we always encourage folks to be fully immersed. We have yet to hear someone say after their baptism, "I sure wish they would have used *less* water."

One woman, who had stepped into the church one millimeter at a time over six years, asked to be sprinkled. Thoughtful, sophisticated, and stylish, she opted for an amount of water to suit her elegance. "I must be kind of a prototype for you," she told me, "someone who is agnostic and becomes a follower of Jesus over time." I assured her that she was. Her two grade-school children followed, both eager for full immersion. Both were cheerfully and dramatically submerged in the front of our sanctuary, rising with faces full of radiating joy.

Next in the baptismal line that day were another brother and sister. The sister, a middle-school student, was first to be plunged under the water. She emerged with a kind of shiny look of belonging. Finally, it was time for her younger brother. In all our prebaptismal conversations, he was clear and consistent: "I want to be immersed." But there, in front of the church, looking at his soaked sister, his dunked, dripping friends, and maybe the horse-feeding trough we used as a baptismal pool, something changed inside. A new perspective dawned. He came to the edge of the tank and said, in front of the entire congregation, "I want to be sprinkled."

Everyone froze. There, before everyone, he had a profound and deep change of mind. Not wanting to make his change any more of a spectacle than it already was, I demurred, playing the wise and compassionate pastor. "Of course," I said. "We can baptize you with sprinkling. But are you sure?"

His sister would have none of it. With her most matter-of-fact older-sister tone she reminded him, "We said we were going to

do this together. We still are. It's your turn." Even his dad, who
seldom attends church but who had arrived early that morning to
snatch a prime seat to view his children's baptisms, offered coaching from the front row: "Come on, do it. Go all the way." But the
boy shook his head and held his (dry) ground. So there, in front
of God and everyone, we sprinkled him.

I still don't know exactly why he changed his mind. The mind
of a ten-year-old is deep water, murky and mysterious even to him.
But I wonder if he didn't suddenly see the suffering symbolized
by the water and consider baptism all over again. Some plunge
headfirst into the faith like high divers unafraid about what's next;
others go step by step, inch by inch, drop by drop.

Can baptism give those of us who follow Jesus a particular
framework for suffering that is neither morbid or morose, not
sullen or brooding or angry? Can it be a way, even *the* way, for
us to steward the pain we encounter and gracefully walk the up-
hill journey of faith? To put it as Jesus did to his disciples, who
at that precise moment were vying for first place but eventually
would understand and embrace the deep meaning of his words:
"Can you drink the cup I drink or be baptized with the baptism
I am baptized with?" After hearing their cheery, naive, unthink-
ing affirmation, Jesus prophesied, "You will drink the cup I drink
and be baptized with the baptism I am baptized with"—suffering
(Mark 10:37–39).

Jesus never tries to hide the road of pain or sorrow. We face hurt
and heartache head-on and drink the cup assigned to us because
that's what Jesus did. Because we are baptized in his name.

*two*

# BAPTISMAL LITURGY FOR LIFE

# FOUR

# Renouncing Evil

## Baptism as Exorcism

---

The Spirit immediately drove him out into the wilderness. And he was in the wilderness forty days, tempted by Satan; and he was with the wild beasts; and the angels ministered to him.

—Mark 1:12–13 RSV

In the baptismal rite, which is an act of liberation and victory, the exorcisms come first because on our path to the baptismal font we unavoidably "hit" the dark and powerful figure that obstructs this path. It must be removed, chased away.

—Alexander Schmemann

---

Pete, Delmar, and Everett are outlaws on the run. Sitting around a campfire, their minds flit from hunger pains to vigilance. Desperate for food, only days from escaping a Mississippi state prison work gang, they dine on the only meal available: gophers. An approaching chorus captures their attention. "It's a congregation!" exclaims Delmar. The three look to see lines of people parading to the water as if in a trance. The scene, from the 2000 Coen brothers movie *O Brother, Where Art Thou?* "is encased by the song 'Down to the River to Pray.' With a siren call her voice sounds like a luring trance as lines of people dressed in white robes make their way in an orderly fashion into the water, where the minister routinely dunks each person."[1] After their baptism, a peace settles on each.

The outlaw onlookers are fascinated. Delmar is particularly taken. His know-it-all companion Everett snidely mutters, "Well, I guess hard times flush the chumps. Everyone is looking for answers." It is, after all, 1937 Mississippi. Everyone is struggling overtime to survive the Great Depression's lack. But before Everett finishes his smug censure, Delmar has run to join the procession. Unable to wait, he cuts to the front of the line and wades into the river.

1. Sarah A. Colwill, "Dying and Rising with Christ," sermon, Church on the Mall, January 11, 2015, https://static1.squarespace.com/static/582 a3a6020099eab9d4d6647/t/58aa56811e5b6ce697e60804/1487558273737 /Sermon+1_11_15.pdf.

"Well, I'll be a son of a bitch," Pete marvels. "Delmar has been saved."

Delmar wades back to his two compatriots, his face awash in delight, announcing, "Well, that's it, boys. I've been redeemed. The preacher done warshed away all my sins and transgressions. It's the straight and narrow from here on out, and heaven everylasting's my reward. . . . The preacher said all my sins is washed away. Including that Piggly Wiggly I knocked over in Yazoo."

Everett is indignant. "I thought you said you was innocent of those charges."

Delmar replies matter-of-factly, "Well, I was lying. And the preacher said that sin's been washed away too. Neither God nor man's got nothin' on me now." He adds an evangelistic invite. "Come on in, boys, the water is fine!" Pete runs to join in.

Films by the Coen brothers often stretch the imagination. Their satires poke fun at everyone and everything. Their own perspective (and that of most viewers) may be articulated in the subsequent scenes, as when Everett drives along saying, "Baptism! You two are dumber than a bag of hammers. Well, I guess you're just my cross to bear." Baptism made them "right with the Lord, but the state of Mississippi is less forgiving." Still, the scene captivates spiritual insiders and outsiders alike as one sinner, then two, both fugitives from the law, interrupt their running and celebrate a moment of grace.

In some way, the rest of the film explores their newfound freedom and salvation. Will these newly redeemed convicts live out their repentance? Or will they, as viewers already suspect, regress to thieving, lying, and betraying? In a real way, that's a question for every baptism and for each of us.

In the case of Michael Corleone, the answer is painfully clear. Michael has spent a lifetime dodging the "family business." But slowly, reluctantly, and skillfully his family woos him until he is ready to take the Mafia godfather role left by his dead father. It's not that he wants to be a crime boss—not at all. It's just that Michael, like most people, finds Vito, the family patriarch and veteran don, remarkably hard to resist. It's the story of *The Godfather*, one of the most influential and watched films of all time.

At a Mafia family meeting set in 1948, "Don Vito Corleone vowed that he would not avenge the death of his son, Sonny, providing an end to the bitter (turf) war." But we soon learn he didn't let go of revenge; he merely postponed it. Now his "son Michael, who had just returned from Sicily, took the burden on himself to eliminate the rival families without breaking Vito's vow."[2]

He has the perfect alibi. In an unforgettable scene, Michael stands as godfather to Michael Rizzi, his sister Connie's son. He's in church for the baptism. On behalf of the child, the priest summons Michael to solemnly renounce the devil and all his works. Three times Michael responds. His hollow words echo off the walls of a largely empty church.

"Do you renounce Satan?"

"I do. I do renounce him."

"Do you renounce Satan and all his works?"

"I do renounce them."

"Do you renounce Satan and all his pomps?"

"I do renounce them."

After confessing his belief in God the Father, God the Son, and God the Holy Spirit, he ratifies the ancient sacrament, pledging to turn his back on evil. Graphically interspersed with his three renunciations are the bloody scenes of Michael's capos avenging Vito and finishing his rivals. As he vows to refrain from evil, murders take place by his order: Victor Stracci is "shot down in an elevator." Moe Greene is "shot in the eye" while enjoying a Las Vegas massage. Carmine Cuneo is shot while trapped in a hotel's "revolving door."[3] And so it goes. The unforgettable scene from the unforgettable film is called "Baptism of Fire."

For Michael Corleone, baptism is a tool, a device to accomplish his agenda. So it is for some. It's no wonder the early church built a trajectory away from evil—and an evil lifestyle—into its baptismal liturgies. They viewed each baptism as a kind of exorcism.

Today many clergy make up their own baptismal liturgies, such as the college chaplain who began, "This is a really big day for us,"

2. "Baptism of Fire," The Godfather Wiki, accessed April 30, 2021, https://godfather.fandom.com/wiki/Baptism_of_Fire.

3. "Baptism of Fire."

or a colleague who answered an inquiring novice pastor by saying, "I make up the words for baptism every time we have one." It's one thing to riff on the carefully crafted ancient words; it's another to ad lib completely.

Daniel Meeter is a pastor with a social worker's heart and a church historian's mind. It's no accident that he serves a four-hundred-year-old congregation in the heart of Brooklyn. While visiting in his two-hundred-year-old, book-laden office in the church's rafters, our conversation was delayed while he tended to an emergency of one of his church's unofficial members. The man needed food and subway fare, which Daniel (with me trailing a step behind) quickly provided after walking briskly to the nearest station. Once back among his books, Daniel began our conversation on baptism by telling me that "the Anglican (baptism) liturgy is designed for beauty, the Orthodox liturgy for transcendence, the Roman Catholic for function, and the Reformed liturgy to be catechetical." Knowing that this subject was a special interest of his, I gladly sat silently as he expounded further. "Education was its goal. It was a catechetical liturgy designed not so much to inspire but to confirm and teach. And when it was good, it was good at that, and it came to be beloved. But over the years, whether it was the length or the culture, it began to fail at its purpose."[4]

Since the second century, baptisms in every region have included some version of the same question the priest asked Michael Corleone: "Do you renounce the devil and all his works, the vain pomp and glory of the world, and all sinful lusts of the flesh?" This ancient practice can seem foreign to modern Christians, especially those who prize impromptu liturgy. But historians tell us this renunciation formula "was used almost universally in the Church in all its branches. . . . Some church fathers argued that it originated with the apostles." In some places this practice is "almost completely forgotten in our day, viewed as a vestige of a more superstitious time," but Presbyterian pastor Steve Wilkins thinks "it may be time to revive it again."[5]

---

4. Author interview with Daniel Meeter, June 2014.
5. Steve Wilkins, "Baptism as Exorcism," Theopolis, March 24, 2015, https://theopolisinstitute.com/baptism-as-exorcism/.

This baptismal theme of exorcism can be seen in the Gospels. All four record Jesus's baptism and link it to his wilderness temptation that immediately follows. Of the baptism account in the Gospel of Mark, veteran preacher Scott Hoezee writes, "Very simply: . . . an engagement with evil is precisely what Jesus' baptism was all about." God sends his beloved Son into our world to reconcile every square inch of the world to himself, and "for that very reason task #1 was to engage the evil that holds our world captive."[6]

The Gospels relay a belief that Jesus's baptism equipped him for immediate immersion into the wild. Consider the language of Mark 1:12–13. Many translations render the original Greek to say the Holy Spirit *sent* Jesus out into the desert. But the original Greek verb (*ekballein*) actually carries the idea of being *thrown* out. "Clearly something cosmic is afoot," Hoezee says.[7] Far from being simply a quaint, traditional naming rite, baptism is a matter of life and death—an exorcism.

Noted Orthodox theologian Alexander Schmemann lamented that even in his own history-honoring tradition, where much of the liturgy of the early church remains in weekly use, many participate in this exorcism rite with "lack of enthusiasm." Some argue that it's time to take these questions out of the liturgy. Others don't argue for the rite's removal but simply cease to use it. Maybe the need to renounce Satan and all his ways and pomp "was obvious in a day of pervasive paganism and idolatry," Wilkins writes. "The presence of disgusting idols, widespread perversion, and gross demonic rituals gave Satan a face and identity that he has lost."[8] Evil was a *presence*, "something dark, irrational and very real."[9] But today many people think like the sneering Everett, even inside the church.

6. Scott Hoezee, "Mark 1:4–11," *Sermon Starters*, January 5, 2015, Center for Excellence in Preaching, https://cep.calvinseminary.edu/sermon-starters/epiphany-1b/?type=the_lectionary_gospel.

7. Hoezee, "Mark 1:4–11."

8. Wilkins, "Baptism as Exorcism."

9. Alexander Schmemann, *Of Water and the Spirit: A Liturgical Study of Baptism* (Crestwood, NY: St. Vladimir's Seminary Press, 1974), 22.

In 2014, the Church of England "quietly voted to drop all future references to the devil in a new baptism service." Formerly, godparents were asked to "renounce the devil and all his works for the sake of the child being baptized"—language that some priests worried "might confuse people who are not regular churchgoers." But now the liturgy "only asks whether parents and godparents will 'turn away from sin' and 'reject evil.'"

Bishop Robert Paterson disagreed with critics who claimed the traditional baptismal rite was being weakened: "We all know that for many people, the devil has been turned into a cartoon-like character of no particular malevolence."[10]

The decision was not universally applauded. On a BBC radio program that week, Peter Stanford, author of *The Devil: A Biography*, reminded listeners that since 1974, theologically and psychologically trained exorcists had been connected to each diocese, and wondered, "If we're never going to mention the devil anymore, what exactly is it that these people [are] going to do?"[11]

Maybe we prefer to think of evil as less personal. But, Schmemann warns, "Behind the dark and irrational presence of evil there must be a *person* or *persons*. There must exist a personal world of those who have chosen to hate God, to hate light, to be *against*,"[12] and for naming such realities, words are frustratingly insufficient. Evil is a "horrifying mystery."[13] All of us struggle in our own experience to fathom and subdue it. We all have an "experience of *fall*: of something precious and perfect deviated and betraying its own nature." If this seems unnecessarily theologically detached, think only of the maddening beyondness of evils such as addiction, racism, alcoholism, poverty, and betrayal. As we all know, and as these historic baptismal themes remind us, evil "is not to be 'explained' but faced and fought" following the example

10. Trevor Grundy, "Church of England Kicks the Devil out of Baptism Rite," Religion News Service, July 15, 2014, https://religionnews.com/2014/07/15/church-england-kicks-devil-baptism-rite/.

11. Grundy, "Church of England Kicks the Devil out of Baptism Rite."

12. Schmemann, *Of Water and the Spirit*, 22.

13. Schmemann, *Of Water and the Spirit*, 23.

of Christ on the cross. Our call is to combat evil by his "love, faith and obedience."[14]

Baptism is "the public act in which the Church declared to the world (and Satan) that the new Christian no longer belonged to the kingdom of evil," so "baptism is inescapably a form of exorcism."[15] At baptisms, Schmemann says, "We may not see [the devil], but the Church knows he is here. We may experience nothing but a nice and warm family 'affair,' but the Church knows that a mortal fight is about to begin."[16] No wonder at baptism the church has always "addressed the devil directly and called on the baptized to denounce him, renouncing all allegiance, loyalty, and service that he may have formerly given; renouncing all the deadly works of darkness and pledging by the power of the Spirit to have no fellowship with them any longer."[17]

Like it did for Pete and Delmar in *O Brother, Where Art Thou?*, baptism marks our liberation. We are saved from the realm of darkness and enter the kingdom of light. Our deliverance from evil and Satan is real. Going forward, the challenge for Pete and Delmar—and for all of us—is to turn our backs on our pet evil practices and to live as new people.

Schmemann suggests that "many Christians are still convinced that there is nothing basically wrong with the world and that one can very happily accept its 'way of life,' all its values and 'priorities,' while fulfilling at the same time one's 'religious duties.'"[18] Writing back in 1974, Schmemann believed most Christians "do not discern the obvious idolatry that permeates the ideas and the values by which men live today and that shapes, determines and enslaves their lives much more than the overt idolatry of ancient paganism. . . . To renounce Satan thus is not to reject a mythological being in whose existence one does not even believe. It is to reject an entire 'worldview' made up of pride and self-affirmation,

---

14. Schmemann, *Of Water and the Spirit*, 23.
15. Wilkins, "Baptism as Exorcism."
16. Schmemann, *Of Water and the Spirit*, 24.
17. Wilkins, "Baptism as Exorcism."
18. Schmemann, *Of Water and the Spirit*, 29.

of that pride which has truly taken human life from God and made it into darkness, death and hell."[19]

Some Christians consider "Satan and his pomps" a trite relic of the past. There are even seasons where some perceive evil as mostly overcome. But a clear look at reality objects to this theological fantasy. Renouncing evil is an essential aspect of a thoroughly Christian worldview. It's vital that those of us who have dropped the pledge from our baptisms and life restore it. News varies, as do social ills. But though their forms change, their reality does not. We are never too polished or sophisticated to renounce Satan.

Listing Satan's "works and pomps" in the life of Michael Corleone takes little time. The movie makes them painfully clear. Though for Pete and Delmar the list is less obvious, their temptations throughout the film are apparent. But it may not seem so easy to recognize Satan's works in our own lives.

John Chrysostom was a lead presbyter in Antioch before becoming archbishop of Constantinople in AD 397. In his "catechetical instructions" for those about to be baptized, he asks our question: "What are the pomps of the devil?" His answer is forthright: "Every form of sin, spectacles of indecency [the theater], horse racing, gatherings filled with laughter and abusive language. Portents, oracles, omens, observances of times, tokens, amulets and incantations—these too are pomps of the devil."[20] In another place he adds, it is "madness to be adorned with pearls," for one receives gold "not to bind your body with it, but to help and feed the poor."[21]

Theodore of Mopsuestia, a contemporary of Chrysostom, proclaims that at baptism, "I abjure Satan and all his angels, and all his works, and all his service, and all his deception, and all his worldly glamour."[22] He reminded those about to be baptized that

19. Schmemann, *Of Water and the Spirit*, 29–30.
20. John Chrysostom, *Baptismal Instructions* 11.25, in *Ancient Christian Writers: The Works of the Fathers in Translation*, ed. Johannes Quasten and Walter J. Burghardt, trans. Paul W. Harkins, vol. 31 (New York: Newman, 1963).
21. Chrysostom, *Baptismal Instructions* 12.48.
22. Hugh M. Riley, *Christian Initiation: A Comparative Study of the In-*

the devil was the cause of "numerous and great calamities" that bring injury to people.[23] Of chief concern was the demonic use of "glamour" experienced as "the theatre, race-course, contests of athletes, profane songs, water-organs, and dances." All such behaviors, he warned, were introduced by the devil under the pretext of "amusement."[24]

Syrian leaders around AD 500, like their global church counterparts, examined baptismal candidates to ensure they were ready: "Each person was presented before the entire church with head bowed. . . . An exorcism was performed to root out the devil and free each from his dominion. All chanted psalms." The baptizands then renounced the devil, indicating that their names "were inscribed in the book of life." They were taught that "the devil's weapons are pleasure and fear" as well as "spectacles" such as "chariot races in the circus, mimes and pantomimes in the theater, and wild animal contests in the amphitheater."[25] These are pomps the devil uses to entice people to pleasure.

We see the theme. These lists may seem bound by time and culture. From a distance of centuries, we may see a temptation toward legalism or even the self-righteous pride they warned against. But following the deep wisdom of the early church that names such dangers, what might be on our list of Satan's "pomps," or behaviors we must forgo for our spiritual health?

In the spring of 2019, I journeyed with a dozen fellow North American clergy to the national borderland of El Paso, Texas, and Ciudad Juárez, Mexico. The group was a dazzling variety of pastoral leaders, gathered from many traditions for a year of reflection.

---

terpretation of the Baptismal Liturgy in the Mystagogical Writings of Cyril of Jerusalem, John Chrysostom, Theodore of Mopsuestia, and Ambrose of Milan (Washington, DC: Catholic University of America Press, 1974), 35.

23. Riley, Christian Initiation, 557.

24. Riley, Christian Intitiation, 43, in Everett Ferguson, Baptism in the Early Church: History, Liturgy, and Theology in the First Five Centuries (Grand Rapids: Eerdmans, 2009), 524.

25. Thomas Macy Finn, Quodvultdeus of Carthage: The Creedal Homilies, Ancient Christian Writers 60 (New York, Newman, 2004), 6–8, in Ferguson, Baptism in the Early Church, 772.

Once in El Paso, we held a worship service along the border fence. Parts of our liturgy that afternoon involved sprinkling baptismal waters along the fence and praying for its removal.

There, over several days, we heard poignant stories of life in those neighborhoods and met a series of captivating people who have given their lives to serving the forgotten. During our stay we met repeatedly with Msgr. Arturo J. Bañuelas. A native of El Paso, Arturo is the dynamic pastor of St. Mark's Catholic Church, a thriving community with members from dozens of nations of origin along with both border patrol agents and recent immigrants. I watched Arturo serve communion on Sunday to an overflowing congregation, saw him hold court in neighborhood cafés, and heard how he catalyzed the start of many much-needed organizations. After earning his doctorate from the Gregorian University in Rome, he returned home to minister in its unique setting. He advocates "on behalf of farmworkers, immigrants, and for justice at the border."

During lunch between services that Sunday, as he urged us to eat more tortillas and dessert, he explained why he cares so much about his home and is doggedly resolved to live a faithful baptized life there. This is the story that, in his words, is the reason he is "focused on ministry and motivated and 'charged,'" even though he's officially past retirement age.

Years earlier, their congregation sent a work team over the border into Mexico. This trip took the team high into the mountains, out of the range of vehicles, cell phones, and running water. They had been there a couple of days when a local mother of four told them she was dizzy. Communication was difficult; her Spanish was limited.

Arturo is not a medical doctor and didn't pretend to be. But with no one else available, he volunteered to help. He looked for obvious physical maladies, but outwardly she seemed OK. Then, in a moment of intuitive clarity, he thought to ask, "When did you eat last?"

She whispered weakly, "Six days ago."

Just then her young daughter entered their meager home, asking, "Mom, will we eat today?" Her children hadn't eaten in five days.

Immediately Arturo, who is clearly not one to sit idly by, told the group, "We are going to feed them with the food we brought for our mission team." Today, if you ask Arturo why he's so motivated to work for immigration reform, he will respond, "So she and her kids can eat."

Here was a Mexican woman who had never been in a car. She had nothing in her house. She lived isolated in the mountains. There was no priest, no electricity, and no running water. Her husband was in *el norte* (the United States), working a migrant job to provide. She didn't know where because they had no phone. Her husband risked imprisonment to feed his family, coming home every three months to give her money for basic needs. Then he would be off to find work again.

Arturo is so committed to immigration justice, and has been for so long, that many border patrol agents work with him. They give him advance notice about raids and let him know when folks will be released from custody so his team can provide them food and clothes.

Arturo, his team, and his congregation renounce Satan and all his works not only in their baptismal liturgy but in their baptized lives. What do you think he might list as Satan's "pomps"? Would his list include poverty, child hunger, and nationalism?

On January 6, 2021, armed vigilantes stormed the US Capitol. It was the first time the building had been occupied by a violent force since British soldiers filled its halls during the War of 1812. Vice President Mike Pence was whisked away to a hidden location, as were many senators. People on the floor of the House of Representatives were issued masks to protect against biological, chemical, or radiation threats. They feared for their lives.

Barry C. Black, chaplain of the US Senate, was there that memorable day. He's always there when the Senate is in session, opening each day in prayer. He offers counseling and spiritual care for the senators, their families, and their staffs—more than six thousand people. He provides guidance on spiritual and moral issues, supports their research on theological questions, and teaches a

Bible study. And on that fraught and fear-filled day, Black denounced Satan and all his pomp and ways.

Black recalls praying in an impromptu group of senators when Capitol Police interrupted and told them to move to safety. Many fretful hours later, after Congress certified the 2020 election in the early morning hours of the next day, Chaplain Black was again asked to pray. His prayer was steeped in Scripture. He prayed in a way that "denounced evil and all its pomp." He prayed, "We deplore the desecration of the United States Capitol building, the shedding of innocent blood, the loss of life, and the quagmire of dysfunction that threaten our democracy." He prayed, "These tragedies have reminded us that words matter, and that the power of life and death is in the tongue." He prayed, pressing for unity instead of division, asking all present to "see in each other a common humanity." He prayed a baptismal prayer of renunciation.[26]

What is on Black's list of Satan's pomps? Lies, hateful speech, incivility, posturing, selfish use of political power, division.

Is it clear why renouncing Satan is an essential part of a baptismal worldview?

David Bailey is the founding director of Arrabon, a ministry dedicated to helping congregations become "reconciling communities." It's based in Richmond, Virginia, the former capital of the Confederacy and until recently a city whose boulevards were lined with statues of Confederate war heroes. Bailey has a lot of work to do, and he does it well.

During Black History Month 2021, David highlighted several saints "whose lives and witness have encouraged" him in his own faith. He ended the month by talking about Frederick Douglass. "He's a huge figure in my life," David wrote. "When you come into my house, his is the first picture you will see. He saved my intel-

26. Megan Specia, "'The Power of Life and Death Is in the Tongue,' Senate Chaplain Says in a Powerful Prayer Calling for Unity," *New York Times*, January 7, 2021, https://www.nytimes.com/2021/01/07/us/politics /senate-chaplain-prayer-capitol.html.

lectual life when I was 16. Then, more than a decade later . . . he played a central role in saving my spiritual life as well." Both times Douglass's famous autobiography, *Narrative of the Life of Frederick Douglass: An American Slave*, gave David the "vital wisdom and perspective" he needed. David often returns to the book's appendix, where Douglass "distinguishes between the 'Christianity of this land and the Christianity of Christ,'" saying, "To be the friend of the one, is of necessity to be the enemy of the other. I love the pure, peaceable, and impartial Christianity of Christ: I therefore hate the corrupt, slaveholding, women-whipping, cradle-plundering, partial and hypocritical Christianity of this land." Douglass, writes Bailey, "was able to live through hard things without giving up hope. He was willing to say hard things without bitterness."[27]

What is on Douglass's and Bailey's list of Satan's works and pomps? Racism. Injustice. Empty promises. Complicity. Betrayal.

My own denomination loves the rootedness that historic confessions provide. Our favorite dates from the sixteenth century. But in the 1970s, wise leaders found themselves longing for something new to help affirm the old. They wanted to offer the wider church a "new seasonal flower next to the perennial plants,"[28] speaking in a language of today with flourish, giving "a hymn-like expression of our faith."[29] The outcome is a poetic gem called *Our World Belongs to God*. It's a beautiful document, soaring in places, yet standing the test of time. Note how this

27. David Bailey, "Sincere Faith and Steadfast Hope: The Life and Witness of Frederick Douglass," *Arrabon Weekly* (email digest), February 27, 2021.

28. Morris N. Greidanus, "The Making and Shaping of *Our World Belongs to God: A Contemporary Testimony*," *Inside Story* (blog), Christian Reformed Church in North America, accessed April 30, 2021, https://www.crcna.org/welcome/beliefs/contemporary-testimony/our-world-belongs-god/inside-story.

29. *Our World Belongs to God* (Grand Rapids: Christian Reformed Church in North America, 2008), https://www.crcna.org/welcome/beliefs/contemporary-testimony/our-world-belongs-god.

section in particular describes the kind of exorcism embedded in baptism:

> Followers of the Prince of Peace
> are called to be peacemakers,
> promoting harmony and order
> and restoring what is broken.
>
> We call on our governments to work for peace
> and to restore just relationships.
> We deplore the spread of weapons
> in our world and on our streets
> with the risks they bring
> and the horrors they threaten.
> We call on all nations to reduce their arsenals
> to what is needed
> in the defense of justice and freedom.
> We pledge to walk in ways of peace,
> confessing that our world belongs to God;
> he is our sure defense.[30]

I'm sure the framers of this document didn't see their work as part exorcism. But I do imagine they wanted to renounce some things, whether they explicitly considered them Satan's pomps or not. Based on these few stanzas, what would be our denomination's list of Satan's pomps? Too many guns. Weapons in the wrong hands. Unjust relationships. Racism. Toxicity between people groups and nations.

What's on your list? Here are a few of mine: Spiritual elitism. Abuse of creation. Narcissistic church leaders. Children in harm's way.

It's far more common to think of baptism as a witness to our personal faith, as a covenant pledge to raise a child, or as solidarity with Christian sisters and brothers around the world. But what if

30. *Our World Belongs to God.*

we also, following the lead of wise Christians before us, see it as a kind of exorcism? To be baptized is to clearly and repeatedly turn our backs against evil and injustice and to denounce them wherever we see them. And, as we shall see in the next two chapters, it is to move toward an Easter-like carnival of full "participation in the life of the Risen Christ."[31]

This big view of baptism is personal enough to guide Pete, Delmar, and all of us toward spiritual flourishing, and it's cosmic enough to make the work of our lifetime an exercise toward global shalom. It is a whole new way of seeing ourselves and our world.

31. Schmemann, *Of Water and the Spirit*, 8.

# FIVE

# An Ordained Life

## Anointing our Missional Identity

---

Then Jesus came from Galilee to the Jordan to be baptized by John. But John tried to deter him, saying, "I need to be baptized by you, and do you come to me?"

—Matthew 3:13–14

Most of us who are Christians underestimate the gifts given us in baptism.

—Dale F. Bruner

All baptized people, whatever their work or rank, location or function, charismatic gifts or personal talents, share in the one ministry of the body of Christ for the world, in the world.

—William Stringfellow

---

All four Gospels tell the story of Jesus's baptism, as if every reader needs to hear it. Jesus's cousin John, outfitted in a garment made of camel's hair and a rustic leather belt, has set up camp in an unmarked wilderness to preach and prophesy. Everyone comes out to listen: The pious and the profane. The bankrupt and the ruined. The broken and the eccentric. Religious misfits and spiritual castoffs. All get a dose of John's caustic threats and stern warnings. Each hears the message of impending judgment. Many confess and are baptized, one repentant sinner after another. And then Jesus, the Messiah, gets in line as if he's in a Costco checkout.

Each gospel offers its own angle on the story. Mark starts his gospel with it, skipping Christmas as incidental and quickly launching into Jesus's ministry. Luke copies much of Mark's detail, following the gist of his telling but refusing to mention the involvement of the eccentric cousin. John emphasizes the Spirit lingering on Jesus like a dove, avoiding any awkward mention of an actual baptism.[1]

The unique feature of Matthew's version is the cousin conversation. John admires Jesus. He believes in Jesus. That's exactly why

1. Scholars say the gospel writers' reluctance and awkwardness are proof that Jesus really was baptized by John. After all, when someone informs you about something not in their best interest for you to know, it's likely they're telling the truth.

he rebuts Jesus. He can't stomach Jesus's baptismal plan. Not one to hold back his opinions, John protests: Jesus shouldn't be in the same line as the dreck of humanity. John's baptismal liturgy is consistent: repent, be baptized, live a new life. Why is Jesus in that line? What does he have to repent of? The baptizer's harsh, prophetic words can't apply to the Savior. So he asserts that Jesus's baptismal plans are backward. If one cousin is to baptize the other, Jesus should baptize *him*. The innocent should be the one baptizing, not the professional baptizer. "I need to be baptized by you," John says, "and do you come to me?" (Matt. 3:14).

Every religion knows humanity needs a fix. Like the humble penitents in John's baptismal line, we know we need a cleaning. It's no surprise, then, that many religions recommend or require some sort of ritual cleansing.

The law of Moses required any material that touched a dead animal to be ritually cleansed. The Greek translation of the Old Testament translates the idea with the word "baptize." Only after a "baptism" can the material be used again (Lev. 11:24–40). Further, any person who touches a dead body was automatically unclean for seven days. On the third and seventh day of uncleanness, a clean person would mix running water with ashes of purification, dip (*baptwo*) hyssop into the bowl, and sprinkle it on the one who wished to be "clean" again (Num. 19:17–20).[2]

A tract from the Mishnah, a collection of the oral tradition of Jewish religious law, described *mikvaoth*, or "immersion pools" devoted to cleansing baths. Each pool represented a level of cleanliness, gradually getting one fully "clean."[3] Moses had people wash their clothes before hearing God speak on Mount Sinai. His subsequent regulations call for washing after intercourse, nocturnal discharge, releasing a scapegoat, or coming in contact with mold. New candidates for the Jewish sect called the Essenes, after a year's probation, were allowed to "share in the purer kind of waters for purity," though they were only admitted fully after

---

2. Everett Ferguson, *Baptism in the Early Church: History, Liturgy, and Theology in the First Five Centuries* (Grand Rapids: Eerdmans, 2009), 61.

3. Ferguson, *Baptism in the Early Church*, 64.

two more years.[4] A group called the Hemerobaptists, who practiced daily baptisms, insisted that "unless they wash, they do not eat" and "unless they cleanse their beds, tables, platters, cups and seats," they don't use them.[5] Ritual cleansing also occurred among Romans and Greeks and later among Muslims.

It's easy to imagine that in dusty first-century Palestine, where water was precious and dirt ever-present, a person might consider ritual cleansing a necessary preparation for meeting God. But when John talked about baptism, he emphasized repentance. And it wasn't just proselytes who needed baptismal washing. Everyone did. Baptism meant repentance. It meant embracing the need for profound moral change. It still does.

One damp and drizzly February I visited Israel. It was amazing to see places I grew up reading about: a Bethlehem sheep pen, the Sea of Galilee, and the Mount of Olives. Like many pilgrims, I planned a stop at the place John baptized Jesus. Months in advance, the tour brochure piqued my interest: I could get baptized in the Jordan River exactly where John baptized Jesus. Like many Israeli tourist sites, there's some controversy about the precise place of the original baptism, but no matter the spot, the experience is for many the spiritual highlight of a lifetime.

Take, for example, the twenty-two marines and sailors from the amphibious transport dock ship *Mesa Verde* who were baptized in the Jordan in 2014. Their chaplains, Lieutenants Bryan Purvis and Michael Monroig, like John before, did the baptizing. "It was such a humbling experience," Purvis said. "To think, this is where John baptized Jesus, and I had the honor and privilege of baptizing so many sailors and marines. It is what ministry is all about. . . . The emotion from the sailors and marines as they understood the significance of what just occurred is something I will never forget." They identified with Jesus in the same river, just as millennia before, he identified with them.

Monroig added, "The opportunity to watch people's personal and spiritual life grow as they participated in the baptisms is an

---

4. Ferguson, *Baptism in the Early Church*, 68.
5. Ferguson, *Baptism in the Early Church*, 72.

honor. . . . Some . . . were recommitting their lives to God; [for] others it was a renewal of their faith. . . . I believe that this experience will be a life-changing event for the sailors and marines who participated."

"This experience left me in awe," said Jalisa Dembo. "To be baptized where my Lord and Savior walked, talked, and delivered his people was an absolutely awesome experience. It was my first time being baptized and one that I will nearly, dearly treasure for the rest of my life."[6]

It felt a bit less magical to those on our tour. The marketing brochure's invitation had already done little to entice my Reformed bones toward rebaptism. On spying the murky Jordan waters, everyone on our bus of pilgrims thought the same. When we drove up to the site at the end of a dreary daylong journey, we all decided *not* to go into the river. The day was winter cold, the waning part of a damp afternoon. Our group, mostly Idaho Lutherans and their much-loved pastor, instead gathered in a circle on the shore. The pastor/tour guide reached into the Jordan for water, which he used to make a wet sign of the cross on each of our foreheads. Gazing tenderly into our eyes as he did so, he echoed Martin Luther: "Remember your baptism." We were happy, and moved, to have our own remembering. But it struck me then, and still does now, what an odd idea it is to enter filthy waters to become spiritually clean.

Missionary-turned-Bible-commentator Dale Bruner calls Jesus's baptism his "first miracle." Standing in line, waiting his turn, dunked into murky water, Jesus forever identifies himself with the shadowy reality of humanity's brokenness and our human need for repentance. His baptism miracle was his first step of humble obedience, setting him on a course to his death and resurrection.[7]

In her sermon "The River of Life," Barbara Brown Taylor says, "Even if [ Jesus] were innocent, even if his intentions were noth-

---

6. "Sailors and Marines Baptized in Jordan River during Israel Visit," *Breaking Christian News*, March 20, 2014, https://breakingchristiannews.com/articles/display_art_pf.html?ID=13543.

7. Frederick Dale Bruner, *Matthew: A Commentary*, vol. 1, *The Christbook, Matthew 1–12* (Grand Rapids: Eerdmans, 2004), 101.

ing but good, it was ruinous to his reputation. Who was going to believe that he was there just because he cared about those people and refused to separate himself from them? Gossip being what it was, who was not going to think that he had just a few teeny-weeny things to get off his conscience before he went into public ministry?"[8]

Baptism always, in a sense, risks your reputation.

Origen, a brilliant third-century scholar and a prolific author, wrote, "He was washed for our sins in order that we might be sanctified in his bath." In the early fourth century, Gregory of Nazianzus, a much-loved pastor and teacher, said, "Jesus submitted to be purified in the river Jordan for my purification, or rather, sanctifying the waters by his purification (for indeed he who takes away the sin of the world had no need of purification)."[9]

At the very first Christian baptism, Jesus identified with sinners. It's what he was ordained to do.[10] Like his cousin, we may prefer that Jesus stay clear of scandalous connection with religious underachievers, but that's how Jesus includes *us*. He didn't need the heavens opened. But we do. As John Chrysostom (his name means "golden-tongued") explains, the heavens were opened to "inform thee that at thy baptism also this is done."[11]

A perhaps apocryphal story is told about Henri Nouwen suffering from the same bad dream for many nights. In the dream, he was visiting another city and bumped into a high school classmate, who said, "Henri, I haven't seen you in years! What have you done with your life?" Nouwen was always shaken by the question because his life, like anyone's, was full of both joys and troubles, yet he felt he was being judged. He didn't know how to respond. Sometime later he had a different dream in which he died and went to heaven. As he waited to meet God, he imagined the Al-

8. Barbara Brown Taylor, *Home by Another Way* (Lanham, MD: Rowman & Littlefield, 1999), 35.

9. Ferguson, *Baptism in the Early Church*, 114.

10. A sinless Jesus receiving from John a baptism to repentance "would not have been invented by Jesus' disciples nor accepted if invented by others" (Ferguson, *Baptism in the Early Church*, 100).

11. Bruner, *Matthew*, 89.

mighty in a cloud of smoke and flames, ready to condemn Nouwen's response to the question: What have you done with your life? When the terrified Nouwen of the dream finally entered the throne room, he found it warmly lit by the presence of God, who gently said, "Henri, it's good to see you. I hear you had a rough trip, but I'd love to see your slides."[12]

A couple of years ago I was talking with a friend going through a divorce. Each divorce is a kind of dying, a personal and public agony. This friend is one of my favorites at church, working behind the scenes, always ready to fix an emergency, a loyal friend who once told me, "If no one else comes to church, I'll be there."

In his own imperfect way he fought for years to heal his marriage. But that morning in my office, he faced the reality he had been fighting and postponing: his marriage was broken beyond repair. What do you say to someone whose twenty-year marriage is crumbling? What do you say now, at the point of no return, when the inevitable he dreaded is now upon him? We talked for a while. We reviewed his options. And then, as we ended our visit in prayer, we leaned into his baptismal identity. We prayed, asking God yet again to heal his marriage and, if it was healed or not, to whisper over him what Jesus heard thundered at his baptism: This is the one I love.

In a 2010 radio devotional, Rev. Joanna Adams reminds her listeners how Martin Luther was often "plagued . . . by a deep sense of unworthiness and despair. To drive back those demons, he kept an inscription over his desk that said, 'Remember, you have been baptized.' Often, he would touch his forehead and remind himself, 'Martin, you have been baptized.'"[13]

Both church insiders and church avoiders are more enamored with Christmas, Easter, or even a football game or shopping mall than with baptism. Baptism seems a cliché by comparison, a ritual

12. Thomas G. Long, "Called by Name," *Day1*, January 11, 2004, https://day1.org/weekly-broadcast/5d9b820ef71918cdf2002429/view.

13. Joanna Adams, "God Believes in You," *Day1*, January 10, 2010, https://day1.org/weekly-broadcast/5d9b820ef71918cdf20028d6/god_believes_in_you.

easy to overlook. Maybe, we might think with such an opinion, the gospel writers, like some freshman English composition students, needed filler to lengthen their essays?

Baptisms today aren't usually accompanied by a voice like thunder or a visible flyover of the Holy Spirit. But the early church believed that the triune fullness of God is present at our baptisms. It's as if heaven opens again. God gets to us. And maybe we get to God. The Spirit of healing and wholeness descends to make an ordinary person holy. And the Father's voice issues another adoption decree; heaven opens and we understand that this is God's beloved child.

Following gospel footsteps, early church leaders taught that Jesus's baptism identified him with forgiven sinners and launched his ministry. It was, to put it in Old Testament terms, his anointing. Jesus publicly recognized and accepted his special relationship with God and so began his public ministry.

Preaching professor Tom Long tells the story of a biblical scholar explaining Jesus's baptism to a group of teenagers. Leaning into his expertise in the original Greek, he informed them that at the baptism the skies did not merely "open up," as some translations say, but violently *ripped* open. "When Jesus was baptized," the scholar explained, "the heavens that separate us from God were ripped open so that now we can get to God. Because of Jesus, we have access to God—we can get close to him."

One teen in the front row had been clearly bored by the lecture, but at this remark he sat up straight. "That ain't what that means," he exclaimed. "It means that the heavens were ripped open so that now God can get at *us* anytime he wants. Now nobody's safe!"[14] That keen young observer might have been reading the early church fathers!

After a far-reaching and meticulous survey of baptism in the earliest centuries of Christianity, Eugene Ferguson summarized the nascent church's teaching about Jesus's baptism: "Although

---

14. Scott Hoezee, "Mark 1:4–11," *Sermon Starters*, January 5, 2015, Center for Excellence in Preaching, https://cep.calvinseminary.edu/sermon-starters/epiphany-1b/?type=the_lectionary_gospel.

in developing the doctrine of baptism different authors had their particular favorite descriptions, there is a remarkable agreement on the benefits received in baptism. . . . Two fundamental blessings are often repeated: the person baptized received forgiveness of sins and the gift of the Holy Spirit (Acts 2:38)."[15]

If we could see a YouTube video of this first Christian baptism, what would most linger in our minds? The thunderous voice? John's "desert chic" outfit? Jesus's lack of clothing? The earnest, anxious faces of the crowd? The self-righteous elitism of the Pharisees? Jesus's face when he is acknowledged publicly as God's Son?

Imagine the YouTuber zooming in on John the Baptist, capturing his face as he sees the last thing he expects: a dove. He'd been threatening judgment, predicting fire. But the Spirit comes as a dove. In that moment, the Gospels and the early church say, Jesus is anointed. At his baptism, he is ordained.

Baptism, not Christmas, starts the story. Baptism is the set of glasses through which we can see all of Jesus's life. His other miracles, his teaching, his friendships, his loving or tough words to broken people, his death on the cross—all are a working out of his baptism. "When the New Testament strikes the note of baptism," Bruner writes, "all the overtones of the great chord of God's salvation can be heard."[16]

Our baptisms too are ordinations. Each baptism, in its specific place and time, marks the beginning of a *life* of baptism. Our entire postbaptismal life is lived under water. Every decision, each career move, and each sentence we speak is an overflow of baptismal waters, the outpouring of the Holy Spirit. In his baptism Jesus links himself to us, and in our baptisms we get linked to him. In faith we work with the Spirit toward humble obedience, to multiply life, to live our anointed calling, just as Jesus did.

That's why, former archbishop of Canterbury Rowan Williams notes, we expect to find the baptized living out their ordination "in the neighbourhood of chaos, . . . near to those places where humanity is most at risk, where humanity is most disordered, dis-

15. Ferguson, *Baptism in the Early Church*, 854.
16. Bruner, *Matthew*, 85.

figured and needy." Williams has witnessed thousands of Christians living their baptisms in ordinary or desperate places. "If being baptized is being led to where Jesus is," he says, "then being baptized is being led towards the chaos and the neediness of a humanity that has forgotten its own destiny."[17]

Like Jesus, the baptized need not fear being *contaminated* by the mess of humanity because "they have a new level of solidarity with them."[18] It seems a contradiction that the baptized could both be in the center of God's joy and pleasure and at the same time the center of mission. "And that of course means that the path of the baptized person is a dangerous one. Perhaps baptism really ought to have some health warnings attached to it: 'If you take this step, if you go into these depths, it will be transfiguring, exhilarating, life-giving and very, very dangerous.' To be baptized into Jesus is not to be in what the world thinks of as a safe place. Jesus' first disciples discovered that in the Gospels, and his disciples have gone on discovering it ever since."[19]

The early church, and still many Christians today, symbolized this spiritual anointing with a literal one. Already in the late second century Theophilus of Antioch wrote, "We are called Christians on this account, because we are anointed with the oil of God." Unable to resist wordplay, he said followers of Christ (*christos*) are to be "useful" (*chrestos*).[20] Along with other liturgical actions, the practice of baptismal anointing "gave expression in literal acts to theological ideas associated with baptism, and it was natural to bring out the associations of Christians with Christ (the 'Anointed One')."[21]

Sometimes this anointing happened before the actual baptism. Sometimes it happened afterward. Cyprian's list of "postbaptismal actions include unction, imposition of hands, and signing." He

17. Rowan Williams, *Being Christian: Baptism, Bible, Eucharist, Prayer* (Grand Rapids: Eerdmans, 2014), 4–5.

18. Williams, *Being Christian*, 6.

19. Williams, *Being Christian*, 9.

20. Theophilus, *To Autolycus* 1.12, trans. Marcus Dods, rev. and ed. Kevin Knight, in New Advent, accessed May 5, 2021, http://www.new advent.org/fathers/02041.htm.

21. Ferguson, *Baptism in the Early Church*, 247.

taught that "a person who is baptized has to be anointed so that by receiving the chrism (*chrisma*), or anointing (*unctio*), he may become the anointed of God and receive within him the grace of Christ."[22] In many cases, the symbolic anointing was joined with the "laying on of hands," another reinforcing Old Testament symbol for commissioning to a life of service.

Rites varied, but all included a renunciation, an anointing, and a taking on of baptismal clothes. Sometimes there were multiple renunciations, sometimes multiple anointings, sometimes a back-and-forth between the two. In every case the anointing symbolized the outpouring of the Holy Spirit, just as happened in Jesus's own baptism. "The post-baptismal chrismation was interpreted as a messianic anointing and a strengthening of the neophyte."[23]

In a series of lectures, Cyril of Jerusalem gives us a window into one kind of anointing taking place in the fourth century: "The ointment was applied to the forehead (so as to remove the shame borne by Adam and to reflect the glory of the Lord—2 Cor 3:18), ears (to hear the Lord Jesus in the gospel—Isaiah 50:4, Matt. 11:15), nose (to be the savor of Christ—2 Corinthians 2:15), and breast (with the breastplate of righteousness to stand against the devil—Eph. 6:11, 14). The invocation of the Holy Spirit made the ointment no longer simple or common but Christ's gift of grace to impart his divine nature."[24]

Consider how far this trio of baptismal renunciation, anointing, and clothing is from many contemporary baptism experiences, both for parents who view baptism as a child's simple naming rite and adults who see it as merely an expression of their personal testimony. Historically, baptism was an elaborate, layered commissioning service much like that designed for priest or pastor, but instead for all believers.

Chrysostom urged all believers to live into this baptismal idea of commissioning. Using 2 Corinthians 1:21, he taught that each baptized person is anointed and sealed by God and is therefore

22. Cyprian, *Letters* 70 (69), 2.2, in Ferguson, *Baptism in the Early Church*, 353.

23. Ferguson, *Baptism in the Early Church*, 480.

24. Ferguson, *Baptism in the Early Church*, 480.

made a prophet and priest and king. His accent on this threefold office later became a stream of thinking on the identity of Jesus, reflected by his followers. In the Old Testament, only a select few were called to an anointed office, and always to a single one— prophet, priest, *or* king. But now, Chrysostom said, Christians are anointed and sealed to hold *all* these offices "pre-eminently."[25]

Fifth-century bishop Fastidius also "linked the anointing of all the baptized by the Holy Spirit to Jesus Christ's own anointing, which was the culmination of the physical anointing of the priests, prophets and kings in ancient Israel. 'All (the baptized) are anointed as prophets and priests and kings,' he wrote, 'Thus we receive the name Christian because we are anointed like Christ the anointed one.'"[26]

For generations, followers of Jesus have received this beautiful gift of anointing and then put it into tangible expressions of concern and sacrificial working for the common good.

Barbara Brown Taylor remembers reading about two paramedics who, on seeing the chaos and misery left by a flood in Honduras, immediately left their home to help. They had no Spanish-language skills. They had no place to stay. They had no illusions. They knew they would be pulling dead bodies out of the mud. But they "thought it might help the families to give them back their loved ones for burial."[27] They were simply living their baptismal ordination.

When I was a pastor in small-town Minnesota, a friend who managed the local hardware store phoned me to say, "You're go-

25. John Chrysostom, 2 *Corinthians homilia* 3.4–5, in Rose M. Beal, "Priest, Prophet and King: Jesus Christ, the Church and the Christian Person," *John Calvin's Ecclesiology: Ecumenical Perspectives*, ed. Gerard Mannion and Eduardus Van der Borght (New York: T&T Clark, 2011), 92.

26. Fastidius, *De Vita Christiana* 1, Patrologia Latina 50:394, in Peter Drilling, "The Priest, Prophet and King Trilogy: Elements of Its Meaning in *Lumen Gentium* and for Today," *Eglise et Theologie* 19 (1988), 189, in Beal, "Priest, Prophet and King," in Mannion and Van der Borght, *John Calvin's Ecclesiology*, 92.

27. Barbara Brown Taylor, "Matthew 11:2–11," Sermon, Washington National Cathedral, December 13, 1998, https://cathedral.org/sermons/sermon-1998-12-13-000000.

ing to want to come and see this." New to small-town life, I was only slowly becoming aware of its tempos and rhythms. Of course, I knew we were in a drought; we had been praying for rain every Sunday for weeks. But the level of desperation had somehow missed me. Only a couple of our attendees were directly involved in agriculture.

When I drove, as directed, to the site of our sister church, I saw a row of semitrailers. A group of men, some of whom I knew but many of whom were unfamiliar, ambled about. Each truck bed was overflowing with hay—food that would feed livestock. Food that would mean these farmers could survive the season. A group of farmers from the other side of the state, which had experienced a few more "lucky" thunderstorms that summer, had heard about the plight of their neighbors from hundreds of miles away and had come to help. There were no news outlets recording the event. There was no public spotlight. There was just a group of unassuming farmers living their baptism ordination.

Again, we are challenged by Rowan Williams, "Baptism does not confer on us a status that marks us off from everybody else" so we might imagine ourselves more elite people who can "claim an extra dignity" or a "sort of privilege." Rather, baptism moves us beyond ourselves. It calls us to an "openness to human need" and a "corresponding openness to the Holy Spirit."[28] The baptized still struggle to be decent human beings. We are still tempted to be less than God created us to be. But in Jesus, God gives us spiritual power to choose a higher and better way. Because of our baptisms, we live inside the promise that we are loved and can live love.

In *A People's History of Christianity*, Diana Butler Bass contrasts two different brands of Christianity. The first she calls "Big-C Christianity." Militant and proficient, morally righteous and right, "it features know-how belief that for centuries has married 'faithful living' with all sorts of excess—crusades and inquisitions, warfare and slavery, blind nationalism and equally blind oppression."[29]

28. Williams, *Being Christian*, 7, 9.
29. Diana Butler Bass, *A People's History of Christianity: The Other Side of the Story* (New York: HarperCollins, 2009), 4.

A second brand of Christianity she calls "generative," which "seeks new possibilities and places to offer God's sprawling grace. In its wake is humble serving, acts of compassionate, thoughtful peacemaking, the kind of faith that welcomes the stirrings of expansive grace."[30] That's baptismal living.

Saint Patrick knew both kinds. Years before he baptized the king of Munster and became the stuff of missionary lore,[31] Patrick had been to Ireland as a slave. Celtic pirates raided his family lands and captured him along with several other young men. The bandits then set sail for Ireland, where they sold their human cargo into slavery. Patrick's owner was a wealthy tribal chief named Miliuc, who assigned Patrick to herd cattle. There Patrick lived, underfed and cold. Six years later, Patrick heard a voice in a dream: "You are going home! Look! Your ship is ready." The voice further directed Patrick to flee the next morning. He obeyed, walking to the coast, found the ship, made his way on board, and returned safely to the comforts of home.[32]

Patrick was born a Briton. As was his father. And his grandfather. And every one of his relatives. Britons in his time were aristocratic and learned, highly cultured and well spoken. And they were Christian.

Back home, free from his enslavement, Patrick returned to life as an aristocratic Briton. He visited popular pilgrim destinations, such as the Saint Martin of Tours monastery and the city of Rome. Then he returned home to live among the comforts of England. But one night, at the age of forty-eight, Patrick had another dream. Celts, the same people who enslaved him, begged, "We appeal to you, holy servant boy, to come and walk among us." On the surface this made no sense. As a true Briton, a Roman, Patrick knew this would be impossible. From a Roman perspective this was a doomed enterprise. Since the second century, no mission to barbarians—Vandals or Franks, Visigoths or Frisians, Huns or

30. Bass, *A People's History of Christianity*, 10.

31. This part of Saint Patrick's story is told in chapter 3.

32. George G. Hunter III, *The Celtic Way of Evangelism: How Christianity Can Reach the West . . . Again* (Nashville: Abingdon, 2000), 13–14.

Celts or Vikings—was effective. The church simply assumed barbarians were impossible to reach. They couldn't read or write. They were unstable and overly emotional. Some participated in human sacrifice.[33]

But Patrick was baptized. He was anointed. And he was commissioned. So he answered the dream, was ordained as a bishop, and set off for Ireland again, this time to offer the unreachable barbarians grace and to invite them all, kings and commoners, to join a life of anointed baptismal living.

33. Hunter, *The Celtic Way of Evangelism*, 17.

# SIX

# *Baptismal Clothes*

## Wearing Our Baptism

---

All of you who were baptized into Christ have clothed
yourselves with Christ.

—Galatians 3:27


I rejoice heartily in the LORD,
   in my God is the joy of my soul;
For he has clothed me with a robe of salvation,
   and wrapped me in a mantle of justice.

—Isaiah 61:10 NAB


[You] have put on the new self, which is being renewed in knowledge in the image of its Creator. . . .
Therefore, as God's chosen people, holy and dearly
loved, clothe yourselves with compassion, kindness,
humility, gentleness and patience. . . . And over all
these virtues put on love, which binds them all together in perfect unity.

—Colossians 3:10, 12, 14


For that purpose Christ instituted holy baptism,
thereby to clothe you with his righteousness. It is tan-
tamount to his saying, My righteousness shall be your

righteousness; my innocence, your innocence. Your sins indeed are great, but by baptism I bestow on you my righteousness; I strip death from you and clothe you with my life.

—Martin Luther

Take off the old self, as a filthy garment, [and] receive the garment of immortality that Christ, having unfolded [it], holds out to you.

—Gregory of Nyssa

There was no reason for Don[1] to be there. Sure, he lived in Hoboken. He shopped there. His barber was there, as was his dry cleaner. And he used mass transit there, crowding with others for the daily commute to New York City. But no one expected to find him—a young, gay, Jewish man—seated in that modest, unadorned, German Reformed church building.

Don started attending worship services there after some Jewish friends told him Jesus was the Messiah. These friends lived in the city but told him he needed to find a congregation closer to home. So he did. It was an unlikely choice. But there he sat, Sunday after Sunday, a new and unlikely convert in a prim New Jersey church.

In the first few months he worshiped there, the congregation baptized two adults: a Parsi man of Iranian descent and a formerly Buddhist woman who grew up in Japan. Baptizing adults was rare in that congregation; much more frequently they baptized infants. Maybe it was witnessing these adult baptisms, or maybe it was the way the time-tested liturgy told the ongoing story of grace, but after regularly worshiping there those months, something made Don tell his pastor one Sunday, "I want to be baptized."

So the pastor, as was his practice with people new to the faith, and following in the footsteps of pastors like Ambrose and Augustine and his own father, began to train this new attendee in

1. Not his real name.

the richness of the Christian faith. He began, the pastor called it, to *catechize* him. Together they talked about sin, salvation, and Christian service. Together they studied the Lord's Prayer, the Ten Commandments, and the Apostles' Creed. Through this ancient curriculum, Don learned more deeply about the contours of grace. When the subject of his upcoming baptism arose again weeks later, Don added to his baptismal request, "I'd like to be immersed."

The congregation didn't typically practice immersion. It had no practical way to do so in its dated building. But the pastor responded with enthusiasm: "Great!" With the hope of renewal, the congregation was already planning that year to add an Easter vigil, a worship service on the eve of Easter that has historically included the baptism of new converts. But they didn't yet have a person to be baptized. Don's request was a gift. Don became, the pastor recalled with a twinkle in his eye, their "Easter vigil victim."

But the church, while glad to immerse him, faced a logistical challenge. They needed to find a suitable baptismal vessel and then get it inside the old German Reformed church building. Their search turned up several possibilities, but finally they chose a child's wading pool, blue with pink fish and whales. Bringing this new baptismal pool inside the vintage sanctuary, placing it before worn wooden pews and a pipe organ, they realized they had several obstacles. The building was old—too old to have running water inside. They would need to fill the pool with water hosed in from an outside spigot. But there was a second challenge to the pastor, who was still enthused but tuned in to the liturgical sensibilities of his congregation: "We need to cover these fish." They tried covering them with canvas. They tried surrounding the pool with potted plants. They tried moving the pool from one side of the sanctuary to another. But nothing they did improved the look of the wading pool or the way its pink fish fit, or didn't, in their setting. So they decided to use it as it was. Don would be baptized with the pink fish.

Readying Don was easier. They ordered a robe for him from a Christian church supplier. It was specially fitted with little lead weights in the hem so the robe would not float up during the moment of baptism.

Don and his pastor met together the afternoon of the Easter vigil. The pastor showed him the blue pool with the pink fish. That was fine. He told him the canvas cover wouldn't work; that was fine. He walked Don through the service elements, and that was fine too.

And then Don asked, "How exactly are we going to do this?" The man requesting immersion had never seen one.

His pastor explained, "I'm going to get in the pool with you and dip you down into the water." And that was not fine.

Don was alarmed, and his face showed it. "You're going to dip me?!"

The pastor, who *had* seen immersions, was startled by the question. "Well, yes. You said you wanted to be immersed. This is immersion."

Don was dazed. He was distraught. The real prospect of a very public humiliation was sweeping over him. "Oh, no," he said, sagging in distress. "Now everyone will know I have a hairpiece! What if it comes off?"

Seminary prepares church leaders for a lot of questions: How many natures does Christ have? What is the difference between supralapsarianism and infralapsarianism? How do you best outline a sermon? Graduates sometimes accuse their alma maters of providing answers to questions no one is asking or ever will ask. But no pastoral training covered Don's specific concern about hairpieces.

The pastor was taken aback by Don's sudden revelation and its implications. With New Jersey directness, he stated, "Don, you should have thought of that before now!" Then, his significant pastoral instincts recovering, he added, "OK, look. You asked to be immersed. So we can do one of two things. We can switch baptism methods and sprinkle you. Or I can try to hold you in a way that will keep your hairpiece on. I can't guarantee it will work. But I'll do my best."

That was good enough for Don.

So that evening, in the inaugural Easter vigil service of that Hoboken German Reformed church, they dunked a gay Jewish man in a blue wading pool with pink fish. Following long-standing church tradition, the pastor dunked him three times, in the name of the Father, and of the Son, and of the Holy Spirit. Though in a strategic face-saving move, they dunked him forward to improve the odds that his hairpiece—and dignity—would remain in place. They did.

"It's a miracle," the pastor reflected years later. He wasn't talking about his newfound expertise at keeping a hairpiece in place. "Each baptism. For some, baptism can be just a ceremony to follow. I have known many people for whom it is meaningless. In the lives of so many people it ends up a nonchalant, 'Oh, yeah, I was baptized.' But God really does something."

It's doubtful any of the earliest followers of Jesus had to worry about hairpieces at their baptisms. It's also unlikely any wore special clothing ordered from a church supply catalogue. The Ethiopian court official (Acts 8) was in his chariot traveling home, presumably with his bags packed. If he had clothes other than what he was wearing, you'd imagine they were in his laundry bag. Did the household of Lydia, that small-business owner the Bible describes as a clothier, wear any of the expensive purple garments she was known to sell (Acts 16)? Or in a sensible move, did Lydia decide such garments were too extravagant to get wet? And what about the three thousand baptized at Pentecost, a spontaneous event? It's hard to imagine them rushing home to get better or more appropriate baptismal clothing.

But relatively soon in the life of the church, wise leaders began to design baptismal litanies featuring the symbolic use of clothing. The clothes of baptism weren't the main feature, nor were they required. But inspired by Paul's words to "put on" Christ,[2] astute leaders designed clothing and an accompanying ritual specifically for those receiving baptism. Pushing Paul's metaphor forward, baptizands would literally put on white linen as a symbol that in their baptisms they had put on a new identity in Christ.

This link between baptismal identity and clothes was a favorite of early church leaders. Aphrahat, a fourth-century bishop called the "Persian Sage," wrote that Christians, on rising out of the bap-

---

2. Gal. 3:27, "All you who were baptized into Christ have clothed yourselves with Christ."

tismal pool, are clothed with what is for them a kind of wedding garment. Receiving baptism, he said, is a way of putting on the "garment of glory"—becoming a new person, taking on a new self: "Light has shone out, resplendent and beautiful, garments not made by [human] hands." Aphrahat also described baptism as putting on military armor: "Whoever has put on armor from the [baptismal] water, let him not take off his armor."[3]

John Chrysostom, archbishop of Constantinople around the same time, wrote to the recently baptized, "You have put off the burden of your sins and put on the shining robe." He employed this clothing imagery repeatedly, highlighting it as a way to accent the new reality baptism brings about:

> We put off the old garment, which has been made filthy with the abundance of our sins; we put on the new one, which is free from every stain. What am I saying? We put on Christ himself.
>
> Identifying with Christ, we are new creatures who have put on a "new and shining cloak, this royal robe" so that "a new creation has truly taken place."[4]

We know what it's like to "put on" an identity. When grade-schoolers play Wiffle ball in their front yard, they "put on" the batting stance from their favorite major league slugger or try the pitching motion of their favorite reliever. A budding preacher "puts on" the voice of her favorite mentor. A young basketball prodigy literally puts on the brand of shoes worn (and hawked) by his favorite all-star. Fans attend football games having put on their lucky jersey; a mayoral hopeful "puts on" the policies of her biggest donor; a Mississippi-born lawyer learns to put on the accent of his San Francisco clients. A child might "put on" the anger or angst or atheism or alcoholism of a parent or peer.

---

3. Aphrahat, *On Paschal Sacrifice* 6.6, in Everett Ferguson, *Baptism in the Early Church: History, Liturgy, and Theology in the First Five Centuries* (Grand Rapids: Eerdmans, 2009), 498.

4. Referring to 2 Cor. 5:17; Chrysostom, *Baptism Instructions* 5.18, in Ferguson, *Baptism in the Early Church*, 561.

Still today, in a pluralistic culture with a smorgasbord of spiritual options, this ancient practice of specific baptismal clothing, if not its full meaning, remains.[5] One Southern California pastor I know keeps baptismal robes ready in a church closet just in case someone spontaneously asks to be baptized. A search for "baptism clothing" online turns up baptismal gowns from everywhere from Nordstrom to Walmart to special Christian discounters. And whether people realize it or not, of course these baptismal clothes are symbolic. They represent the baptizand's new identity, received from Christ as a gift. They now are *in* Christ. And we know from our own experience that clothes are *always* symbolic.

On a baptism day or any day, we clothe ourselves with an identity. Intended or not, the apparel we put on sends a hundred signals about us; it is a kind of billboard message about our identity and character that people can read instantly and intuitively. Sociologists such as Julia Twigg study this built-in connection between clothing and identity. "Identity and dress are intimately linked," Twigg writes. "Clothes display, express and shape identity, imbuing it with a directly material reality." Attire shapes our identity as adolescents and adults, and even affects how we work through the effects of aging.[6]

We know it's true even before sociologists such as Twigg confirm it: clothing shapes our perception. In one quick glance we receive and read a hundred unspoken signals that instantly tell us if a person "fits" or not. Clothes can tell us a stranger must be a cowboy, a hipster, a nerd, a prostitute, or an aging hippie. Specific apparel that enables a person to belong in suburban Indiana might not work the

5. The verb form in Greek is *enduō*, used in the Gospels to mean "putting on" or "wearing" clothes or even "sinking into (clothing)" (https://www.biblestudytools.com/lexicons/greek/nas/enduo.html). John uses it in Revelation (Rev. 1:13; 15:6; 19:14), where he clearly intends the clothing to be a symbol of purity and righteousness.

6. Julia Twigg, "Clothing, Identity, and the Embodiment of Age," in *Aging and Identity: A Dialogue with Postmodernism*, ed. Jason Powell and Tony Gilbert (New York: Nova Science Publishers, 2009), https://www.researchgate.net/publication/326254641_Clothing_identity_and_the_embodiment_of_age.

same way in urban Newark. Fashion signals that say "I belong" in trendy Amsterdam might give a different message in Hoboken.

My friend Tim has an American father and a European mother. Today he looks like a model straight from a Nordstrom catalogue. Casual or classy, his attire suits him. He has a knack for dressing exactly right for every occasion. Once, he remembers, when he and his two brothers were in the intense throes of adolescent anxiety, the family traveled from Europe, where they were living, to America for an extended visit. Tim's mother prepared for the trip by buying new clothes for her fashion-savvy young sons—clothes she assured them were the latest in American fashion. They disembarked from their transatlantic flight wearing pleated plaid golf pants. They were instantly dismayed. The clothes they had put on sent all the wrong signals. In silent code their spanking-new fashion shrieked, "I don't belong here."

The American fashion scene for men in the 1980s had some very distinctive features, such as acid-wash jeans and pastel blazers over T-shirts. But plaid golf pants were not on that list. If only Tim's mom had heard of Air Jordans.

We all know Tim's sense of shame. How many of us have believed we purchased or assembled "the perfect outfit," only to walk into a dinner party, a new country, or a girlfriend's parents' country club and quickly realized our clothes were in fact a fashion disaster that screamed "I don't belong here"?

Historically, sociologists suggest, wardrobes have formed identities that separated people by social class. Style sorted people of the same city or neighborhood by economics. The rich elevated themselves by adopting fashions to show their elite status. By the time these fashion statements were available to or imitated by lower-income groups, the elite would have abandoned them for a new exclusive fashion. Clothing served as a way for the elite to create, keep, and increase influence and power. Clothes were put on to feed patterns of dominance and subordination.[7]

In the *New York Times*, journalist Rachel Swarns illustrated the way clothing can create new opportunities that lead to a new

7. Twigg, "Clothing, Identity, and the Embodiment of Age."

future identity by telling the story of Joseph Campbell. "He had admired the sleek suits, starched shirts, and gleaming cufflinks" of those passing by as he looked for work in Manhattan. People of purpose strolled all around him, "wearing pinstripes or herringbone, seersucker or linen," their wardrobe "signal[ing] success and prosperity," looking like people who want to "take care of some serious business."

But "he didn't have a suit hanging in the homeless shelter where he lives." No credit card allowed him to join those strolling confidently through Manhattan. So Campbell "arrived at a job placement agency . . . in a black T-shirt, green canvas shorts and Nike boots." But before his job interview that afternoon, his first in months, his case managers "told him he had one last appointment to keep."

They sent him to Suited for Work, where Campbell "felt as if he had stumbled into a new world. Brand-new suit jackets from designers like Calvin Klein, Perry Ellis and Michael Kors hung from the racks. A kaleidoscope of ties beckoned. Dress shirts sat neatly stacked on the shelves, their pearly buttons calling for nimble fingers." Campbell left for his interview wearing "a charcoal gray Michael Kors suit, a mauve dress shirt and a purple striped tie." Before leaving, "he adjusted his collar in front of the floor-length mirror and marveled at the transformation. . . . Asked how he felt, Mr. Campbell smiled: 'Like new.'"[8] It was a baptismal-like transformation.

In our youth-tilted culture, the connection between identity and clothing shifts endlessly. To use another sociological term, fashion is now "democratized." Clothing trends can start anywhere before going mainstream: in Boystown in Chicago, on the streets of Brooklyn or East Los Angeles, or in a rural family that owns a duck-call business. One college basketball team can singlehandedly make it desirable for an entire nation to shift to black athletic socks and shoes. Still, this thwarting of conventional

8. Rachel L. Swarns, "Nonprofits Provide Jobless Men with a Fitting for a Second Chance," *New York Times*, August 3, 2014, https://www.nytimes.com/2014/08/04/nyregion/a-fitting-for-a-second-chance.html.

class distinctions doesn't solve every fashion downside. A hoodie might be read as "I'm a dangerous person." Heels and hemlines can "objectify or limit women, locking them into defensive and inauthentic forms of presentation, and reinforcing their cultural association with narcissism and triviality."[9] When it comes to clothing, people often operate reflexively, viewing clothing as an indication of workplace ability, whether a person should be valued or discarded, and something that enhances or diminishes one's sense of self-worth.

In a world of steadily shifting fashion, clothing becomes one more identity management exercise. Our age of shopping malls (or thrift stores) insists that we create a unique and fetching version of our self. Even opting out of these unspoken demands is itself a statement of identity.

Our culture's fashion fluidity, say the people who study us, produces as much anxiety as pleasure or self-confidence, a fact many of us already know. Women especially feel pressure to choose the *correct* clothes, Twigg says. Anxiety rises because we know clothes are a set of markers that signal the boundaries of belonging or being excluded from a group. We might fear looking old, or overweight, or Republican, or Pentecostal, or like a preacher. (If someone said, "You dress like a preacher," how many of us would have our sense of identity affirmed?)

Our wardrobes send messages about who is in and who is out. Something as simple as a particular color sock, or a length (under the ankle, over the ankle, knee-highs, invisible), sends a hundred signals about your age, gender, and economic class.[10] And like my friend Tim, many know the shame that comes with not fitting in. Dress smart and be youthful and hip. Lose your hairpiece and be thought a fool.

To sense this deep, often unconscious link between our identity and our clothing choices, try wearing what feel like clearly "wrong" clothes for your own sense of self. Do that for a week,

9. Twigg, "Clothing, Identity, and the Embodiment of Age."
10. See the Twigg essay for an extended discussion of the sociology of clothing.

all the while saying with Martin Luther, "No worries, I am baptized!" Go to a Bears game at an overflowing Soldier Field wearing a Packers jersey. Or imagine late one evening donning a hoodie and walking through a predominantly upper-middle-class white neighborhood.

In many ways this link between clothing and identity is something we *feel*. We may feel shame, or our outsider status, or a fragile sense of inclusion. Ironically, "the increasing emphasis on individuality does not encourage us to create uniquely beautiful looks for ourselves" but instead puts us in a box.[11]

If fashion can stir anxiety and establish identity—an identity that can divide or unite groups, that can signal social status and value—what might it mean (*feel* like) to "put on" Christ? How might we "put on" the reality of our baptismal identity in a world that accepts or discards us according to whether we have the right T-shirt or shoes or purse?

Hudson Taylor wore his Christian identity literally. British by birth, his parents had from his youngest years trained him to be a missionary to China, even teaching him the language. "One day a Chinese man asked Taylor to explain why he had buttons on the back of his coat!" That day he saw clearly how "his Western style dress was distracting his listeners from his message." So from then on, breaking with the custom of most missionaries at the time, "he decided to dress like a Mandarin, a Chinese teacher. He was amazed at how dressing Chinese allowed him to travel more freely and be accepted more readily by the people. Taylor's goal was not to have the Chinese become like English Christians, but to have them become Chinese Christians."[12] He lived his baptismal

11. Twigg, "Clothing, Identity, and the Embodiment of Age," 4. Drawing on sociological and anthropological studies, Twigg also says clothing and identity can be studied in "semiotic terms," that is, clothing serves as a "linguistic code—a means whereby people send messages about themselves" (2).

12. Diane Severance, "Hudson Taylor's Heart for China's Millions," *Christianity.com*, May 3, 2010, https://www.christianity.com/church /church-history/timeline/1801-1900/hudson-taylors-heart-for-chinas -millions-11630493.html.

identity by learning the semiotics of Chinese fashion and adopting visual cues to make himself appear believable and understandable in his new context.

Is it too much to say that his baptism, his dying and rising with Christ, his deep identification with a gospel-formed identity enabled him to let go of his own culture to serve a greater good? His baptismal identity dictated his clothing selection!

Exploring this link between clothing and identity, we feel again the liberating gift of baptism. We experience again the wisdom of these ancient baptismal practices. Imagine a Germanic slave and a Roman aristocrat putting on the same baptismal clothes. Imagine a Jewish woman and an Ethiopian eunuch doing the same. Or picture an urban teen and an aged farmer, a Somali immigrant and a Google executive dressing *alike*. And radiating glory! The fourth-century bishop Gregory of Nyssa suggested that those being baptized "take off the old self, as a filthy garment," and "receive the garment of immortality [or incorruption] that Christ, having unfolded, holds out to you."[13]

Is it any wonder a robing ceremony was a treasured part of the baptismal event? Since the very beginning, with Adam and Eve in the garden of Eden, our connection to clothing has been deeply emotional, touching the core of how we see and express and focus ourselves. We see the wisdom and emotional impact of literally "putting on" Christ to symbolize our new identity.

Didymus (313–398), an Alexandrian teacher who prepared people for baptism, said most early Christian baptismal rites included these components: those desiring to join the congregation were "enrolled, catechized, exorcised, scrutinized and given sponsors. . . . Their sincerity of purpose was judged as they fasted, refrained from bathing, kept vigils, and gave alms. . . . When their baptismal day arrived, they were required formally and publicly to renounce Satan and to declare their allegiance to Christ. They were stripped, anointed over their whole bodies, and then"—like Don in Hoboken—"dunked three times in cold, fresh water as

13. Gregory of Nyssa, *Against Those Who Defer Baptism*, Patrologia Graeca 46.420C, in Ferguson, *Baptism in the Early Church*, 614.

they affirmed faith in the trinitarian God." As they emerged, all were given new white garments. Then the bishop, to confirm their baptism, anointed them (*chrism*) and washed their feet (yes, the bishop), and they celebrated communion.[14]

It's easy to imagine how this clothing exercise created an indelible memory, a profound and deepening sense of belonging and of sharing a kind of spiritual wardrobe as a way to symbolize the baptizands' new baptismal identity. Each act in the baptism ceremony served an identity-building purpose. "Recipients were corporally bathed and spiritually cleansed by the water. . . . Their initial nudity indicated their lack of shame" and a return to the purity of the garden of Eden. The white garments symbolized their new life as recipients of grace. "The scented chrism imparted the gift of the Holy Spirit. The lights they carried represented their newly enlightened minds and souls . . . now free from the stain of original sin. Gathering with their new siblings [in Jesus], they celebrated their new identity. They had become a people set apart."[15]

When leaving the baptismal pool, the baptizands likely dressed again in their own clothes. "But over them now were draped ceremonial vestments of white." Leading the procession into the church, "these newly initiated Christians must have felt very special indeed as they were anointed by the Father, clothed in Christ, and rinsed by the Spirit and showered with his gifts."[16]

These stories from the early church are not designed as a plea for people to wear specific clothes for their baptism. We've been asked countless times, "What should I wear to my baptism?" Our standard answer is, "Whatever makes you comfortable as you get wet." The results have been a startling variety of ensembles: Floral-patterned bathing suits. The board shorts favored by teens. One early retiree wore an elegant white linen caftan over her swimsuit. Of course, when less water is involved, the dress

14. Ferguson, *Baptism in the Early Church*, 467–70.

15. Robin M. Jensen, *Baptismal Imagery in Early Christianity: Ritual, Visual, and Theological Dimensions* (Grand Rapids: Baker, 2012), 3.

16. Garry Wills, *Font of Life: Ambrose, Augustine, and the Mystery of Baptism* (New York: Oxford University Press, 2012), 118. Hereafter, page references to this work will be placed in the text.

changes: it might be polo shirts or, in the case of one adolescent profoundly weak from cancer and unable to stand, a Christian-themed T-shirt.

But maybe it's worth rethinking the early church's baptism clothes. The point, of course, both with the apostle Paul's original statement and with the early church ceremony, was a spiritual fashion statement. As is true of the best dressers, regardless of style, the clothes of the early Christians reflected their true identity and not something they were pretending to be.

All the early church's baptismal practices were designed for the candidate to hear and learn the "mysteries of the faith"— renouncing the devil, exorcisms, profession of faith, anointing, making the sign of the cross, memorizing the Apostles' Creed and the Lord's Prayer—which, all together, are called *mystagogy* (150–51).

There were two basic approaches to the final training of new believers as they "put on" Christ. Some early church leaders, such as Ambrose and Cyril of Jerusalem, "put the principal instruction *after* baptism"—mystagogy as postexperiential catechesis (151 [emphasis added]). To be sure, candidates participated in a rigorous process of preparation that included Lenten fasts, examinations, and extensive personal instruction from the bishop himself. But sometimes we learn best retrospectively: "Remember what happened on Good Friday? Here's what was going on . . ."

Delaying instruction also allowed Ambrose to indulge his flair for the dramatic. He wanted God's astounding truth to be a wonderful revelation, so in his mystagogy he often repeats enthusiastically, "Look!" and "See!" He reveled in "the drama of a group undergoing a long tutelage together" (151).

But others, like Augustine, John Chrysostom, and Don's pastor in Hoboken, thought people should know *beforehand* what they were committing themselves to. So Augustine outlined and taught "competencies" for spiritual athletes-in-training as part of his Lenten sermons. Candidates under his care were to "fast, wear sackcloth, and not bathe (they would be given a session at the baths on Holy Thursday). When they underwent their *scrutamen* [examination], they removed the sackcloth and stood on a goatskin . . . as a renunciation of the goats who will be separated from the sheep in the last judgment." Augustine's approach was "less mystagogy than pedagogy" (152).

In some times and places the difference between postbaptismal and prebaptismal training was a practical consideration. Augustine was against delaying the sacrament simply to coincide with Easter, the customary day for celebrating the rite. Though he did often follow the tradition of Lenten instruction and Easter baptism, Augustine taught that we could celebrate Easter any day, and people ought to be baptized whenever they're ready (150–52).

These ancient teaching strategies became powerfully relevant again the day I conversed with five Navajo pastors. They told stories of the early missionaries trying to make young Navajos act like them, forcing children to wear white shirts and khaki pants and making them march to classes in their private Christian school. If the children spoke in their native language, the missionaries would wash their mouths with soap. It's no wonder one pastor whose children went to the mission schools said wistfully, "Somehow [they] turned against Christianity after they left."

These pastors were raised Augustinian-style. From an early age they learned the catechism's rudiments of faith and that such instruction was a prerequisite for baptism and a life of faith. Because many within their tribe believe that being a Christian means you're not really a "true Navajo," their evangelistic and discipleship strategy is to openly talk about all aspects of the faith from the beginning with adults and to train baptized children systematically. Among a people who have been repeatedly deceived and marginalized, even in the name of religion, they work to avoid anything that might appear secretive. So, rather than waiting to give further explanation after baptism (or any aspect of the Christian faith), they immediately reveal its meaning. The pastors are the spiritual descendants of John Calvin, who "called for a vigorous program of post-baptismal catechesis to rehearse the gospel promises signed and sealed in baptism. Those baptized, especially those baptized in infancy, had to be instructed in the faith." Baptism is to be a "cornerstone of the Christian life."[17]

17. John Witvliet, *Worship Seeking Understanding: Windows into Christian Practice* (Grand Rapids: Baker Academic, 2003), 159.

Our baptism summons us to grow up, to put aside the ill-fitting or vain or self-centered clothes of our own making and to "put on" Christ and his virtue. In the long run, whether we receive training before or after our baptism isn't the most important thing. The most important thing is that we get fully dressed in love. That was modeled so well by Don's pastor and his empathy for Don and his hairpiece.

This doesn't happen all at once.

A veteran pastor tells about a man in his congregation who overflowed with the qualities of baptismal grace. He was "an example of all things good and decent and helpful." People sought him out for his wisdom. He was known for his selfless love for the church. But he wasn't born that way.

No, for a long time he was a rascal, mischievous in mind and ability. He recalls, "I was always looking for trouble. And if the trouble were really bad, I'd look for it twice!" Everything changed one day when love walked into his life. He was used to mayhem. He was comfortable with chaos. He was a person of contagious disarray. "But then," he said, "I met Elizabeth—a kind, sweet, moral, smiling girl who loved me no matter how big a scoundrel I was. And little by little, because I wanted to live up to her love, I became less and less a scoundrel. Finally we married, and I've spent my whole life trying to make her as happy as she made me."

Everything changed the day he received a new vision for his life, one embodied in a person. "The truth is," he said, "Elizabeth loved me into loving."[18]

Atheist-turned-believer C. S. Lewis talks about a child who likes to play dress-up. He has a favorite box of clothes full of all sorts of interesting outfits. He can be a train engineer, a soldier, or a ballplayer. He can be a prince, a painter, or a pirate. The box is full of grown-up clothes. All are too big. The child is only pretending to be grown up. But someday he will be an adult. His pretending and preparing are steps along the way. In the same way, none of us "fit" into our baptismal clothes. Baptismal radiance is more often aspirational than a reflection of current reality. But the

18. Michael Brown, "Does Baptism Matter?" *Day1*, January 13, 2013, http://day1.org/4406-does_baptism_matter.

clothes point the way. They tell us who we are and who we one day shall become. The most bedraggled and unrepentant scoundrel can become by grace an embodiment of contagious virtue. We get clothed with Christ.[19]

Don was baptized that day. In a pool with pink fish. Wearing a baptismal robe and his hairpiece. But the main event wasn't that he looked smashing in his robe or that his hairpiece and dignity remained, but who he was becoming. He wasn't first of all Jewish. Or from Hoboken. Or snappily dressed. Or gay. None of those was his main identity. In the kiddie pool, he was clothed with Christ. And whatever other labels people give him, that clothing was a sign of his belonging. In his baptism he had "put on" Christ.

19. C. S. Lewis, *Mere Christianity* (New York: Macmillan, 1960), 161.

*three*

# Baptismal Abuse

# SEVEN

# *Identity Politics*

## Living as Citizens of Heaven (and Earth)

---

You are a chosen people, a royal priesthood, a holy nation, God's special possession, that you may declare the praises of him who called you out of darkness into his wonderful light.

—1 Peter 2:9

Here there is no Gentile or Jew, circumcised or uncircumcised, barbarian, Scythian, slave or free, but Christ is all, and is in all.

—Colossians 3:11

Christ is the true *patria*.

—Augustine

---

One of my friends was born in South Korea but now lives in California. One day he told me he considers himself a misfit. I was surprised. Each week after worship, after a service he helps to lead, he stands in the atrium bantering with friends or laughing with the high school students he helps teach. A misfit? I protested, pointing out his trendy phone, hip jeans, up-to-date cultural lingo, and many friends. He acknowledged his multicultural aptitude but explained, "In my native language I'm funnier. My jokes are better, my stories are more entertaining, and everyone 'gets' me."

"Still," I objected, "you fit."

He nodded but said, "All immigrants are 'misfits.'"

I found myself considering this again on the Fourth of July, when America celebrates its independence. Fireworks explode, children and military bands parade, and we retell favorite stories from the nation's founding. Canadians celebrate similarly on Canada Day, and the French on Bastille Day. Our nationality or ethnic identity seems profoundly fundamental to our individual identity. We are Canadian. We are French. Or we are Korean.

A philosopher might tell us that patriotism, our soulful sense of national identity and pride, is a recent phenomenon, and that our expanded city-states often have little bearing on actual cultures. And it's true that for many, their national identity is awkward and ill fitting (think of Canada's First Nation people or the Kurds in

Iraq). Still, many of us swell with pride when we see our country's flag or soccer team or military parade.

Once, while teaching a seminary class on spiritual disciplines, I illustrated memory's powerful role in identity formation by spontaneously starting to sing the Canadian national anthem. The class was held in the United States, but instantly the Canadian students, a minority, burst into song with me, swelling with an enthusiasm and pride that surprised even them. It was as if they levitated as they sang. Their identity as Canadians was lodged deep in their soul.

How might our national or cultural identity affect the way we experience and live our baptism? Or how might our baptism affect the way we experience our national or cultural or ethnic identity?

All through the Bible, God identifies himself as the God of all peoples. All nations come to him (Pss. 47:9; 72:17). Abram is renamed Abraham, the father of many nations (Gen. 17). While the Israelites are God's chosen people, their identity is not to promote ethnic pride or privilege but to represent and extend God's love for all peoples.

Each nation and people group has a place in God's geography. Contrast this with Homer's classic Greek tales, in which Ethiopians are "the stuff of mythology and tall tales . . . uniquely visited by the gods who join their banquets." They "live longer than others, avoid sickness [and] . . . thrive on exotic diets."[1] But the Bible treats them not as myth but as people loved by God, those who will one day bring him special offerings (Zeph. 3:9–10). Isaiah tells us that in God's amazing grace, at the end of time, when Jesus returns to make all wrongs right, nations and people won't lose their cultural identities. They will be redeemed, swept up into the new heaven and new earth (Isa. 66:18–19).

Included in Jesus's family tree are Ruth the Moabite and Rahab the Amorite. He talks extensively with a Samaritan woman. It's

1. Richard Bauckham references this in *Bible and Mission: Christian Witness in a Postmodern World* (Grand Rapids: Baker, 2005), 62.

no accident that we read about Philip explaining the gospel to an Ethiopian eunuch or that a Roman centurion professes, after Jesus's death, "Surely this man was the son of God!" (Mark 15:39). The Bible's multilayered affirmation of cultures in God's kingdom shapes the way we view and live out our own national citizenship and our identity as baptized people.

In the Bible, baptism doesn't nullify our cultural or national identity, but it does renew and redeem it in Christ. Paul tells the Colossians that in Christ they have put on a new self, that "there is no Gentile or Jew, circumcised or uncircumcised, barbarian, Scythian, slave or free, but Christ is all, and is in all" (Col. 3:11). The baptized will still be circumcised or uncircumcised. They will still be Greek or Jew. They may even be Scythian.

Scythian?

The ancient Greeks had a term for all non-Greeks: barbarians. But Scythians were the most barbaric of the barbarians. They were uncivilized savages. One ancient writer said they were "little better than wild animals." (It reminds me of some middle schoolers I once knew!) One commentator says Paul used the word "barbarian" to describe those from the south of Greece and "Scythian" to mean those from the north, along the Black Sea. Even Scythians can belong, Paul tells us. They, too, along with their language and culture and favorite beverages, can be swept up in the gospel story.

Baptism doesn't flatten or erase our national or cultural identity. The kingdom hope of the Bible is not to wipe out nations but to have them be fully alive, to enable each of us to experience the delight Lamin Sanneh described when the gospel came to his neighborhood: people "sensed in their hearts that Jesus did not mock their respect for the sacred nor their desire for an invincible Savior, so they beat their sacred drums for him until the stars skipped in the skies." Jesus helped Africans "to become renewed Africans, not remade Europeans."[2]

2. Lamin Sanneh, *Whose Religion Is Christianity? The Gospel beyond the West* (Grand Rapids: Eerdmans, 2003), 43.

Baptism reminds us that we—*with* our cultural experience and country of origin—are deeply included in this new community called the church. We are a new people. Together. All of us—no matter our birth country—are now part of a new race. Our culture isn't diminished, but our heart and soul are only at home in God. We are first of all citizens of heaven. To put it another way, in a balkanized world where politics or nationality or ethnicity demands to be our main identity, we are first the baptized. We belong primarily to the group Jesus calls out to become his church, the community that spans all times and all places, one that includes "misfits" from every continent.[3] The early church accented this with its baptismal rituals and by living into the multifaceted biblical images of church as family, a group of athletes or soldiers, a school of fish, a flock of sheep, or a new third race.[4]

A thousand voices call to us asking, even demanding, to be our first love. Each is a kind of siren song offering a beauty and a belonging it claims we cannot enjoy anywhere else. We are begged, cajoled, flattered, and then finally enslaved by these songs insisting that we be first of all consumers or employees or family members or Mets fans. Perhaps the most inviting of the enchanting voices is that of our ethnic or national identity.

For someone like me, a majority-culture male who grew up in the United States of America, this offered identity seems especially tempting. After all, our national stories proclaim, we are a city on a hill, a chosen nation, a people with "manifest destiny." After all, if we ask God in "America the Beautiful" to "shed his grace" on our nation, who are we to not shed some grace on her as well through robust love of country?

This political siren song, one that of late has mixed faith and love of country until they are indistinguishable, did not originate

3. Much of this section is adapted from Kevin Adams, "Scythian Worship? Nations and Cultures at Worship," *Reformed Worship* (blog), accessed April 30, 2021, https://www.reformedworship.org/blog/scythian-worship-nations-and-cultures-worship.
4. Robin M. Jensen, *Baptismal Imagery in Early Christianity: Ritual, Visual, and Theological Dimensions* (Grand Rapids: Baker, 2012), 54.

with the United States. Many countries see themselves as God's peculiar and favorite people. It began with ancient Rome—the same Rome who fed some Christians to lions and crucified others. The same Rome who called Christians atheists (asking, "Who follows a god they cannot see?") or cannibals ("You eat your savior's body?") and devalued their citizenry.

Powerful Roman emperors found it convenient to blame Christians for all sorts of societal ills and for Rome's diminishing glory. So, in a time when the masses needed "bread and circuses" to keep them satisfied and compliant, inventive ways of persecution were just the ticket. Toss Christians to the lions or beasts or gladiators—or simply torture them. But all that changed in AD 306 when Constantine (officially, Flavius Valerius Constantinus) was "acclaimed as emperor by his troops in York" and then officially appointed "deputy emperor of the West."

Successful as a general, he won a series of battles in Italy as he marched on Rome. He was a disciple of the sun god Sol Invictus (Apollo), and the afternoon before a crucial battle outside the walls of Rome he and his troops saw a lighted cross above the sun with the words *In hoc signo vinces* ("In this sign conquer"). That night in a dream, "Christ told him he should use the sign of the cross against his enemies." He woke with such conviction that he ordered his soldiers to mark their shields with the cross. After his commanding victory, Constantine credited his success to the "god of the Christians."[5] His predecessors had cruelly persecuted Christians. But in 313 Constantine's Edict of Milan declared that "no one whatsoever should be denied the opportunity to give his heart to the observance of the Christian religion."[6] His faith was "still imprecise, but few questioned its authenticity."[7] For the rest of his life Constantine aimed to be a loyal citizen of Rome *and* the

5. Richard Cavendish, "The Battle of the Milvian Bridge," *History To-day* 62, no. 10 (October 2012), https://www.historytoday.com/archive/battle-milvian-bridge. The story was first told by Eusebius of Caesarea, a Christian biblical scholar and historian who wrote the first biography of Constantine after the emperor's death.

6. Cavendish, "The Battle of the Milvian Bridge."

7. "Constantine: First Christian Emperor," *Christianity Today*, accessed

church. He appointed Christians to "high office and gave Christian priests the same privileges as pagan ones. . . . He also built magnificent churches, including [the original] Santa Sophia in his capital of Byzantium, renamed Constantinople." And in less than fifteen years, "the birthday of Sol Invictus on December 25th had become the birthday of Christ."[8]

Constantine also worked personally to sort out theological disputes that threatened church and state unity. He convened and presided over the Council of Nicaea, at which the church articulated the doctrine of the Trinity. "You are bishops whose jurisdiction is within the church," he said. "But I also am a bishop, ordained by God to oversee those outside the church."[9] At his death in 337, the Christian faith was "well on its way to being the state religion of the Roman Empire." Never lacking in confidence, he considered himself the thirteenth apostle of Jesus Christ,[10] a title even the most pious Christian leaders dare not presume.

Constantine did all this, living his dual church-state citizenship, without being baptized. Like many worldly men of his era, especially those with potentially compromising and unvirtuous job-related demands, he postponed baptism, believing "one could not be forgiven after baptism."[11] He had hoped to be baptized in the Jordan River, as Jesus was. But when he realized he was dying, he "requested the baptism right away, promising to live a more Christian life should he live through his illness."[12]

This intermingling of civic and Christian citizenship has taken many forms over the centuries. Charlemagne, who conquered much of Europe, expanded his kingdom "in the name of the Lord and mandated that his soldiers be baptized into the church. In several incidents, whole armies were plunged into a river so that

April 30, 2021, https://www.christianitytoday.com/history/people/rulers/constantine.html.

8. Cavendish, "The Battle of the Milvian Bridge."
9. "Constantine."
10. Cavendish, "The Battle of the Milvian Bridge."
11. "Constantine."
12. Joseph A. Dow, *Ancient Coins through the Bible* (Mustang, OK: Tate, 2011), 285.

they became God's servants before they went into battle." But
even during this unorthodox baptism, he "allowed his soldiers to
hold their sword out of the water so they were free to be as 'un-
Christian' with that hand (and sword) as they desired."[13]

King Olaf of Norway was one of many national leaders who
walked in Constantine's footprints. Olaf was at first a reluctant
convert to Christianity. It interfered with his pillaging. But once
converted, he demanded that his generals convert as well. Given
his propensity for violence, mayhem, and one-on-one combat,
his chieftains had little choice but to comply.[14] At various points,
rulers of England and France, Spain and Portugal, Germany and
Mexico considered themselves God's own favored rulers, confident that God himself gave them power to use for his cause.

But in the last centuries, few countries have conflated national
identity with Christian identity as habitually, publicly, or religiously as my homeland, the United States of America. It's true
that no president or governor has been audacious enough to em-
ploy the title "thirteenth apostle of Jesus" or "bishop for those outside the church," but it's also true that many ordinary Americans
assume they live in a Christian nation.

I experience this regularly while teaching an undergraduate
course in philosophy. The Christian university where I teach requires a course on worldview. We discuss a galaxy of subjects,
including economics and science, apologetics and pop culture,
and politics.

During the sessions on politics we consider the intersection of
faith and patriotism. Often I begin the session by asking, "Should
churches have an American flag in their sanctuary?" My tone is
neutral. Using the Socratic teaching style, I want to begin a discussion that allows participants to consider various viewpoints.
But often the discussion implodes immediately, and even raising
the issue is incendiary. I don't insist that any or all churches re-

13. Nick Honerkamp, "What Are You Holding Out of the Water?" *Nick
Honerkamp* (blog), March 6, 2017, http://nickhonerkamp.com/what-are
-you-holding-out-of-the-water/.
14. A more extensive account of Olaf appears in chapter 8.

- Identity Politics 125

move the national flag from their sanctuary. I simply want the class to consider what the flag's presence symbolizes. Each semester students protest, vociferously and pointedly. How can I suggest such a thing? How can we even consider such a thing? Several times I thought students might walk out or storm my very modest and unprotective podium. They cannot even entertain the idea; to them it's sacrilege. And they tell me so in the most forceful way they dare address a professor. I try to wonder with them if their baptism might take precedence over their patriotism. But many can't even discuss the idea civilly. The flag, through various and oft-repeated national liturgies, has become for them a powerful, electric, and deep-seated symbol of their identity. I wonder if they would react as strongly to the possibility of removing the baptismal font or communion table from a church sanctuary.

In 1967, sociologist Robert Bellah explained this conflating or blending of faith and national citizenship with a term he borrowed from Jean-Jacques Rousseau: "civil religion," defined by *Encyclopedia Brittanica* as a combination of "quasi-religious attitudes, beliefs, rituals, and symbols that tie members of a political community together."[15] Bellah wrote: "While some have argued that Christianity is the national faith, and others that church and synagogue celebrate only the generalized religion of 'the American Way of Life,' few have realized that there actually exists alongside of and rather clearly differentiated from the churches an elaborate and well-institutionalized civil religion in America."[16]

Bellah's fellow sociologist Dr. Stjepan Meštrović wrote, "Civil religion is neither bona fide religion nor ordinary patriotism, but a new alloy formed by blending religion with nationalism."[17] It mixes agreeable parts of the Christian faith and pious-sounding patriotism into a polished amalgam many Americans find alluring. Captivated, they participate with heartfelt devotion. Bellah

15. *Brittanica Concise Encyclopedia* (London: Encyclopaedia Brittanica, 2006).

16. Robert N. Bellah, "Civil Religion in America," *Daedalus* 96, no. 1 (Winter 1967): 1–21, http://www.robertbellah.com/articles_5.htm.

17. Stjepan Meštrović, *The Road from Paradise: Prospects for Democracy in Eastern Europe* (Lexington: University Press of Kentucky, 1993), 125.

uses John F. Kennedy's 1961 inaugural address as an example. Kennedy began:

> We observe today not a victory of party, but a celebration of freedom—symbolizing an end, as well as a beginning—signifying renewal, as well as change. For I have sworn before you and Almighty God the same solemn oath our forebears prescribed nearly a century and three quarters ago.
>
> The world is very different now. For man holds in his mortal hands the power to abolish all forms of human poverty and all forms of human life. And yet the same revolutionary beliefs for which our forebears fought are still at issue around the globe—the belief that the rights of man come not from the generosity of the state, but from the hand of God.[18]

Kennedy ended with this: "Finally, whether you are citizens of America or of the world, ask of us the same high standards of strength and sacrifice which we ask of you. With a good conscience our only sure reward, with history the final judge of our deeds, let us go forth to lead the land we love, asking His blessing and His help, but knowing that here on earth God's work must truly be our own."[19]

Bellah admits that identifying civil religion is "not a simple or obvious task and American students of religion would probably differ widely in their interpretation of these passages." But, he claims, it could be argued that "the passages I have quoted reveal the essentially irrelevant role of religion in the very secular society that is America." Religious references in the address "as well as more generally in public life" indicate that religion "has only a ceremonial significance."[20]

18. "Inaugural Address of John F. Kennedy," Avalon Project, Yale Law School, January 20, 1961, https://avalon.law.yale.edu/20th_century/kennedy.asp.

19. "Inaugural Address of John F. Kennedy."

20. Robert N. Bellah, "Heritage and Choice in American Religion," *Sociologica* 4, no. 3 (2010). Reprinted at http://www.robertbellah.com/articles_5.htm.

He suggests, "A cynical observer might even say that an American President has to mention God or risk losing votes." But the way "Kennedy made his reference reveals the essentially vestigial place of religion today. For he did not refer to any religion in particular. He did not refer to Jesus Christ, or to Moses or to the Christian church" but only to "the concept of God, a word that almost all Americans can accept but that means so many different things to so many different people that it is almost an empty sign."[21]

Kennedy, of course, was the first Roman Catholic elected president of the United States. But in using vague, nonoffensive religious terminology, he followed Dwight Eisenhower, the commander of the Allied forces in World War II and one of the most publicly religious presidents in US history. Eisenhower once declared, "I am the most intensely religious man I know," and on another occasion said, "Our form of government has no sense unless it is founded in a deeply felt religious faith, and I don't care what it is."[22] One might fairly wonder how those beliefs might connect to the central image of baptism as dying and rising.

As the Cold War intensified, "Christian leaders encouraged Americans to turn to God and away from secularism." Eisenhower "showed his commitment by joining the Presbyterian Church, in which his wife, Mamie, had been a longtime member, just weeks after taking office. He became the first"—and still the only—"president to be baptized while in office."[23] Eisenhower's "work to link faith and American identity has influenced political debate in the country for half a century since."[24]

---

21. Bellah, "Heritage and Choice in American Religion."

22. Dwight D. Eisenhower, "Address at the Freedoms Foundation, Waldorf-Astoria, New York City, New York," December 22, 1952.

23. "God in the White House," PBS, *American Experience*, accessed April 30, 2021, https://www.pbs.org/wgbh/americanexperience/features/godinamerica-white-house/.

24. William I. Hitchcock, "How Dwight Eisenhower Found God in the White House," History Channel, updated August 22, 2018, https://www.history.com/news/eisenhower-billy-graham-religion-in-god-we-trust.

If civil religion is one rival to living out baptismal identity, nationalism is another. Historian Ernest Renan offered a defining outline of nationalism in 1882. He described the "frequent confusion between the idea of nationhood and of racial or linguistic groupings," a confusion that doesn't seem any clearer now. Renan believed "a nation is a 'living soul, a spiritual principle' that binds people together by 'common consent' and shared 'memories' and shared forgetting."[25] The siren song of nationalism doesn't proclaim its plan to push baptismal identity to second place. It doesn't overtly announce a "cult of the nation," political scientist David Koyzis writes. Rather, imitating the Christian faith, nationalism offers "its own liturgical ceremonies, Te Deums, sacraments, icons, and feast days. Like YHWH, the God of Israel, the nation is a jealous god whose worshipers are likely to be intolerant of all dissenters, including adherents of rival religions. Nationalism is a bloody religion whose victims dwarf in number the casualties of the late medieval crusades. And as a rival 'religion,' nationalism 'represents a reaction against historic Christianity, against the universal mission of Christ; it re-enshrines the earlier tribal mission of a chosen people.'"[26]

Baptismal identity seeks to draw people together—even barbarians, Scythians, and seventh graders from rival schools—based on selfless love and humble service. By contrast, nationalism "drives [people] apart on the basis of pride and tribal selfishness." In that way, Koyzis writes, nationalism (or assertions of ethnic or racial superiority) is, at its core, idolatry: "Even if it were to lack such trappings as national anthems, holidays, parades, oaths of loyalty and the like, nationalism would still be religious insofar as it sees a nation as a transcendent reality infusing ultimate meaning into the rest of life."[27]

25. Carlton Hayes, *Essays on Nationalism* (New York: Macmillan, 1960), 100.

26. David T. Koyzis, *Political Visions & Illusions: A Survey & Christian Critique of Contemporary Ideologies*, 2nd ed. (Downers Grove, IL: InterVarsity Press, 2019), 98; interior quotation from Hayes, *Essays on Nationalism*, 100, 124.

27. Koyzis, *Political Visions & Illusions*, 98.

Nationalism leads to thinking like that of US president William McKinley. His was an era when many American Christians believed the nation was called to "usher in [God's] millennial kingdom and thus be a blessing to the rest of the world."[28] McKinley, after "several nights of anguished prayer to God" during the Spanish-American War, concluded "that the United States had a divine calling to annex the Philippines for the purpose of uplifting, civilizing, and Christianizing its population."[29] This logic seemed only natural, a living out of what John Winthrop, the first governor of Massachusetts Bay Colony, described as the "aspirations of his fellow Puritans to establish 'a Citty [*sic*] upon a hill,' which would be a shining example of a godly commonwealth to the rest of the nations."[30]

With that heritage, American believers have a "tendency to fall prey to the appeal of ideologies, despite their commitment in principle to the exclusive claims of the gospel. It is not surprising, therefore, that many believers have willingly embraced nationalism. Moreover, some have so closely tied their faith to nationalism that the two have become almost indistinguishable in their minds."[31] People who can see through the pretensions and false promises of the political party to which they don't belong often are unable to see the particular nationalism or hubris of their own.

Still, Koyzis reminds us, "Christians can hardly be faulted for wishing to correct their nations' deficiencies." What citizen doesn't want better schools or optimal health care or pothole-free roads or world-class universities or captivating museums and iconic sporting stadiums? But remembering and rehearsing our baptism can keep us from falsely applying biblical promises meant for the church to our country.[32]

28. Koyzis, *Political Visions & Illusions*, 121; based on A. J. Betzinger, *A History of American Political Thought* (New York: Harper & Row, 1972), 31.

29. Koyzis, *Political Visions & Illusions*, 121; based on G. J. A. O'Toole, *Spanish War: An American Epic 1898* (New York: Norton, 1984), 386.

30. Koyzis, *Political Visions & Illusions*, 121.

31. David T. Koyzis, *Political Visions & Illusions: A Survey & Christian Critique of Contemporary Ideologies*, 1st ed. (Downers Grove, IL: InterVarsity Press, 2003), 119.

32. Koyzis, *Political Visions & Illusions*, 1st ed., 117–19. I wish to acknowl-

Let's contrast baptized patriotism with the rivals of civil religion and nationalism. How can we have a healthy loyalty to and affection for our country (or ethnicity or state or neighborhood)? Is it possible to love our nation or neighborhood without unknowingly idolizing it? And if so, how? What strategies can we use to keep patriotism "in bounds," subordinate to our baptismal identity?

The tension in these questions is as old as Saint Augustine. Admired and loved by Protestant, Orthodox, and Roman Catholic theologians alike, he loved his home, the (eventually) faith-friendly Roman Empire. He wrote from inside it, three generations after its Constantinian conversion. In *The City of God*, Augustine writes, "a people is an assemblage of reasonable beings bound together by a common agreement as to the objects of their love."[33] Love, not law, he says, is what binds a society together; he wrote, "the soul takes on the character of what it loves" and "to see what a people is like, we should look at what they love."[34]

So how do Christian citizens join together to love their neighbors? How do we live our baptism *and* love our country? This may be less a problem to be once and forever solved and more a tension to be lived in every generation and geography. Perhaps we can best live the tension in our unique time and place by asking instead: How does the baptismal life enable us to live our truest selves as citizens?

We've already considered Augustine's example. He writes that every Christian, through baptism, lives in two cities—the city of human building and the truer city of God's own building. To put it another way, our baptism allows us to be authentic patriots, good

---

edge in this discussion of nationalism the long, regrettable history of "baptizing" conquered peoples in the name of Christendom, a reality we will explore in the next chapter.

33. Augustine, *City of God* 19.24.

34. John Doody, Kevin L. Hughes, and Kim Paffenroth, eds., *Augustine and Politics* (Lanham, MD: Lexington Books, 2005), 6; Augustine, *City of God* 19.24.

citizens of our earthbound country but all the while registering our first and primary heavenly citizenship.

As we explored in chapter 1, early Christians saw another example in the Old Testament story of Naaman, which they considered a baptismal text. A much-admired general in one of the world's most powerful militaries of his day (Syria), Naaman has everything going for him. He's rich, successful, popular with the king and the political establishment. And he has leprosy. In that context, the highly contagious, often visible disease was a devastating diagnosis that would separate him from family, vocation, and eventually life itself.

Following a servant's suggestions, Naaman visits Elisha, a humble Israelite prophet (2 Kings 5), who tells him he will be cured if he bathes seven times in the Jordan River. At first Naaman refuses. Rivers back home are pristine and inviting. This one is a foul, muddy mess. But when he reconsiders and bathes, he becomes clean. He gets his life back. He will still be a general. He will still have the trappings of the successful. And he will still report directly to the king, who doesn't share his faith. So he returns to Elisha, craving reassurance. Will the true God forgive him if even in this newly "baptized" state he bows with the king in his national temple? Yes, the prophet answers.

Simone Weil is another example of baptized citizenry. She was a French philosophy writer and political activist who struggled with many spiritual questions, including a long-standing personal question about whether she should be baptized. She slowly came to love Jesus, or more accurately, to believe she was deeply loved by him, but she viewed herself as a perpetual church outsider, destined (or called) to spend her days at the doorway of the church rather than fully inside.

Weil was suspicious of any social group—including the church and her country. Still, while living in the United States, she worshiped most Sundays at a Baptist church in Harlem, "where she was the only white person in the congregation"; she also attended Mass on the Upper West Side. Through her "deep Christian convictions" she saw "prideful expressions of national identity" as "spiritually offensive." Though "repelled" by what she called "a patriotism founded upon pride and pomp-and-glory," she saw how nations offered a kind of belonging, and she "considered a sense of rootedness to be a profound human necessity" and did not want to "live with the experience of alienation from the land of her birth." Before her untimely death at thirty-four, she wrote *The Need for Roots*, in which "she reflected on how best to cultivate a genuine sense of rootedness in her French identity."[35]

The unbaptized Weil suggested a baptized patriotism "inspired by compassion"—a patriotism that requires loving one's country as "something beautiful and precious" but also "imperfect, . . . very frail and liable to suffer misfortune," and "necessary to cherish and preserve."[36]

Just as helpful as Weil's insights are those of another young poet who spoke eloquently into the tension of loving her imperfect country without making it her highest love. Articulating a contagious conviction beyond her twenty-two years, the nation's first ever youth poet laureate spoke at the inauguration of President Joe Biden. On that clear, crisp Washington day, Amanda Gorman invited listeners to be honest about their country's shortfalls but to be hopeful about what it can become, to live the kind of hope willing to sacrifice in order to move a nation toward its unfinished work and aspirations. Gorman presented her poem "The Hill We Climb," which includes this passage:

> We will not march back to what was,
> but move to what shall be:
> A country that is bruised but whole,
> benevolent but bold,
> fierce and free.[37]

35. "Richard J. Mouw: It's Time for America to Embrace a Patriotism of Compassion," *Dallas Morning News*, October 4, 2020, https://www.dallasnews.com/opinion/commentary/2020/10/04/americans-need-a-patriotism-inspired-by-compassion/.

36. "Richard J. Mouw."

37. Amanda Gorman, "The Hill We Climb: The Amanda Gorman Poem

With her stirring poetry Gorman urged her listeners—those of her own nation and those eavesdropping from around the globe—to bring their best selves to the exercise of patriotic love. Leveraging her own spiritual (baptismal) freedom, she called us to live the same, to dodge the inertia and lethargy and cynicism brought on by decades of decadence and self-serving sin. Her verse spurred citizens everywhere to live their country's ideals. Echoing the wisdom of Weil and Augustine, she summoned national leaders and humble citizens to make their homeland better for everyone.

Her inspiring brand of baptized patriotism is no accident. This poem and its poet were shaped by a baptized community. Gorman's blend of hope and humility is the fruit of communal life at Saint Brigid Catholic Church of South Central Los Angeles, "an Afrocentric Catholic church . . . overseen by the Josephites . . . formed in 1871 to meet the needs of newly freed people after the Civil War."

She "grew up singing in the youth choir, taking her sacraments and reciting her poetry." Seeing Amanda in the inauguration spotlight, a fellow parishioner remembers Gorman's mother taking her twin daughters, Amanda and Gabrielle, to church "with the hope of exposing her children to a Catholic faith 'that was relevant to their identity as African American.'" The sisters "became part of the religious education program and stayed throughout their preparation for baptism, first Communion and confirmation."

Gorman's parish priest said the inaugural poem "was about 'democracy and unity,' and the importance of 'living in the country as one people, recognizing one another and respecting one another,' adding, 'That is the spirit of St. Brigid.'"[38]

---

That Stole the Inauguration Show," *Guardian*, January 20, 2021, https://www.theguardian.com/us-news/2021/jan/20/amanda-gorman-poem-biden-inauguration-transcript.

38. Alejandra Molina, "At Amanda Gorman's Black Catholic LA Parish, 'It's like Everybody Here Is a Freedom Fighter,'" *Religion News Service*,

My friend Richard Mouw has spent a lifetime studying and living faith in the public square. During World War I, he says, "a well-known Reformed pastor in the Midwest refused to allow the American flag to be displayed in his sanctuary. This caused such an uproar in his . . . community that he was physically attacked one night as he walked home from the church."[39] That sounds a lot like my university students. Apparently, even after a hundred years, emotions about national symbols still run hot.

Mouw understands this: "Christians need to work hard at keeping patriotic feelings within proper bounds. There is nothing wrong with my loving my country simply because it is my country—just as I love my parents, simply because they are my parents. But this does not put my country beyond criticism. To honor our nation in a godly manner is to want it to contribute to the cause of Christ's kingdom. To love our country with a Christian love is to want our nation to do justice and love mercy and walk in humility before the face of the Lord."[40]

He indicates the Navajo nation takes such a path: "The sense of tentativeness in the Navaho's commitment to the American nation, coupled with his genuine desire to participate in that nation, is instructive for the church."[41] Navajos contribute to the nation, seeking its good, but their first allegiance lies elsewhere.

Each of these examples reminds us that through baptism we are tied to fellow kingdom citizens who currently live under very different governments. Our baptismal bonds "transcend and override our commitments to governments and groups

---

January 28, 2021, https://religionnews.com/2021/01/28/at-amanda-gormans-black-catholic-l-a-parish-its-like-everybody-here-is-a-freedom-fighter/.

39. Richard Mouw, "The Danger of Alien Loyalties: Civic Symbols Present a Real Challenge to the Faithfulness of the Church's Worship," *Reformed Worship* 15 (March 1990), https://www.reformedworship.org/article/march-1990/danger-alien-loyalties-civic-symbols-present-real-challenge-faithfulness-churchs.

40. Mouw, "The Danger of Alien Loyalties."

41. Richard Mouw, *Political Evangelism* (Grand Rapids: Eerdmans, 1973), 48–49.

outside the church."[42] In the words of Augustine, Christ is the true fatherland.[43]

Built into our baptism is the reality that our earthly citizenship is, at best, a second-rate allegiance. As part of their baptism preparation, new converts were taught by John Chrysostom to consider themselves "strangers" in the world—participants for sure, but with one eye on their kingdom citizenship. He told them that "by their behavior they should demonstrate their loyalty to and citizenship of a different nation."[44] They should not consider their country their true home. Rather, they should live as a distinct race or people. Their true identity is "more boldly marked" by their "heavenly parentage" and their "birth from the womb of their spiritual mother"—a favorite baptismal image of the early church.[45]

Our last example is a gem of early Christian writing. It describes believers who withstand the siren call to be excessively enamored with their homeland. It embraces the "misfit" feeling my young Korean American friend feels every day. The author is unknown. The recipient, Diognetus, was curious about the Christian faith. At the time Christians were a tiny minority, but the church lived as a new people, a new nation, with a mission offering healing and hope. They lived as a "third race" (after Jews and gentiles). The letter offers a priceless picture of lived baptismal identity among second-century believers:

> They dwell in their own countries, but simply as sojourners. As citizens, they share in all things with others, and yet endure all things as if foreigners. Every foreign land is to them as their native country, and every land of their birth as a land of strangers. They marry, as do others; they beget children; but

42. Mouw, *Political Evangelism*, 49.

43. Augustine, *Confessions* 7.21.27.

44. John Chrysostom, *Catecheses ad illuminandos* 7.23 (Stavronikita 7), in Jensen, *Baptismal Imagery in Early Christianity*, 56.

45. Chrysostom, *Catecheses ad illuminandos* 7.23 (Stavronikita 7).

they do not destroy their offspring. They have a common table, but not a common bed. They are in the flesh, but they do not live after the flesh. They pass their days on earth, but they are citizens of heaven. They obey the prescribed laws, and at the same time surpass the laws by their lives. They love all . . . and are persecuted by all. . . . They are poor, yet make many rich; they are completely destitute, and yet they enjoy complete abundance. . . . They are reviled, and yet they bless. . . . When they do good they are punished as evildoers; undergoing punishment, they rejoice because they are brought to life.[46]

He might have summarized, "They are baptized."

---

46. Mathetes, "Epistle of Mathetes to Diognetus," in *Ante-Nicene Christian Library*, vol. 1 (1867), trans. Alexander Roberts and James Donaldson.

# EIGHT

# Forced Baptism

## Tales of the Unwilling

Peter replied, "Repent and be baptized, every one of you, in the name of Jesus Christ for the forgiveness of your sins. And you will receive the gift of the Holy Spirit. The promise is for you and your children and for all who are far off—for all whom the Lord our God will call." With many other words he warned them; and he pleaded with them, "Save yourselves from this corrupt generation." Those who accepted his message were baptized, and about three thousand were added to their number that day.

—Acts 2:38–41

Baptism, then, is about celebrating the incomparable gift we receive as creatures beloved of God. . . . Baptism is our call to the community of the church. . . . Baptism is a blessing, not a bludgeon. It is a sacrament, not a weapon of mass destruction.

—Kathleen Norris

Harvey grew up Baptist. Loose Baptist. A kind of unbaptized Baptist that never went to church. A church-dodging Baptist like him would never marry a churchgoing girl from a strict, churchgoing family. Especially one from a close-minded, tough-skinned, circle-the-wagons immigrant church cantankerous to their own kind, let alone an outsider. But, in a move stunning to his family and himself, he did.

Harvey and his wife, Micah, heard about the new, young pastor at her strict immigrant church. They couldn't bear the previous minister, but they thought they'd give this new one a try. And to their surprise, and to his, they found they could not only bear each other, they actually liked each other. So Harvey and Micah started attending church.

Their attendance didn't mean the blunt, demanding congregation had grown soft. The rookie clergyman recalls that most of his members would "rather shoot you than pray with you." Church insiders shared their homeland's language, strict conformity to tradition, and fierce arguments about the sort of clothing appropriate for Sunday services. They were unbending and difficult. The pastor remembers it was almost impossible for anyone who didn't speak the language of the motherland to fit in. The odds of an unconverted, Canadian-born Baptist entering their uptight family with its uptight theology and uptight practices seemed less than zero. Who would want to worship with this tough-minded band of immigrants? Still, something tugged on Harvey and Micah to join in.

In their conversations, the new pastor discovered Harvey's status as an unbaptized former Baptist. Soon after, they agreed that he and their two daughters, a four-year-old and an infant, would be baptized together. As the day approached, they developed a plan: Harvey would be baptized first; in strict adherence to church expectations, he would profess his faith. Then Harvey and Micah would together bring their daughters forward for baptism. It would be a kind of family baptism, a delight to all who knew them. Over the next months the couple met with their pastor and learned the basics of the faith, all becoming good friends along the way—Harvey and Micah, the two little girls, and the pastor.

Then came baptism day. Harvey was introverted—extremely so. It's no surprise, then, that standing in the front of church, exposed before God and all these interrelated, hyper-demanding, emotion-burying immigrants, he started sweating. Visibly. Profusely. Generously. Then this giant of a man started shaking. It became a spectacle: he and his wife and their two small daughters together before an overflowing sanctuary of unyielding immigrants.

Still, Harvey knelt and was baptized, water and sweat mingling on his skin and clothes and then on the floor. All the while, Micah held their infant daughter and the hand of four-year-old Devon. When Harvey's baptism was over, he stood, still shaking, and the pastor reached to receive Devon for her baptism. Over months of preparation, they had repeated conversations about this moment. First Daddy would get baptized, then Devon and Sissy. But at that moment, after watching sweat pour down her dad's face, Devon jumped back and screamed, "I don't want to be baptized! I don't want to be baptized!" And she escaped in a dash down the center aisle.

Many of these immigrant churchgoers were farmers. They could deftly corner a heifer or nimbly corral a runaway calf. But when that about-to-be-baptized girl ran down the aisle screaming, they froze in place, as if a giant bale of hay pinned them fast in the pews. Most had not seen an adult baptized in years, never mind a four-year-old. This was clearly outside their baptismal expectation and experience. So it was up to the rookie pastor, in his church suit and tie, to chase Devon down the aisle. She ran. And he ran.

A Baptist baptism-dodger's daughter and her determined baptizer. Finally, with the help of a woman who sprang up as Devon reached the back row, the pastor caught this second-generation baptism-dodger and carried her in his arms forward to the font. Devon cried through every part of her baptism—while running down the aisle, while being captured, and as the water touched her head. Still, the pastor baptized her, in the name of God the Father, God the Son, and God the Holy Spirit. And then Sissy, who remained held—tightly—in her mother's arms.[1]

I've never had to chase a baptizand down the church aisle, but once I came close. Our congregation began as a "nonnucleus" church plant. That's a way of saying my wife and thirteen-month-old son and I parachuted into an area without any sure congregants and began to gather a new church. For the first nine months we met in small groups. Then we started worshiping together on Sundays. To our great amazement and delight, people came. Eleven months after that first Sunday worship service, we celebrated our first baptism. Twenty-three people were baptized that day: A single professional woman raised agnostic who, when she stepped over the line to faith, warned, "OK, I'm a Christian now, but don't get weird with me!" A mom and her middle-school daughter. Several teenagers. Our own daughter.

One mom and her two boys had become regulars, key partners in beginning the new congregation, the kind of wonderful volunteers every new church depends on to start and survive. Like Harvey, she'd had some church connections as a child. But it had been decades since she attended a church. When a friend invited her to our fledgling congregation, she came, grew in faith, and became part of the church. On that amazing first baptism day, we baptized her. Then I was to baptize her two boys. When I reached for her oldest, about six years old, he expertly slid away, beyond my arm and the waters of baptism. He didn't run down the aisle, but you could see by the look in his eyes he was powerfully tempted. Thankfully, his mom—a bit less shaky than Harvey and more like the Canadian immigrant farmers who were experts at corralling

1. Author interview with Daniel Meeter, June 2014.

strays—nabbed him before he fully escaped. So I baptized him as he wriggled uncomfortably in the front of church, and after him, his kid brother. To this day it remains the most reluctant baptism at which I've ever officiated.

Even TV shows know about reluctant baptism. In an episode of *The Simpsons*, the long-running animated series, Homer Simpson's children Bart and Lisa appear to be suffering from neglect. As a result, they are sent to a foster home, ending up next door at the home of their neighbor Ned Flanders. Ned is a bit socially awkward; some might call him a doofus. He's an honest, well-intending, nonhypocritical evangelical Christian whose spiritual zeal sometimes goes too far. When Bart and Lisa move in, Ned discovers neither is baptized, so he decides to conduct an emergency rite. Alarmed, their parents, Homer and Marge, rush to the Springfield River to stop Ned. Just as Ned is about to pour holy water to baptize Bart, Homer shoves Bart over to prevent the water from hitting him. And of course, Homer is baptized mistakenly instead.

"Wow, Dad, you took a baptism for me!" said a startled Bart. "How do you feel?"

Homer, temporarily aglow from his unintended baptism, replies with heavenly-sounding vocabulary, "Oh, Bartholomew. I feel like Saint Augustine of Hippo after his conversion by Ambrose of Milan."

Neighbor Ned is stunned and asks, "Homer, what did you say?"

But the spiritual glow quickly recedes, and Homer returns to his normal self. "I said, shut your ugly face, Flanders!"[2]

Unwanted baptisms happen in real life too. A mom in our congregation began to explore the faith, hesitantly daring to attend because of the integrity and nonchalant joy of the neighbors with whom she shares a backyard. Years before, her mother-in-law had arranged for her children to be baptized without her permission

2. *The Simpsons*, season 7, episode 6, "Home Sweet Homediddly-Dum-Doodily," directed by Susie Dietter, written by Jon Vitti, original air date October 1, 1995, on Fox.

or knowledge. This grandma, who lives in the Midwest, schemed with her son to have his children baptized, against their mom's wishes, while she was out of town. The plan was to take the kids to San Francisco on a "weekend getaway," then sneak them into a church for a quickie ceremony. Mom discovered the plot, put an immediate stop to the unapproved baptism, and gave her chagrined husband a tutorial in marital expectations. Now, unexpectedly attending church because of her neighbors' kindness, she and her children and her now-estranged husband aren't at all sure what to think about church. Or baptism.

Two thousand years removed, New Testament baptism can sound tidy and pristine. It can seem particularly formal and religious. Participants' motives seem far less mixed than our own. Baptism episodes in the Bible are diverse, for sure: A high-ranking Ethiopian court official receives an impromptu baptism after a one-session, on-the-road Bible lesson from Philip. A small-business owner named Lydia is baptized with her entire household, as is a Philippian jailer who hours earlier was overseeing the incarceration of Paul and Barnabas. And on Pentecost, Peter concludes his talk to a huge gathering of spiritually curious listeners by saying, "the promise [of baptism] is for you and your children and for all who are far off" (Acts 2:39).

One wonders if a closer view of those baptisms would show a less orderly process, closer to the tangled mess we often experience. Did a four-year-old in Lydia's home, facing her own baptism, dash for the exits shouting, "I don't want to be baptized"? Might a teenage child of the jailer protest his baptism into a faith he likely knew nothing about but was about to join as a result of his father's near-death experience? Should we imagine a Bart Simpson–like smart remark: "Dad, I'm glad for your early morning conversion and rescue, but what about my right to choose here?"

Given what we know about the strong authoritarian role of the *pater familias* in the first century, likely not. Fathers had absolute sway over their families, and on a whim or because of an emotional fit, could arrange a child's marriage, sell a child into slavery, or put a child to death. They wouldn't expect or receive any resistance to any decision. Most things—jobs, household tasks, and marriages—were forced in such a culture. It's doubtful a child in such a world considered protest or imagined choosing one's own spiritual identity.

Even Billy Graham seemed susceptible to pressure to be baptized. Eventually he became a cross-denominational luminary, with doors around the world open to him. He spoke to millions of people in dozens of countries. He counseled United States presidents of both political parties. But early in his career such opportunities were rare. That's in part why Graham was baptized three times. The first time, he was an infant brought forward by his Presbyterian parents. The second time he was an adult, immersed by John Minder, dean of the Florida Bible Institute. His third and final baptism was officiated by Cecil Underwood, pastor of Peniel Baptist Church in East Palatka, Florida. His last baptism was done "mostly to satisfy the requirements of local Southern Baptist pastors who were sponsoring Graham's first revival meetings." Apparently even an evangelist needs to submit to a compulsory baptism.[3]

We usually think of baptism as a simple binary choice. Someone either wants to be baptized or doesn't want to be baptized. But life is more complicated than that. Sometimes, in a land of infinite choices, we don't even know what we want. Even for those who believe baptism should happen when a person reaches an age of discernment, the precise line of discernment gets murky. I have a friend who remembers walking down the aisle at her (first) wedding repeatedly thinking, as if singing a refrain, "This is a mistake." Her parents didn't arrange the marriage. Her siblings weren't pressuring her to tie the knot. Neither she nor her family was, like the young protagonist Rose, who faces an awful engagement in the movie *Titanic*, on the verge of financial ruin. She was simply unsettled in her own mind. Isn't life, and aren't our decisions, often like that?

How many people have thought something similar at a baptism they chose to receive? How many of those baptized in the

3. "Billy Graham (1918–2018)," Regular Baptist Ministries, February 21, 2018, https://www.garbc.org/ministry-highlights/billy-graham-1918-2018/.

past months or years appear to an honest pastor or churchgoer to be really sincere and to fully know what they are doing? How many people over the centuries were baptized under some influence, whether that influence is the loving concern of a spouse, emotional or financial pressure from a controlling grandparent, or a parent's expectation? And to what degree does such influence affect the viability of baptism? Theologians say a key to baptism is "receiving by faith." OK. But what quality of faith? What makes "true" faith—99 percent pure, 51 percent pure?

A few years ago on the Yahoo! Answers website, "Anonymous" posted a plea from a desperate teen titled "Youth Forced to Get Baptized by Parents." The post read, "I'm getting forced to get baptized, HELP PLEASE!??" And the teen filled in touching details: "I'm 15 years old and my mom is very religious and she told me 3 days ago that this sunday I'm getting baptized, and I don't want to. I tried reasoning with her and talking but she said no, you are getting baptized end of story. WHAT CAN I DO? I DON'T WANT TO BE BAPTIZED!"

The now-defunct website allowed anyone to answer peer-submitted questions about everything from how to change a flat on your bicycle to how to obtain discount wedding flowers to how to prepare sweet corn in the microwave. Responses to the teen's problem poured in from a variety of sources. "Dudley M," sounding alternately like a savvy, sympathetic teenager or a narcissistic life coach positing himself as a sage voice of experience, weighed in with a rambling, typo-laced, self-assured path forward. He began, "Ok . . . I am gonna assume you are in an oppresive 'REGIME' house hold . . . the bible is the law or supposedly." Then, wholly confident he had properly diagnosed the situation, he prescribed two main remedies. The first he titled simple "honesty": "With the honesty approach you simply explain to you family that you do not wish to participate with this and that should you be forcibly put into this you will fight in any and all fashions possible." He added, "PLEASE call you Preist/pastor or what ever you congregation has."

Next, savvy realist that he was, or maybe with firsthand experience of his own, he suggested a backup plan, one he advised to implement with caution: this strategy he called "Shock and Awe." Here's the plan: "Go into the church dressed in the most henious out fit you can find. . . . Die your hair with a temporary hair color" (he suggested "bright orange or red") and threaten to "stand up infront of every one and say that you are being forced into this by your parents and tht you have not been give the choice." Dudley explained: "Above all else in religion it can not be forced upon you . . . and in a babtism this is most definetly the case."

Later Dudley came to his most drastic and dramatic advice: "And if your mom still insit at the end . . . SHOW YOUR *** AT THE CHURCH . . . be quiet and calm all the way to the church. and as soon as you walk into the church yell loudly and proudly I DONT GIVE A DAM WHAT YOU WANT MOM I DONT WANT TO BE BABTIZED!!." But he advised his counselee to be out of arm's reach when he made this move, and that he should try other methods first.[4]

This fifteen-year-old's heartbreaking question and the responder's capricious, overreaching answers only accent our complicated pilgrimage through the murky world of involuntary baptism. In a culture that emphasizes personal choice, who isn't unsure or unsettled at times, too mixed up to be confident about every feeling or decision? People once fiercely determined to do something can change their minds. People reluctant to do something may later be happy that someone talked them into it—or out of it. The apostle Paul, who speaks so clearly and confidently about baptism's amazing promises, in the very next chapter describes his own inner tangle of motives and behavior: "I do not understand what I do. For what I want to do I do not do, but what I hate I do. . . . I have the desire to do what is good, but I cannot carry it out. For I do not do the good I want to do, but the evil I do not want to do—this I keep on doing" (Rom. 7:15, 18–19).

We, who live in a culture that prizes individual choice, want to celebrate our decision in all things, baptism included. Theologi-

4. Anonymous, "I'm Getting Forced to Get Baptized, HELP PLEASE!??" *Yahoo!answers*, Pregnancy & Parenting Board, 2011, https://answers.yahoo .com/question/index?qid=20080819232200AAsKHzF&guccounter=1.

cally, most Protestants believe baptism needs faith to "take." But just how important are human motives or certainty in baptism? How far does the impact or beauty or grace of baptism rest on one's own sincerity, or one's strength of faith? Baptism is tied to all sorts of things: the motives of people in authority (including parents), the expectations of those around us, and the captivating grace of God. Why, we might ask, must we leave this completely up to personal choice anyway?

William Buckley was born sixth in a family of ten children. He grew up in New York City in a family where faith was taken seriously. Lent, for example, was a time of reflection, even for the children. The piano was "locked on Good Friday," and he and his siblings "collected in their mother's room to talk about and reflect upon the Passion of our Lord."

His "eclectic childhood" included time in France, Venezuela, England, New York City, and then Sharon, Connecticut, where his father purchased a huge estate they named Great Elm. Some of the great house "was converted into a private school and tutors were hired to teach the children . . . everything from apologetics to piano woodcarving." Buckley "spoke fluent French and Spanish before mastering English."

For the entire family, "the Church was at the center of their lives." Bill and his young sister Patricia once "overheard their father and mother saying two sisters (and family friends) were fated to go to hell because they had not been baptized." When the women next visited, the children patiently "waited until the sisters took an afternoon nap and then sneaked into the guest room and baptized them with holy water." This became a pattern for the resourceful siblings. "Whenever non-Catholic guests stayed the night, Bill and Patricia would get up in the middle of the night and silently baptize the visitors." Eventually their mother learned of their clandestine baptisms and put a stop to it. But in their minds, they were saving souls.[5]

5. Lee Edwards, "Catholic Maverick: A Profile of William F. Buckley, Jr.," *Crisis*, February 1, 1995, http://www.crisismagazine.com/1995/catholic-maverick-a-profile-of-william-f-buckley-jr.

No one would consider these actual baptisms. But what makes a baptism authentic? Is it the faith of the one being baptized? Or the faith of the one baptizing?

Sherry Braithwaite's eight-year-old daughter came home from Bible school crying. Between sobs her daughter reported, "They made me take off all my clothes, put on a church robe, and they dunked me." Later Braithwaite and the mother of a ten-year-old boy also baptized without parental permission told local police. Soon the police chief made appointments to talk to the children involved.

The girl had boarded a church bus with three cousins to go to a new church for Bible school. The children—ages four, seven, eight, and twelve—were baptized by Rev. Lamar Breedlove, the church's pastor. Only the twelve-year-old came home pleased to participate. The younger children were distraught at having been told they must "disrobe and be put into the water to 'save their souls.'"

Braithwaite said, "They took away mine and my husband's rights to see my daughter baptized, and my daughter has no idea what baptism is all about; they didn't tell her anything." Her daughter felt uncomfortable undressing in front of other children. "It's one thing to come to my door and tell me about God, but don't do this to my child."

One church member, who helped the pastor begin the congregation, said the church has done more than 1,500 baptisms of adults and children since its founding: "According to the Bible, it says that people can be baptized immediately. We don't usually wait because they didn't do it that way in the Bible."

The ten-year-old boy had slept at a friend's house one Saturday night, and together they went to church the next morning. "He came home and said he was saved," his mom said, "but then he started crying and told me they wanted him to take off all of his clothes." Afterward, her son refused to go to his family's Episcopal church for several weeks. "He was baptized in our church as an infant," she said, asserting that the church isn't "saving souls [but] harvesting children."

A few days after the baptism, Breedlove and a church member came to her home and apologized. But how should a parent or an unwittingly baptized child think about this? Does the pastoral apology make the child "unbaptized"?[6]

In fact, what makes a baptism forced? Who has the proper authority to approve a baptism? Parents? *Both* parents? A king? An individual? Or a couple of enterprising children? What might seem charming coming from the Buckley children was not charming to those baptized by Reverend Breedlove.

Breedlove's unwanted baptisms were a clear misuse of his authority and trust. Regrettably, he's not the first to do this. Church history records many who abused their power to baptize people without their consent, even forcing baptisms at the point of a sword.

For instance, the warring Saxons hated Christianity. They "hated the foreign yoke of the Franks; they hated the tithe which was imposed on them for the support of the church" in distant Rome. "They looked at Christianity as the enemy of their wild liberty." Missionaries were unable to persuade them of the gospel. Their conversion came only by Charlemagne's threats. He was determined to "unite all German tribes in one great empire and one religion" and thought that anyone who was baptized—even against their will—would be transformed into Christians. Those who protested too much would be killed.[7]

In the cinematic farce *Nacho Libre*, Ignacio (played by Jack Black) lives and works as a cook in the Mexican monastery where he was reared. Motivated by his love for wrestling, he "dons a mask and a cape" and enters a local competition, hoping to win the two hundred dollar prize to "buy better food for the kids and

6. Charlene Hager-Van Dyke, "Parents Protest Unwanted Baptisms: Two Families Say a Lake Helen Church Baptized Their Children without Parental Permission," *Orlando Sentinel*, August 29, 1996.

7. Philip Schaff, "The Conversion of the Saxons. Charlemagne and Alcuin. The Heliand, and the Gospel-Harmony," in *History of the Christian Church*, vol. 4, *Mediaeval Christianity, A.D. 590–1073* (Oak Harbor, WA: Logos Research Systems, 1997), http://www.ccel.org/ccel/schaff/hcc4.i.ii.xxii.html.

achieve respect." Every wrestler needs a partner, so Ignacio picks
Steven, a scrawny, homeless man who steals tortilla chips left for
the orphans. Nacho believes lack of success in the wrestling arena
is due to Steven's lack of faith. Before an important match, Nacho
says to Steven, "I'm a little concerned right now about your salvation and stuff. How come you have not been baptized?"

"Because," Steven answers defiantly, "I never got around to
it, OK?"

Nacho weighs this, circling the room in his wrestling tights. All
the while Steven continues talking. "I don't know why you always
have to be judging me because I only believe in science."

Nacho is listening. But he has quietly filled a bowl with water
and approaches Steven from behind, replying, "Because tonight
we are going up against Satan's Cavemen. And I just thought it
would be a good idea if you . . ." His voice trails off as he forcefully
plunges his friend's head into the bowl while saying, "Praise the
Lord," in Spanish.[8]

Stories of forced baptism are plentiful, and most often not as
comic as the one portrayed in *Nacho Libre*. The list seems endless: Charlemagne's soldiers; European Jews wanting to keep their
livelihood or lives; Navajos wanting their next meal; a young, up-
and-coming evangelist wanting his new denomination's support;
children who wish to remain in their parents' will.

One of the most dramatic stories of forced baptism is the "be
a Christian or die" campaign of a person history calls a saint:
Olaf, whom we met briefly in the chapter on patriotism. When
it comes to forced baptism, few match the exploits of King Olaf
Trygvesson of Norway. A superb athlete as a young man, Olaf
turned his physical abilities to combat. He plundered the Netherlands and France, then England, Scotland, Ireland, and Wales,
leaving misery in his wake. "The young king drove a bloody
game," a poet wrote. "The Irish fled at Olaf's name, fled from a
young king seeking fame."[9]

8. *Nacho Libre* (2006), directed by Jared Hess, written by Jared Hess
and Jerusha Hess, featuring Jack Black.
9. James Reston Jr., *The Last Apocalypse: Europe at the Year 1000*

Even Olaf's baptism was violent, if not forced. After his own successful raids, Olaf allied with the Danish king Svein Forkbeard. Together they stormed England, torching small villages, "sparing neither the women nor children of tender age." As they waited to make a deal with the weak King Ethelred, who worked to purchase peace, Olaf waited off the British coast, weary and anxious. Hearing of a local hermit with the gift of prophecy, Olaf visited, and was so taken he asked about the odds of success.

"Thou wilt become a renowned king and do celebrated deeds," the hermit told him. But he also foresaw a mutiny among Olaf's crew. Olaf would be injured and "carried back to the ship on his oblong shield." But in a week, he would recover and be baptized. "Many men wilt thou bring to faith and baptism, and both to your own and others' good," the seer concluded (16–17).

The hermit was spot-on. After the mutiny and the recovery, Olaf asked the man about the origins of his gift. He told Olaf, "The God of the Christian has blessed me so that I can know all that I desire."

Olaf was immediately baptized.

Learning of Olaf's sudden conversion, King Ethelred planned a baptism party for him, including plenty of extravagant gifts, and Olaf then "promised never again to visit war upon England."

For Ethelred, baptism did what warriors and gold could not: get Olaf to stop pillaging his land. And for Olaf, baptism bestowed on him "a dignity and stature among kings that he had lacked" (17–18).

Sailing home as king, Olaf returned to Norway with a "holy mission." He was "a hybrid of Odysseus and Michael the Archangel, avenger, exile, and zealot all in one." In a national assembly he was "proclaimed the king of all Norway. One by one, the petty earls and chiefs of the country paid him homage" (24–25). Then the new king, in a style more heathen than baptismal, "gathered his relatives together and deputized them" as part of his holy mis-

---

A.D. (New York: Doubleday, 1998), 14–15. Hereafter, page references from this work will be given in parentheses in the text.

sion. "I shall make you great and mighty men for doing this work," he told them. "All Norway will be Christian or die" (30).

Some, compelled by his demand and sword, agreed to immediate baptism, but others resisted. To their great pain and regret, Olaf "treated the holdouts without mercy, killing some, mutilating others, and banishing the rest." Soon, between "his sword and his axe, he had claimed all of the [region] for Christ and dared anyone to claim otherwise" (30–31).

Through his "be baptized or die" strategy, "Christ's supreme hatchet man had conquered all of Norway for Christianity" (33), though its residents were not quite converted. Conversion, as historians and parents and pastors know, "is a slower process." But even in "Olaf's violent way, the process of conversion was begun."[10]

What about you? Was your baptism involuntary, compulsory, required, or even forced? Was it a choice?

Even those fully convinced in theory or by theology that baptism must always be a free choice, an adult believer's decision, can lose hold of their convictions, overwhelmed by zeal. Baptism carries such strong emotions that its proponents can be tempted to force compliance. Especially in the 1500s, it seemed difficult for those with power—parental, royal, or economic—to trust their children or subjects to be baptized according to their own beliefs.

Some followers of the Swiss reformer Ulrich Zwingli (historian Stephen Tomkins calls them "Zwingli's unwanted children,"[11] but they are better known as Anabaptists) took his ideas further, insisting on believer's baptism instead of infant baptism.[12] These long-suffering people of deep piety had to flee from authorities to live true to their faith. One Anabaptist leader, Michael Sattler,

10. James Reston, "Norway Part 1: 'Be Christian or Die,'" *Christian History* 63 (1999), https://www.christianhistoryinstitute.org/magazine/article /norway-part-1-be-christian-or-die/.

11. Stephen Tomkins, *A Short History of Christianity* (Oxford: Lion Hudson, 2005), 142.

12. Tomkins, *A Short History of Christianity*, 142–43.

"a former monk married . . . to a former nun, was arrested by imperial forces in the Black Forest in 1527 and tried for denying transubstantiation, infant baptism, and last rites, as well as for despising the Blessed Virgin and saying that it was wrong to fight the Turks."[13]

But they were not always the victims. Though Anabaptists were generally pacifists, a group led by Jan Matthijs "overthrew the government of the German city of Münster and in a bizarre inversion of Anabaptist ideals, forced the whole population to undergo baptism." The town became a haven for Anabaptists from all over Europe. "Leaders took all property into common ownership . . . and burnt all books but the Bible." They "instituted the death penalty for adultery, . . . and they ended up allowing polygamy and quickie divorces."[14]

The tangle of forced or enforced baptism may be a puzzle that needs an entire book to address. Who can redeem the violent disrespect for a people's right to own faith for themselves? Who can undo the trauma inflicted by forced baptism, a spiritual toxicity so damaging it poisons the faith of persons and families and nations for generations?

Baptism is supposed to bring healing.

While visiting the Monastery of the Holy Archangel Michael in New Mexico, I had vibrant conversations with a Pentecostal-turned-Orthodox couple of profound spiritual vitality. They had formerly been part of the Vineyard movement, which claims that the ongoing and electric healing of Jesus and his disciples is powerfully available now. Sent from Colorado to Baltic nations to convert those who were "Christians in name only," they returned a year later converted themselves. One was now an Orthodox priest.

When I asked how they came to believe in the healing power of baptism, they told me what I later learned was a favorite Orthodox story. Aresnios Eznepidis, a famous Orthodox theologian and monk, was a radio operator during the Greek Civil War of

---

13. Tomkins, *A Short History of Christianity*, 148.
14. Tomkins, *A Short History of Christianity*, 148.

the late 1940s. Over and over his radio broke down. And over and over, for the sake of those listening to coded messages essential for their well-being, he repaired it. Eznepidis compared our lives to a radio. Sin rips up all the radio wiring, and the radio no longer works. But baptism is a rewiring, a healing, so it functions again. We still have to use the radio—that is, we need to practice a life of faith, but baptism heals us so new life is possible. To withhold the radio, he said, would be to put people at risk, to withhold life itself. Just like people with disease need medicine, so people with sin need baptismal grace.

Natalia and Nicolas, the young couple at the monastery, explained, "If your child is sick, you don't wait until they're old enough to want the medicine to give it to them. You give it to them as soon as you can. Baptism heals the sickness of our soul. You give it to your kids as soon as you can. Just like—in a lesser sense—you teach them to brush their teeth or play baseball or practice piano and take French lessons, you give them baptism."

Who, they wondered, would want to withhold healing from their child—or anyone else? Or, we might ask, who would want to administer baptism in a way that is toxic?

Devon, the child who nearly escaped her baptism, had a profound change of heart immediately afterward. At the family celebration later that afternoon, and walking around her small town for weeks after, she would announce in her squeaky, four-year-old voice, "I am baptized!" It was a badge of honor, news she wanted to proclaim to everyone she met. So she enthusiastically informed the grocery store clerk, the bank teller, her preschool teacher, and a crossing guard, most of them not knowing the context or meaning of her words. They could only surmise that, like Martin Luther before her, baptism defined her very existence. And she was delighted to be baptized, from head to toe.

# NINE

# Widow Waters

## Unknown Hearts Baptizing Unknown Hearts

---

"Well, but the nations, who are strangers to all understanding of spiritual powers, ascribe to their idols the imbuing of waters with the self-same efficacy." (So they do,) but they cheat themselves with waters which are widowed.

—Tertullian

When Simon saw that the Spirit was given at the laying on of the apostles' hands, he offered them money and said, "Give me also this ability so that everyone on whom I lay my hands may receive the Holy Spirit." Peter answered: "May your money perish with you, because you thought you could buy the gift of God with money! You have no part or share in this ministry, because your heart is not right before God. Repent of this wickedness and pray to the Lord in the hope that he may forgive you for having such a thought in your heart."

—Acts 8:18–22

---

The epic film *There Will Be Blood* is, as they often say about movies, "loosely based" on a book, in this case Upton Sinclair's novel *Oil!* The main character, a miner-turned-oilman, pursues wealth with religious fervor during the Southern California oil boom of the early twentieth century. It's a story of greed versus ambition, family versus freedom, justice versus exploitation, and of abusive baptism.

All through the film, oilman Daniel Plainview (Daniel Day-Lewis) and Pastor Eli Sunday (Paul Dano) battle for power. In move after move, clash after clash, each tries to vanquish the other. Each is fueled by his desire. Each sets the other on edge. Each betrays, and each is betrayed. Each is aiming to be a god. "Eli believes God controls each oil well. Daniel is convinced the oil well makes him God."[1]

We see all this in Daniel's baptism. Viewers have already witnessed Pastor Eli slap "the 'devil' out of a woman, getting her to walk again." But this particular Sunday the pastor's lethal rival strides into his sanctuary. And, like a lion in his den, the pastor prowls, then pounces. Former liturgy is tossed aside. He has his rival in his claws.

1. Commentary on the movie comes from Patrick Kirkland, "Know Your Ending: There Will Be Blood," *TheScriptLab*, April 6, 2011, https://thescriptlab.com/features/screenwriting-101/script-tips-applied/1010-know-your-ending-there-will-be-blood/.

Eli longs to diminish Daniel, to control him. Daniel is in church—not to worship, not to meet God, not to satisfy his spiritual curiosity, but to expand his empire. An elusive property, a place for which he longs and lusts, an oil-rich field for which he will do anything, is about to become his, if only, his seller promises, Daniel offers himself to be baptized.

Knowing this, Pastor Eli circles his prey, humiliating the first-time attendee. Eli lunges at his chance. "Now, is there a sinner here looking for salvation? A new member? I'll ask it again: Is there a sinner looking for God?"[2]

"Again and again, Eli calls Daniel a sinner." Again and again he forces Daniel to repeat his word in response to his verbal thrashing.

"Daniel," Eli spouts, "are you a sinner?"

"Yes," Daniel responds.

"The Lord can't hear you! Say it to him louder. Go ahead and speak to him; it's all right."

"Yes!"

The shaming repeats in a savage liturgical refrain. Steadily, relentlessly Eli suffocates his victim, forcing Daniel to his knees. Fully in charge, in his own ecclesiastical lair, Eli commands, "Down on your knees and up to Him. Look up to the sky and say it!"

Back and forth they go, Eli summoning Daniel to echo his toxic baptismal liturgy. Emotion builds, their noxious combat intensifies, and still Eli eggs him on, pressing him further and further into humiliation. Catlike, he plays with his prey, making him repeat the incantation, demanding he repeat his pastoral abuse word for word as he veers from the baptismal liturgy to a lethal one he ad-libs, determined only to punish his quarry.

Finally, Eli shouts, "I abandoned my child. Speak to him and say it, sinner!"

---

2. For this and following dialogue, see *There Will Be Blood* (2007), written and directed by Paul Thomas Anderson, featuring Daniel Day-Lewis and Paul Dano.

Daniel responds without hesitating. There is no turning back now, "I abandoned my child. I abandoned my child." And then, through tears, "I abandoned my boy."

The promise of the one elusive property got Daniel into church. It was enough incentive to get him to yield, even to his opponent, even to be baptized. But maybe that's not how baptism is supposed to work.

Baptismal abuse comes in many forms. Sometimes, as with Eli, baptism is corrupted by clergy, the very ones called to administer grace, not animalistic abuse or narcissistic conceit or finely tuned manipulation or judgment. Otherwise their words are hollow. Baptism becomes what Tertullian called "widow water," empty of its design.[3]

In *The Preaching Life*, Barbara Brown Taylor describes being raised in "a contentedly secular" home. Her dad, a midwestern Roman Catholic, and her mom, a southern Methodist, together had almost nothing to do with church. A lone exception was the day they brought Barbara for infant baptism. But what happened so traumatized her parents that they avoided church the next seven years. Her mother said, "That priest took you out of my arms, going on and on about your sinfulness, my sinfulness, everybody's sinfulness, and I thought, 'This is all wrong.' You were the best thing I had ever done in my life, and I could not wait to get out of there."[4]

Taylor's family—and Taylor herself—were deprived of the grace of baptism. Their local priest didn't offer a winsome invitation to shape her identity, her young emerging self, by the reality of being profoundly loved by the Infinite One. He didn't highlight the life-sustaining themes of forgiveness and grace, the core of baptism since John immersed Jesus in the Jordan River. What he did was drive away two parents who had at least enough spiritual curiosity to bring their squirming infant to church. What he did

3. Tertullian, "Use Made of Water by the Heathen. Type of the Angel at the Pool of Bethsaida," in *On Baptism*, https://www.sacred-texts.com/chr/ecf/003/0030727.htm.

4. Barbara Brown Taylor, *The Preaching Life* (Lanham, MD: Rowman & Littlefield, 1993), 15.

was turn them away with his one-dimensional God. What he did was impose his and the church's overly serious piety in a way that bullied this young couple into years of staying safely away.

Many congregations and many church leaders offer a similar version of a life-flattening, soul-suffocating God. They present a God quick to condemn and slow to accept. They describe a God carefully and relentlessly searching for our faults, or one available to us only in the clutches of some self-promoting, manipulative, opportunistic, or overreaching minister.

Megachurch pastor Steve Furtick was already criticized for his expensive house and flamboyant style. Then news leaked that his congregation's mass "spontaneous baptisms" were not actually spontaneous. Named by *Outreach* magazine as one of the nation's fastest-growing churches, Elevation Church draws fourteen thousand attendees a week. "Part of that growth has been attributed to Elevation's flashy baptism ceremonies"—but the "supposedly spontaneous baptisms are carefully planned ahead of time."

Elevation strategically places church insiders throughout the building to be the first to respond to the pastor's invitation to "walk down the aisle." A detailed guide originally posted on the website for one of Furtick's books instructs these plants to rise at the offer to be baptized and to "move intentionally through the highest visibility areas and the longest walk." That's how the church "activated our faith to pull off our part in God's miracle." The guide further instructs that the baptisms are to be completed in just thirty to forty-five seconds: "Think of the (changing) room in terms of a NASCAR pit stop. It has to be quick in and quick out." The church also "provides everything a new convert could need to get ready for baptism, from dark-colored T-shirts and shorts in various sizes to sports bras, hair ties, deodorant, flip-flops and make-up remover. Cheering volunteers man the doors to usher the 'traffic' of new believers toward the front, and another set preps the converts for a dip in the baptismal pool."[5] Every detail is meticulously staged.

5. Sarah Pulliam Bailey, "Megachurch Pastor Steven Furtick's 'Spontaneous Baptisms' Not So Spontaneous," Religion News Service, Febru-

Rev. David Key, who teaches Southern Baptist studies at Emory University's Candler School of Theology, says Elevation's mass baptism service is like a show at Walt Disney World. "This church has obviously discovered what we in the industry call the 'Disney-fication' of religious services." And Tony Merida, preaching pastor at Imago Dei Church in Raleigh, North Carolina, and professor at Southeastern Baptist Theological Seminary, said this: "We have a history in a lot of revivalism and evangelicalism in that type of planning to get numbers," but added, "I can't imagine [the apostle] Peter saying, 'Hey, 15 of you get up and we'll see if 1,000 will join.'" He contrasted Elevation's assembly-line approach with something the apostle Paul wrote: "Rather, we have renounced secret and shameful ways; we do not use deception" (2 Cor. 4:2).[6]

Several years ago I interviewed a group of Navajo pastors to learn about baptism in their Native American context and congregations. As we talked over a leisurely lunch, one told us of the time he baptized a medicine woman. Every week for months, she and her son drove from Arizona to his congregation in Red Valley, New Mexico. They even studied the church's catechism to prepare for their baptism. So, the pastor told us, "When it was time for me to baptize them, I did." But not too long after that she went back to her old religion, and the pastor never saw her again.

Why did she want to be baptized? I asked. After some quiet consideration, he responded, "I think her son told her she had to be. And I think she did it just for him." Here was a faithful pastor who didn't seek to cajole or offer false incentive. Here was a pastor a thousand miles from prearranged "spontaneous" baptisms. This baptism wasn't in any way a NASCAR pit stop. He had provided the woman with historic baptismal training. Together they had studied the Bible. They had compared and contrasted her religion with Christianity. He had tutored her in the faith. But, he remem-

---

ary 24, 2014, https://religionnews.com/2014/02/24/megachurch-pastor-steven-furticks-spontaneous-baptisms-spontaneous/.

6. "How Elevation Church, Pastor Furtick Produce 'Spontaneous' Baptisms," WCNC, February 20, 2014, https://www.wcnc.com/article/news/investigations/i-team/how-elevation-church-pastor-furtick-produce-spontaneous-baptisms/275-292975851.

bers, "when I was sitting down with her, I knew that she was not very serious. And her son, he sounded phony to me."

So why did he baptize them? He first answered with thoughtful silence. Then he said, "You never really know. They wanted to be baptized, and so I did." Apparently not even a wise, experienced, and faithful pastor can know what's in a human heart. Neither can an apostle.

Some dreamy days we imagine that those in the times of the apostles had stronger and steadier faith. We imagine the early church having white-hot spirituality. But that mirage is romantic and naive, unlike the true biblical story. Already in the Acts of the Apostles there was baptism abuse. Soon after the first Pentecost, and immediately after Stephen's martyrdom, Philip travels to Samaria. There he meets every definition of ministry success: crowds gather, the sick are healed, the lame walk, and evil spirits are cast out. The crowds put their faith in Jesus. It's no wonder the author Luke sums it up like this: "So there was great joy in that city" (Acts 8:8).

But then Luke tells us about Simon. Simon is on a roll. He's a popular magician. His self-confidence is sure; his self-assessment is flattering. Comparing himself to everyone else he knew, he proclaimed himself "great." (He was indeed known as Simon Magna, or Simon the Great. He did tricks. He impressed men and women, rich and poor. Some considered him divine. Perhaps he even spoke about himself in the third person.)

Then Simon meets Philip. Seeing Philip's miracles, Simon knows he's outclassed. He knows he's in the presence of one greater than he. His first instinct is to join the fledgling group of believers. Luke tells us, "Simon himself believed and was baptized. And he followed Philip everywhere, astonished by the great signs and miracles he saw" (Acts 8:13).

Not much later the A-team arrives. Peter and John, the apostolic reinforcements, are called in to aid and expand Philip's ministry. When they lay hands on people, the Holy Spirit comes. Witnessing the supernatural made something click inside Simon.

When Simon saw that the Spirit was given at the laying on of the apostles' hands, he offered them money and said, "Give me also this ability so that everyone on whom I lay my hands may receive the Holy Spirit."

Peter answered: "May your money perish with you, because you thought you could buy the gift of God with money! You have no part or share in this ministry, because your heart is not right before God. Repent of this wickedness and pray to the Lord in the hope that he may forgive you for having such a thought in your heart. For I see that you are full of bitterness and captive to sin." (Acts 8:18–23)

What was happening? Is Simon's story like that of the Navajo medicine woman? Was he converted? Or was he simply and only on the take? The early church thought the latter. Tradition teaches that Simon went on to become the first heretic.

In a sermon on this beguiling passage, W. A. Criswell, for fifty years pastor of the historic First Baptist Church in Dallas, says, "You will be surprised how much and how greatly this man Simon plays in post-apostolic Christian literature. . . . He plays an unbelievably extensive part" and appears in a number of "fantastic fables." It's said that he was briefly a disciple of John the Baptist, that he "murdered a boy" and then used his spirit to predict the future, and that he once "boasted that he could turn himself and others into brute beasts" and "cause statues to speak." He is even said to have proclaimed, "I am the Word of God. I am the Comforter. I am the Almighty. I am all there is of God." He is viewed as "the heretic of all heretics."[7]

That sounds condemning. And yet Luke says, "Even Simon himself believed." Could it be that his believing was not genuine? Could it be that his faith was like what Jesus described in the parable of the sower? In Luke 8:13 he talks about four types of "soil," or people who hear the "seed" of the good news. About the second type he says: "Those on the rocky ground are the ones who receive the word with joy when they hear it, but they have no root. They

7. W. A. Criswell, "Simony in the Sanctuary," W. A. Criswell Sermon Library, August 14, 1977, https://wacriswell.com/sermons/1977/simony-in-the-sanctuary/.

believe for a while, but in the time of testing they fall away." Could it be that Simon has what the apostle James describes as "useless" faith (James 2:20, 26)?

Roman Catholic scholar Joseph Fitzmyer thinks Simon's misguided intentions might be based on the practice of buying priesthoods in the pagan world, which often went to the highest bidder. He also wonders if this was Luke's way "to interject apostolic authority into the whole mission to verify its authenticity." He suggests, "Luke's intent is also to make an argument that faith and baptism are not the only things necessary for salvation, but right conduct is essential too."[8]

Noted evangelical thinker John Stott puts it this way: "Simon's response to Peter's rebuke is not encouraging. He showed no sign of repentance. . . . What really concerned him was not that he might receive God's pardon, but only that he might escape God's judgment."[9]

What we do know is that Simon came to be associated with abuse in the church. His eponymous word, "simony," refers to all kinds of abuse, particularly buying positions in and favors from the church. Including baptism.

England's King Henry VIII ordered his advisors to justify his desired divorce from Catherine of Aragon—and from the Roman Catholic Church. Willing to use almost anything to bolster their (weak) legal case against Catherine and the church, they focused on church abuses. They reasoned that if they could "convince the English public that the church needed wholesale reform," they could win the popular approval Henry needed for separating himself and the country from the pope's authority "without provoking any sort of backlash."[10]

8. John W. Martens, "Simon Magus Tries to Buy the Holy Spirit," *America*, August 28, 2015, https://www.americamagazine.org/content/good-word/acts-apostles-online-commentary-24; Joseph Fitzmyer, *The Acts of the Apostles: A New Translation with Introduction and Commentary* (New Haven: Yale University Press, 1998), 401.

9. John R. W. Stott, *The Message of Acts: The Spirit, the Church, and the World* (Downers Grove, IL: InterVarsity Press, 1990), 132.

10. C. N. Trueman, "Church Abuses," History Learning Site, March 16,

In a victory for Henry's case, and eventually for his bank account, they pointed to the church's tawdry double standard. The church in England was wealthy and owned lots of land. Yet it still made ordinary people pay for rites they should receive freely, including baptisms. The fees were modest but still beyond what the poor could afford. The irony, of course, was that King Henry was pointing out this church abuse (simony) for his own gain.[11]

Every pastor has stories of baptismal abuse. One of my neighbors showed a keen interest in faith during the earliest days of our fledgling church. She attended membership classes, asked thoughtful questions, and got her infant and toddler baptized. Thirty years later I vividly remember the after-worship baptismal celebration at her house. There was laughter and celebration. Lots of picture taking preserved the moment. Free-flowing alcohol and fine food added sparkle. Then, as the afternoon waned, her brother-in-law said to her across the room, at a volume designed so everyone could hear, including her pastor, "You don't really believe all this, do you?" She seemed stunned at his public scoffing. Taking it in, she answered with a silence that couldn't be clearly interpreted. Was it agreement? Shame? A good front? After the baptism she returned to worship several more times, and then we never saw her again. In the neighborhood, yes. But never in church.

Rene LeBouvier didn't just drift away from church. He consciously decided to be unbaptized. He grew up in a small French village and was baptized in the local church. He attended regularly with his family as a child. His mother even imagined he'd become a priest. Church expectations were so all-encompassing, "you couldn't even get credit at the bakery if you didn't go to mass every Sunday."

But he doesn't believe in God anymore. He certainly doesn't believe in the church. The recent church scandals are "criminal,"

2015, https://www.historylearningsite.co.uk/tudor-england/church-abuses/.

11. Trueman, "Church Abuses."

he says. So, believing it "more honest to leave, . . . he wrote to his diocese and asked to be un-baptized."

"They sent me a copy of my records, and in the margins next to my name, they wrote that I had chosen to leave the church," he says. But it wasn't enough for him. He wanted to be untied completely and decided to take the church to court.

He's not alone. To date the "de-baptism" movement is small. But it's growing. Thousands in France, Belgium, and Germany are asking "to have their baptisms annulled."[12]

In the United States some have gone to an atheistic convention to be ceremonially unbaptized. A prominent atheist wielded a hair dryer he calls "Reason and Truth" and "symbolically dried up the offending waters that were sprinkled on their foreheads as young children."[13]

There's even a website where you can print (and they encourage you to frame) your own unbaptism certificate.[14]

Before 2018, if you were an Irish parent hoping to get your child registered for school, you wouldn't want the child to be un-baptized even if you were a skeptic or doubter or atheist. In a relic from the nation's religious past, a baptism certificate greatly increased a child's chance of getting into a local school. The parents may not have been religious. The child might not have been religious. It may be that none of them went to church or confession or recited the rosary, but if they wanted their child to be enrolled in the public school, they needed them baptized. Ninety percent of primary schools in Ireland had this "Catholic ethos" prioritizing enrollment of Catholic children over non-Catholics "in a crowded system."

12. Eleanor Beardsley, "Off the Record: A Quest for De-Baptism in France," NPR, *Weekend Edition Sunday*, January 29, 2012, https://www.npr.org/2012/01/29/146046428/on-the-record-a-quest-for-de-baptism-in-france.

13. Dan Harris, Eric Johnson, and Mary Flynn, "Atheists Break Out New Ritual Tool: The Blow-Dryer," ABC News, July 10, 2010, https://abcnews.go.com/Nightline/atheists-conduct-de-baptisms/story?id=11109379.

14. http://unbaptism.org/unbaptismorg.html.

Some parents found themselves driving "halfway across Ireland to baptize their children at their families' community parishes" to help their child get a spot. The so-called baptism barrier gave parents incentive to go through the motions of religious observance. During one prebaptism meeting, a priest asked one mother why she wanted to baptize her daughter, "noting that she and her husband weren't regular churchgoers."

"He prodded if we were doing it for school reasons," the mother said. "I pretty much lied through my teeth."

The Irish government changed the law in 2018. But at least one parent, a self-described atheist, resented being pressured to baptize her son. "If he chooses to be Catholic later in life," she said, "I would support him. But that has to be his decision." Another worried, "You can't unbaptize your child."[15] Or can you?

Several years ago a large cargo ship made port in Mobile, Alabama. Fresh from months at sea, the largely Algerian crew was eager for rest and relaxation. They were so eager that when a group invited them for free food and a place to relax, they gladly accepted, only to discover during the evening that the group expected them to accept the Christian faith as a condition of their meal. Not wanting to offend their hosts, they obliged and were baptized on the spot. But the next day they realized their baptism in the name of food and hospitality betrayed their Muslim faith and might put their families in danger. When their ship made port at their next stop in Corpus Christi, Texas, they immediately inquired upon docking, "How do we become 'unbaptized'?"[16]

Can you simply walk away? Is there a ceremony? Can you walk away from your baptism the same way you walk away from a university, or neighborhood, or marriage? Is baptism always permanent? Does it always "take"? Or is there only, after time, a sense that you were baptized in "widow waters"?

15. Kara Fox, "They Baptized Their Children for School Places. Now Regret Is Setting In," CNN, August 25, 2018, https://www.cnn.com/2018/08/25/europe/ireland-baptism-barrier-education-intl/index.html.

16. Author interview with Michelle DePooter, chaplain of Ministry to Seafarers (M2S), Montreal, Quebec, June 2014.

On the same New Mexico trip that I dined with my Navajo friends, I was a guest at the Monastery of the Holy Archangel Michael, where Eastern Orthodox monks gather each morning at 4 a.m. for several hours of prayer, offering intercession for both people they know and those they have just met, even a Protestant pastor.[17] I felt deeply honored when they invited me to join them for their noon meal. In their two-hundred-year-old adobe home, I felt marked hospitality—even more so after a monk asked me, "For dinner, would you like 'light or dark'?" I assumed he was talking about chicken, however unlikely it seemed, but seeing my confused expression, he clarified, "I meant for beer."

I was honored too, to take that private walk with Father Silouan. Along the way, as we stood near a stream that flowed along the trail, he teased me, offering to give me an Orthodox baptism then and there—to make me a real Christian. He meant it playfully. But then he became serious and added the belief we considered earlier. "Baptism is ontological," he said. "It changes our very being. We become new, different, restored people. We are put back together. We get healed."

I found him very convincing as we walked that red dirt path. I wanted to believe as confidently as he did. But I don't live day to day with monks. My neighbors, on a good day, are more like the Navajo medicine woman, and sometimes I wonder if I am too. My faith tradition, my Christian accent, is Reformed. On most days we'd be uncomfortable saying baptism is ontological, that it changes our very being. We are more comfortable using the language of covenant. Baptism, we Reformed folk like to say, is, like the Eucharist, a sign and a seal. But even then, can seals be broken? Undone? Can you simply walk away?

Theologian N. T. (Tom) Wright is one of the wisest people you could ever meet. I've seen him engage in conversations in large halls and in living rooms. Wherever he is, you get the sense he carries a whole seminary curriculum in his head and can draw on its treasures at a moment's notice. He calls these questions about baptism a "pastoral problem." He explains, "People who have

---

17. I first describe this visit in chapter 1.

been baptized can choose to reject the faith, just as the children of Israel could rebel against YHWH after having come through the Red Sea." But, he adds, "they can't get unbaptized: God will regard them as disobedient family members rather than outsiders."[18] No, you can never leave God.

What does that mean practically? What does it mean for those wooed to the front at Elevation Church and my baptized neighbors I haven't seen in twenty years and the Navajo medicine woman? "That," Wright says, "needs pastoral working out. . . . It's the kind of work that happens when you have to look people in the eye and pray with them and struggle with them about who they are and where they are."

Sometimes this problem leads people and pastors "only to baptize people who are absolutely sure of their faith." But don't we all know people who at one point in their lives were absolutely certain about their faith, only to find themselves struggling with doubt years or months later? One horrible moment can violently erode the most vibrant faith. For Rene LeBouvier, it took decades before he wanted to separate himself from the church. For others, it doesn't take nearly as long, whether or not they ever work to get themselves unbaptized.

What do we say in the face of people who want to use or abuse baptism? Some, like Simon and King Henry, have obviously corrupt motives. Others possibly have good intentions, like those feeding the Algerian sailors, but exercise those intentions in the worst way.

Historically, thoughtful churches and Christian leaders established elaborate and sometimes extensive prebaptismal preparations designed to sort the wheat from the chaff, the sincere from the disingenuous. Forty days of Lenten preparation followed by fifty days of follow-up might give those simply posing some pause.

18. N. T. Wright, "Space, Time, and Sacraments," lecture at Calvin College, January 6, 2007, in "N. T. Wright on Word and Sacraments: Baptism (Part 2 of 3)," *Reformed Worship* 90 (December 2008), https://www.re formedworship.org/issue/december-2008. The quotations from Wright from here to the end of the chapter come from this lecture.

In fact, some prebaptismal preparations expanded into a three-year curriculum. It's a practice any wise pastor or congregation may want to consider. Still, as the two-thousand-year history of the church shows, the motives of our heart are often secret, even to ourselves.

Wright "once heard a Roman Catholic cardinal say, 'The world is full of baptized non-Christians.'" We all know what he's talking about. Still, we also "have the testimony of people like Martin Luther saying that when all else fails and when the world seems dark and black, I have been baptized, and that is the chief anchor." We hold these two realities in tension, says Wright; the pastoral problem every church experiences. He says:

> I meet people who say to me, "Oh, I'm a Christian; I was baptized when I was a baby, and uh, got married in the church, and . . . I went to church a couple of Christmases ago but haven't been back since." In what sense are such persons Christians? They may think they are Christian because they are part of that culture. They are not agnostic or atheistic. Somewhere in there is a belief. Such people are probably a loose kind of deist, if truth be told—certainly not Muslim, nor Buddhist, nor Jewish. So they think they're Christian.

Paul, the church planter and pastor par excellence, also faced insincerity within the church. In 1 Corinthians 10, writes Wright, "he is addressing people who've been baptized, who are regular attendants of the Eucharist, and who may not have true faith." Maybe people in the Corinthian congregation, like ours, "drifted into the church because family or friends had done so." Maybe they were "hangers-on." Speaking with profound, Spirit-filled pastoral authority, Paul says, "Watch out, you're playing with fire." When we discard what is sacred, we "are courting disaster." He sounds like Peter speaking to Simon.

Some situations need gentle encouragement. Others, as the Bible shows, need stern confrontation. What is required is pastoral discernment among specific people in a specific community. "It's the kind of work that happens when you have to look people in the eye and pray with them and struggle with them about who they are and where they are," Wright says.

There is no magic formula to ensure sincerity. What's the difference between the Philippian jailer and Simon? Only time will tell. Sometimes the Daniel Plainviews of the world surprise you. They come to church halfhearted, to satisfy a spouse or a boss or out of vague guilt, only to be swept up in grace. That's what makes every baptism worth celebrating. For all of us, "It takes a lifetime to figure out what your baptism means."

Maybe the best we can do in a fallen world is to consider, with the New Mexican abbot and with Tom Wright, the nature of baptism itself and to trust its grace, no matter the human agents. In a world where baptism abuse is real, disorienting, and often painful, in a world of spiritually dishonest and insincere Simons, in a world where even the best of us abuse baptism unintentionally, we are gently and repeatedly invited into the mysterious and healing grace of God.

# TEN

# *Race*

## Failure and Faith

---

Do to us what you will, and we will still love you. . . . Put us in jail and we will go in with humble smiles on our faces, still loving you. Bomb our homes and threaten our children, and we will still love you. Send your propaganda agents around the country and make it appear that we are not fit morally, culturally, and otherwise for integration. And we will still love you. Send your hooded perpetrators of violence into our communities at the midnight hours, and drag us out on some wayside road and beat us and leave us half dead, and we will still love you. . . . One day we will win our freedom, but not only will we win freedom for ourselves, we will so appeal to your heart and con- science that we will win you in the process. And our victory will be a double victory.

—Martin Luther King Jr.

For we were all baptized by one Spirit so as to form one body—whether Jews or Gentiles, slave or free— and we were all given the one Spirit to drink.

—1 Corinthians 12:13

---

The white Anglican men who made up the Virginia General Assembly in 1667 had a problem—or so they believed. They had transplanted much of the culture and customs of their (and their parents') English homeland, simply implementing what was familiar in their new context. But what should they do about their slaves? In England, spiritual sisters and brothers could not enslave each other. Now, on a new continent, financial expediency prompted these settlers to change their minds, their theological convictions, and eventually their laws. They wanted to have it both ways, hoping to satisfy their Christian conscience by offering their slaves the gospel but satisfying their monetary hunger by keeping them enslaved. They had to decide, and decide they did, opting to shape their new state's laws to honor profit more than people, even if these new laws blatantly contradicted the Bible's clear teaching to honor people of every race.

Assembled together, these white men set a new direction for their families, their country, and their slaves. They determined that "the conferring of baptism does not alter the condition of the person as to his bondage or freedom."[1] This decision, and its corresponding new statute, was a marked departure from their English framework.

1. Jemar Tisby, *The Color of Compromise: The Truth about the American Church's Complicity in Racism* (Grand Rapids: Zondervan, 2019), 25.

So these Christian landowners allowed their slaves to hear the gospel, to sing the gospel, in some cases to preach the gospel, and even to be baptized in the name of the gospel. But they meant to keep these spiritual equals, these brothers and sisters in the faith, separate and enslaved. Rather than risk economic loss, they instead chose to risk the authenticity of their faith and that of generations after them.

Four decades later, in 1706, an Anglican mission agency sent missionary Francis Le Jau to South Carolina. His "sincere desire to convert" local people was evident from his journal entries. But he had inherited this new law and wanted to make sure there was no misunderstanding among his enslaved converts. Prior to their baptisms, he added a never-before-used question to the historic baptismal liturgy: "You declare in the presence of God and before his congregation that you do not ask for holy baptism out of any design to free yourself from the Duty and Obedience you owe to your master."[2] This is a sharp contrast to the almost universally used baptismal question of the second century and beyond: "Do you renounce Satan and all his ways?"

Though new to English settlers, the spirit of such laws was not new to the Christian faith. Already in the New Testament, racial favoritism took place between Jews and gentiles. In the fourteenth and fifteenth centuries, converted Jews (called *conversos*) and converted Spanish Moors (called *Moristos*) were treated wildly differently than fellow citizens with a pedigree of multigenerational faith. And European conquistadors brought a toxic brew of faith and racial superiority to the southern part of the Americas, making native converts second-class citizens in their own homeland. Now the Virginia Assembly and a missionary to South Carolina were making it official in North America.

When Benhi was baptized in his homeland of Namibia, the republic was structured by apartheid, an Afrikaans word meaning "apartness." For decades this policy administered affairs between white minority and nonwhite majority citizens, separating citi-

2. Tisby, *The Color of Compromise*, 38.

zens into four groups: Bantu (Black Africans), Coloured (those of mixed race), Asian (Indian and Pakistani), and White. Laws were instituted to create business and residential sections in urban areas for each race. Citizens were barred from living, operating businesses, or owning land in areas not designated for them. Soon the great majority of land was controlled by the White, mostly Christian, minority. Dozens of laws diminished life for non-White citizens. Apartheid laws required that non-Whites carry documents in restricted areas, outlawed most social contact between races, segregated public facilities, created separate educational standards, and denied non-Whites roles in the national government.

Benhi was baptized in his church. He was also baptized into apartheid. The Evangelical Lutheran Church in the Republic of Namibia required his parents to give him a "Christian" name. Lutheran theology teaches that all are equal because of Jesus's atoning work on the cross. This equality is symbolized in the sacrament of baptism. But for Benhi and his twelve siblings, their Christian identity came at the price of taking European names. Though his baptized name (James) and those of his siblings may have been based on names familiar to Bible readers, that did not make them inherently Christian. No, they were just names familiar to White colonists with European roots. Benhi's wife, Angela, writes, "God's gift of baptism [was] being controlled by a system that is unjust. People were forced to abandon their culture and language in the name of the very God who created them."[3]

Unfortunately, this is a story as universal as the Christian faith.

Thomas Merton was as famous as a Trappist monk could be. He wrote dozens of books, most after taking a vow of silence and entering the Abbey of Our Lady of Gethsemani in the late 1940s. His subjects included contemplation, spirituality, and social justice. His autobiography, *The Seven Storey Mountain* (1948), became a

3. Angela T. Khabeb, "Troubled Waters: Our Baptismal Identity," *Café*, August 6, 2018, https://www.boldcafe.org/troubled-waters-baptismal -identity/.

best seller, inspiring hundreds of men to join monasteries across the United States and others to seek his advice.

One advice seeker was a young Black priest from Alexandria, Louisiana. August Thompson visited Gethsemani, like so many, to spend time with Merton and seek wisdom. A short while after their visit, he wrote Merton for spiritual and practical direction. His bishop had disciplined him for "speaking out on the poor treatment of Black people in the Catholic Church." Blacks had to wait to receive the Eucharist until the Whites had already received it. White parishioners were paying drivers to take Black Catholics to another parish to worship rather than sharing their local church. Thompson was "prohibited from saying mass at White parishes," and "some White Catholics refused to call him 'Father.'" Life inside the church was as degrading as it was outside. Merton had offered spiritual direction to dozens of people inside and outside the monastery, providing biblical insight and spiritual wisdom. What, Thompson wondered, would Merton suggest in this situation, for both priest and parishioners?[4]

Willie James Jennings could answer Father Thompson based on Jennings's own study on the realities of race and the Christian faith. Jennings's "theological education began in the living room of his childhood home, where he learned the art of Christian discipline from his mother and an eclectic hospitality for multireligious and ecumenical ideas from his father." He remembers growing up with an acute sense of racial divide, of neighborhoods where he was welcome with his black skin and others where he was not. Many of the environs with the most distinct racial hostility were ones with serious, churchgoing homeowners. It's no wonder, then, that as a graduate student Jennings "fell in love" with the robust kind of theology that featured a broad, multidisciplinary perspective, one that helped him engage especially with the question that has "consistently troubled him: how to put

---

4. Sophfronia Scott, "I Want to Talk to Thomas Merton about Race," *Christian Century*, March 11, 2021, https://www.christiancentury.org/article/first-person/i-want-talk-thomas-merton-about-race.

together the ideas of Christian identity, Christian existence, and race." He reflects, "I couldn't understand how folks could be so serious about Christianity and so racist at the same time."[5]

In a compelling essay on race and baptism, Jennings points to the way Black bodies "presented a serious question" to White Christians.[6] It's been that way since the Virginia Assembly of 1667, and long before. Still, he says, "the emergence of racial identity" as we now experience it, especially in the United States, "could only have come about with the powerful conceptual support of Christianity" (284). Christians formed racism as we now know and experience it. Jennings writes, "The racial condition shows us a deformed doctrine of creation, what Dietrich Bonhoeffer would call an example of *sicut deus*, a false image of God at war with the *imago Dei*, the authentic image of God." This pervasive and often unconscious worldview, including the way it separates races, "has stolen from the Church its revolutionary power of belonging to Christ" (284). The White church's unawareness of its innate biases and its default love for homogenous faith "robbed the baptisms we perform of their message of death and rebirth into Jesus Christ" (286).

Baptism, says Jennings, echoing the early church fathers, is supposed to be an "event of disruption." What's supposed to happen is that the "newly baptized are set on a journey that will bind them to peoples they have not yet seen, to ways of life they have not known, and endow them with a holy desire to love other people different from the people who brought them to those waters." He adds, "A baptism that does not frighten us is a baptism invisible to us" (286), and "A church comfortable inside its boundaries—socioeconomic, educational, racial, special—is a church formed to

5. Leah Silvieus, "Confronting Whiteness in Theological Education: Q&A with Prof. Willie Jennings," Yale Divinity School, October 8, 2020, https://divinity.yale.edu/news/confronting-whiteness-theological-education-qa-prof-willie-jennings.

6. Willie James Jennings, "Being Baptized: Race," in *The Blackwell Companion to Christian Ethics*, ed. Stanley Hauerwas and Samuel Wells, 2nd ed. (Hoboken, NJ: Blackwell, 2011), 280. Hereafter, page references to this work will be placed in the text.

protect those boundaries at any cost. Such a church has forgotten its real baptism" (287).

In these convictions, Jennings stands in a long line of pastors, theologians, and Bible readers. The lineup of determined and sturdy-minded believers who hold this conviction about baptism begins with the apostle Paul, who warns that baptism is a "dying and rising," and with Peter, who describes the days of Noah's flood as a baptism in which only a few people "were saved through water, and this water symbolizes baptism that now saves you also" (1 Pet. 3:20–21). And it includes two fourth-century bishops. One, Cyril of Jerusalem, wrote, "You were plunged in the water and came forth, signifying Christ's burial for three days. By this action you died and you were born, and for you the saving water was at once a grave and the womb of a mother."[7] Another, Ambrose of Milan, declared, "In baptism you are, as it were, specially crucified with Christ."[8] And, "Your old man plunged into the font was crucified to sin, but rose again to God. . . . Whoever is baptized is baptized in the death of Christ."[9] The list also includes the late pastor John Timmer.

We met Timmer in the chapter on baptism as a script for life. Timmer, who shared Jennings's hometown, preached a sermon in which he appears to be coordinating his message with Jennings: "When you were baptized, you drowned to your old advantages. When you were baptized, you rose to the kind of life in which no one has advantage over another. When you were baptized, the whole business of privileged status went by the board. All racial, social, and sexual distinctions were deprived of their advantage."[10]

7. Cyril of Jerusalem, in Olivier Clement, *The Roots of Christian Mysticism: Texts from the Patristic Era with Commentary* (New York: New City Press, 1993), 105.

8. Ambrose, *On the Sacraments* 6.2.8, in Everett Ferguson, *Baptism in the Early Church: History, Liturgy, and Theology in the First Five Centuries* (Grand Rapids: Eerdmans, 2009), 643.

9. Ambrose, *On the Sacraments* 6.2.7, in Ferguson, *Baptism in the Early Church*, 643.

10. John Timmer, "Owning Up to Baptism," in *A Chorus of Witnesses:*

Timmer goes on to reorient his congregation to baptism's clout. In that rite we are all "drowned" to our "old, pagan way of life." As "new Christians [rise] from the baptismal waters their social relationships [rise] along with them." Being baptized "has profound *social* implications. It leads to a breakdown of racial, social and sexual barriers. It has a healing effect on all human relationships."[11]

Jennings and Timmer, Cyril and Ambrose, Peter and Paul: church leaders of different races and classes, from different religious backgrounds and generations, each with profoundly different experiences of race, all profoundly agreeing that baptism must change how the baptized treat people unlike themselves.

To further explore baptism and race, and to deepen our vision of God's intent, let's revisit the three major practices of the ancient baptismal liturgy surveyed in section 2: renunciation, anointing, and putting on our baptismal clothing. First, renunciation.

Jennings affirms the deep baptismal wisdom we explored in chapter 4, that renunciation is "part of the rite of baptism,"[12] and always needs to be. Anyone living a baptism alert to the gospel will renounce old, corrupt, and corrupting realities like racism that cause us to diminish, devalue, or disdain another human simply because of skin color.

Retired seminary president Martin Copenhaver reminds us that sometimes the news is so terrible that we want to turn our backs and shut it out. Another unarmed black man is shot in the back by a police officer who swore to serve and protect the citizens of her city. A person of color is accosted by a local homeowner because, he judges, the shiny bike she's riding doesn't seem to fit her skin tone. "Did you steal that?" he accuses. Another refugee parent has fled her tortured homeland to seek peace in a new country. She arrives at the border with her three malnourished, bedraggled children only to hear an officer say, "We have to put your children

*Model Sermons for Today's Preacher*, ed. Thomas G. Long and Cornelius Plantinga Jr. (Grand Rapids: Eerdmans, 1994), 282.

11. Timmer, "Owning Up to Baptism," 283.

12. Jennings, "Being Baptized," 288.

in a special detention center apart from you," but what this mother senses is a deeper, unspoken feeling that the officer (and the country) doesn't trust people like her to do what's right.

Some days we have the option to turn off the TV, set aside our phones, and avoid other screens. Some days we can try to reroute our attention away from violence and ruin. But on other days it's too close to home. We are the ones suffering the violence, the vandalism to the image of God we bear.

Over the millennia God has seen it all. But he doesn't change the channel. He doesn't move to the suburbs. Instead he renounces evil, and he calls us to the same.[13]

Consider the story of Noah. It's often recast as a children's story featuring a parade of animals walking two by two into the ark as a pleasant and well-groomed Noah looks on approvingly. But the early church read it as a baptism story showing God's clear renouncing of evil and calling all who are baptized to share in God's divine renunciation of our own sin and the sin of the world.

Sure, God ends this renunciation story with a covenant promise. While Noah and family "were still wobbling around on sea legs," God said, "I am establishing my covenant with you." He commits to stick with us "no matter what." But we know the other dark truth, one that appears in the biblical text soon after the flood account, that "when Noah and his family got on the ark, something was smuggled on board with them, tucked away in their hearts, and that is the seed of violence."[14] It's still in us, in our children, and in our world. We see it in the Anglican Christians of the 1667 Virginia Assembly; it is a violence that does mayhem to people of other races and to our own souls.

That's why every baptism needs to echo the story of Noah and the flood. The baptismal form of my childhood congregation assured this by reciting this story within a long framing of baptism designed to educate and remind congregants that we need God's

13. Martin B. Copenhaver, "Starting Over: Genesis 9:8–17; 1 Peter 3:18–22; Mark 1:9–15," *Christian Century*, February 21, 2006, https://www.christiancentury.org/article/2006-02/starting-over.

14. Copenhaver, "Starting Over."

cleansing. It never mentioned the word "renunciation," but that sturdy old liturgical form reminded us that we need to follow God's renunciation of all that is evil. A more recent and poignant way to phrase this truth is that "sin in all of its personal and social forms should be in the process of being asphyxiated in the baptismal waters."[15]

Abraham Kuyper is one of the theological icons of my childhood church, shaping my own Christian faith, John Timmer's, and that of millions of others. Kuyper was a genius who founded a newspaper, a university, and a political party. He became prime minister of the Netherlands. And he was a racist. His opinions on race and people groups led, in some way, to the rise of the apartheid into which Benhi was baptized.

In his 1898 lectures on Calvinism delivered at Princeton University, Kuyper outlines what would become one of his most captivating ideas: the notion of God's common grace, by which we see his glory in art and science, government and business, and the general goodness of people who are not his followers. But in the very same lectures he wonders how people from China, Mexico, or Peru contribute to human flourishing. He says his question "applies more strongly still to the life of the colored races on the coast and in the interior of Africa—a far lower form of existence."[16] The same captivating theologian who offers the electric notion of seeing God's glory "in all that's fair" cannot see what is "fair" in the treasures of various culture groups. Even worse, he seems to believe that abilities of humanity can be seen in their skin tone.[17] If you want to argue that his speech was typical for a late-nineteenth-century context and no longer guides the thinking

15. Andrew Wymer and Chris Baker, "Drowning in Dirty Water: A Baptismal Theology of Whiteness," *Worship* 90 ( July 2016): 335, https://www.academia.edu/29630768/Drowning_in_Dirty_Water_A_Baptismal_Theology_of_Whiteness.

16. Abraham Kuyper, "Calvinism as a Life System," in *Lectures on Calvinism* (Peabody, MA: Hendrickson, 2008), 22.

17. Daniel José Camacho, "Common Grace and Race," *Reformed Journal* (blog), January 10, 2015, https://reformedjournal.com/common-grace-and-race/.

of his adherents today, remind me to tell you sometime about the comment our church work team heard from a Dutch Canadian (Kuyperian) missionary serving in the Dominican Republic just ten years ago. Kuyper's biases live on.

Every baptized person needs to renounce old enemies like racism and its pernicious structures, even when it's tangled with other, helpful work. In each of us, in all of us, in seen and unseen social and economic structures, we renounce what is evil and foster what is good.

Thomas Merton seemed to have talked about racism in a way that was "enough for the leaders of the civil rights movement to mark him as an ally. . . . As the civil rights movement gained steam, Merton came to the table with credibility."[18]

Sophfronia Scott explains:

> One might doubt whether a cloistered White man who lived in Kentucky in the middle part of the last century would have anything useful to offer, but this particular monk knew that such a conversation is never about race alone. Talking about race means, among many things, sharing our fears and frustrations about our place in the world, about how people are treated, about a hope for better opportunities that never seem to materialize. In other words, it's about dignity, respect, a shared humanity, and ultimately our hearts and souls. Racism is not just about White people treating people of color badly; it is about how the repercussions of that treatment reverberate for everyone, to the detriment of us all.[19]

While teaching at St. Bonaventure's College in New York State, Merton met Catherine de Hueck, "who visited the school to speak about the conditions in Harlem and the community center she ran there, Friendship House." When he later visited her center, Merton was overwhelmed. He described what he experienced in his 1948 memoir *The Seven Storey Mountain*:

18. Scott, "I Want to Talk to Thomas Merton about Race."
19. Scott, "I Want to Talk to Thomas Merton about Race."

Here in this huge, dark, steaming slum, hundreds of thousands of Negroes are herded together like cattle, most of them with nothing to eat and nothing to do. All the senses and imagination and sensibilities and emotions and sorrows and desires and hopes and ideas of a race with vivid feelings and deep emotional reactions are forced in upon themselves, bound inward by an iron ring of frustration: the prejudice that hems them in with its four insurmountable walls. In this huge cauldron, inestimable natural gifts, wisdom, love, music, science, poetry are stamped down and left to boil with the dregs of an elementally corrupted nature, and thousands upon thousands of souls are destroyed by vice and misery and degradation, obliterated, wiped out, washed from the register of the living, dehumanized.[20]

Then in clear, explicit terms, Merton did renounce racism: "Harlem is there by way of a divine indictment against New York City and the people who live downtown and make their money downtown. The brothels of Harlem, and all its prostitution, and its dope-rings, and all the rest are the mirror of the polite divorces and the manifold cultured adulteries of Park Avenue: they are God's commentary on the whole of our society."[21]

Every baptism is a renunciation. And it's an anointing, a call to live as prophet, priest, and king. It's a summons to relate in the Spirit of the One whose story forever immortalized a good Samaritan (Luke 10), who healed ten lepers and noted the only thankful one was a despised minority (Luke 17), who redrew the boundaries of inclusion in his community, disregarding genetic bloodlines. Anyone can be a child of Abraham, John the Baptist says to those with false piety but racial pedigree: "Do not begin to say to yourselves, 'We have Abraham as our father.' For I tell you that out of these stones God can raise up children for Abraham" (Luke 3:8). The poor, bent woman of Luke 13 is a "daugh-

---

20. Thomas Merton, *The Seven Storey Mountain* (Boston: HMH Books, 1998), 378.

21. Merton, *The Seven Storey Mountain*, 378–79.

ter of Abraham" (Luke 13:16), just as rich Zacchaeus is a "son of Abraham" (Luke 19:9). And so are the lame man (Acts 3), the Ethiopian eunuch (Acts 8), and all those gentiles who respond to the gospel message declared by Paul and his companions. In the Gospel of Luke and in his Acts of the Apostles, "God's covenant people can be a blessing to the nations only by overcoming the walls of separation."[22]

Viewing race through the lens of the ancient baptismal liturgy, we see how to enact renunciation and live an anointed life. Baptism is our commissioning for a life of service, guided and shaped by the Holy Spirit. What can that mean? What does an anointed life look like?

Imagine Minneapolis police officer Derek Chauvin, when called to investigate a minor disturbance, intuitively seeing George Floyd through the lens of his baptism, someone made in the image of God. Imagine the first European settlers viewing the indigenous people of the Americas as people of equal giftedness and value. Imagine Abraham Kuyper delighting in the "common grace" contributions from the people of China and Peru and Namibia. Imagine the first Christian missionaries to the Navajo nation seeing their first converts as fellow baptized citizens of Christ's new kingdom rather than as inferior projects who needed to have the Native American ways trained out of them. Imagine Christians of every racial and cultural background seeing their fellows as one because of their baptism.

Gregory of Nyssa was seeing this way already in the late fourth century. He "spoke out against the oppressive institution of slavery in a way that none had before, . . . vilifying the institution as incompatible with Christianity."[23] In a homily on Ecclesiastes, thought to be the earliest antislavery writing of the early church

22. Mikeal C. Parsons, "All the Families of the Earth Shall Be Blessed," *Christian Reflection: Racism* (2010), Center for Christian Ethics at Baylor University, 4, https://www.baylor.edu/content/services/document .php/110994.pdf.

23. Kimberly Flint-Hamilton, "Gregory of Nyssa and the Culture of Oppression," *Christian Reflection: Racism* (2010), Center for Christian Ethics at Baylor University, 26.

fathers, Gregory urged Christians to take a clear stance against the institution. It was accepted in his day, tolerated by pagans and Christians alike. Gregory's own colleagues, the Cappadocian Fathers, argued that slavery was an "unfortunate" and unavoidable reality in this world of sin, or that it was a useful institution in a world where some humans were inferior to others. But Gregory vehemently disagreed. Slaves, like their masters, are created in the image of God, and the "practice of one human enslaving another is immoral in the eyes of God."[24] Gregory had a baptized imagination. Did Merton read Gregory?

Thomas Merton returned to the Friendship House again and again. In his volunteering he "looked after children, led prayer services, sorted through clothing donations," and "thought seriously of making Friendship House his own life's work."

Merton did, by the way, reply to Father Thompson's question about racism in the church. He "appealed to the priest's loving heart and not his indignant mind." He advised Thompson to reply to the bishop "with compassion," writing, "You have to take into account the absolute blindness and absolute self-righteousness of people who have been scooled [sic] by centuries of prejudice and injustice to see things their way and no other."[25]

Scott isn't satisfied with Merton's response. It feels weak and accommodating. Like the easy answers, we might say, of those who don't understand the radical nature of their baptism. She responds as if Merton were in the room with her, and they are talking together as old friends, able to speak with searching honesty and camaraderie:

To tell you the truth, Thomas, I would have taken this as a condescending word from an out-of-touch White monk. It sounds too much like the White moderates of the day. But I realize I need to be patient with the words in your response and understand that what you were trying to do for Thompson is what I need to do for myself. You wanted him to take care of his heart

24. Flint-Hamilton, "Gregory of Nyssa and the Culture of Oppression," 27.
25. Scott, "I Want to Talk to Thomas Merton about Race."

first. If he kept bashing himself against the stone wall of the bishop's blind racism, it would only lead to disillusionment and then anger and pain. But if he led with a loving heart, he could instead seep into the stone, like water trickling down a mountain, and eventually crack the mountain open from within, all without compromising his own emotional health. You sought to teach Thompson the essence of nonviolence.[26]

Baptismal identity is a gift, a grace we receive. But it's also a gift we put into action as called people in the often tangled and thorny work of life. We can hear Scott wrestling with what Merton's baptismal anointing means. He is offering spiritual and practical guidance to someone he barely knows within a broader cultural moment that forms the backdrop to what he says. Merton's words, though imperfect and time-bound, were enough to inspire one man who "carried one of Merton's books in his pocket when crossing the Edmund Pettus Bridge in Selma in 1965 and a Black woman who said she 'felt alienated by her church and religious community for her civil rights work in the 1960s' but that 'Merton got it when few others did.'" Black Panther leader Eldridge Cleaver said he would often "reread Merton's Harlem pages whenever he felt his resolve weakening. The passages helped him 'to become once more a rigid flame of indignation.'"[27]

Baptismal living always includes a renunciation, an anointing, and a "putting on." We wear our baptism in a way that makes us new—including the way we speak and think and rearrange our finances and value people in a racially charged world.

Jesus once told a puzzling story about a great ruler throwing a party for his son's wedding (Matt. 22:1–14). The original invitees were summoned but at the last minute made mundane and uninteresting excuses. One had pressing business; another had real estate issues. Perhaps their real concern was that there would be people of the "wrong sort" in attendance. If so, the infuriated king acted on their fear, expanding his guest list to include anyone

26. Scott, "I Want to Talk to Thomas Merton about Race."
27. Scott, "I Want to Talk to Thomas Merton about Race."

and everyone—"the bad as well as the good." His banquet now overflows. But Jesus's story pivots again, and the spotlight now shines on the single attendee without a new wedding robe. The king's servants quickly toss the offender outside "into the darkness, where there will weeping and gnashing of teeth." What can this mean?

Samuel Wells, vicar of St. Martin-in-the-Fields in London, admits the robe "has proved troubling to every generation of interpreters. Augustine saw it as love; Luther unsurprisingly derided those who saw it as anything other than faith; Calvin tweaked it to mean both faith and works." Now commentators consider culturally conditioned interpretations. But the early church, Wells says, knew exactly what this meant: "When they heard the word *robe*, they thought of one thing: the baptismal robe. Baptism meant not just a ceremony with words and water, but also a new social location and putting the rest of one's life in jeopardy in order to enjoy being at the wedding banquet. If you weren't prepared to take steps to show that being at that banquet meant everything to you, then you'd best not be there."[28]

We sometimes crow about "making a difference in the world." Our graduation talks, birthday celebrations, and funeral reminiscing focus on the difference people make. But, says Wells, baptism is the "definitive moment" when Christians allow God to make a difference in them. "The robe signifies baptism," he explains, and baptism "signifies not making a difference, but being made different, being remade, being reshaped in accordance with the difference made by Christ."[29] Going back to the unified theme from the long line of pastors, we can be certain that in baptism social privilege and hierarchy forever change.

In a 2019 sermon given near the ninetieth anniversary of Martin Luther King Jr.'s birth, the Right Reverend Robert C. Wright, bishop of Atlanta for the Episcopal Church, reminded congregants what those early Virginia politicians needed to hear. He

28. Samuel Wells, "Remade: Matthew 22:1–14," *Christian Century*, October 7, 2008, https://www.christiancentury.org/article/2008-10/remade.

29. Wells, "Remade."

called them to baptismal living. "We ought to practice now," he said, "how to be what we are. Family. What we are, and that is, family." He quoted Dr. King for inspiration, urging his listeners to move beyond "sentimentality" to "the hard work of today." Interpreting King, Wright said, "Justice is love. Overthrowing everything, that is not love." And that, he said, is an "understanding for the baptized."[30]

Wright recalled his very first conversation with Andrew Young, former mayor of Atlanta and ambassador to the United Nations. Surprised and delighted to have Young all to himself, Wright couldn't resist asking him about "the strategic plan." He had to know. He asked, "How did you accomplish it all? Montgomery and desegregation and civil rights, and what was it like to deal with the Kennedys? J. Edgar Hoover, and all of that?"

Young responded with an exasperated expletive before explaining "Plan? There was no plan. . . . It was love. Every day, we rose, we kissed our wives, and tried again. We ran experiments. We exercised a portion of faith we had, and walked in love."[31]

It takes all the baptismal courage and grace we can muster to walk in love.

My friend Jonathan is the executive pastor of a large, thriving congregation. Whenever he describes the way their love works for the good of their neighbors, I am amazed. Long- and short-term programs abound—ministering to folks with developmental challenges and to people experiencing homelessness, for example, by providing long-term care or simply providing food or clothing. That might not be surprising for a church named Evergreen. But it might be more surprising if you knew the name of the congregation when it started in 1925: the Japanese Baptist Church of Los Angeles.

Seventy-three days after the attack on Pearl Harbor, President Franklin Roosevelt signed Executive Order 9066. It authorized

---

30. Robert C. Wright, "Martin Luther King Jr's 90th Birthday," sermon at Christ Church Grosse Pointe Episcopal Church, Jan. 20, 2019, https:// www.christchurchgp.org/worship-music/sermons/martin-luther-king-jrs -90th-birthday.
31. Wright, "Martin Luther King Jr's 90th Birthday."

the evacuation of Japanese Americans from Pacific Coast states. Soon more than 120,000 Japanese American men, women, and children—many of whom were US citizens—were removed from their homes, allowed to take only what they could carry, leaving behind homes, friends, businesses, and churches, to live in "relocation centers guarded by armed troops and surrounded by barbed wire fences."[32] In a matter of weeks, Japanese Baptist Church was closed, and remained that way throughout World War II.

Earl Warren was in a position to do something about this dreadful order. Warren was then attorney general of California and a regular attender of First Baptist Church of Oakland. Warren did act—by pressing for quick compliance with the order. Warren "acted in an unconscionable manner, apparently foreseeing that if he gained local popularity by inflammatory acts against the Japanese he stood a good chance of being elected governor later on."[33] He acted in the spirit of the Virginian lawmakers, putting his personal ambition above the welfare of his fellow citizens, including many fellow Christians.

Warren did become governor of California. He later became chief justice of the Supreme Court of the United States. He lived to regret his actions, writing in his memoirs, "I have since deeply regretted the removal order. Whenever I thought of the innocent children who were torn from home, school friends, and congenial surrounding, I was conscience stricken."[34] Warren later "became a stalwart defender of individual freedoms, a crusader for social justice."[35] But what about his moment of truth?

Defining moments—specific times we need to make critical, life-altering decisions— seldom come with second chances. But

32. National Park Service, "Japanese American Memorial to Patriotism during World War II," last updated May 6, 2021, https://www.nps.gov /places/japanese-american-memorial-to-patriotism-during-world-war-ii .htm.

33. James A. Michener, introduction to *Years of Infamy: The Untold Story of America's Concentration Camps*, by Michi Weglyn (New York: Morrow, 1976), 30.

34. *The Memoirs of Earl Warren* (Garden City, NY: Doubleday, 1977), 149.

35. Michener, introduction to *Years of Infamy*, 31.

what if Warren had stood up for justice? What if he had stood up for his Christian principles? What if he had lived his baptism, renouncing evil, living as someone called and anointed, someone who is always putting on the clothes of justice and righteousness?

We will never know, of course. But we do get to consider how we will live *our* baptism.

*four*

# BAPTISMAL HOPE

# ELEVEN

# *Healing Waters*

## Parkinson's and Other Unholy Ailments

---

He saved us, not because of righteous things we had done, but because of his mercy. He saved us through the washing of rebirth and renewal by the Holy Spirit.

—Titus 3:5

The Holy Spirit renovates us in baptism, and in union with the Father and the Son, brings us back from a state of deformity to our pristine beauty and so fills us with his grace that we can no longer make room for anything that is unworthy of our love.

—Ephraem of Syria

Give to [the baptismal water] the grace of redemption, the blessing of Jordan. Make it a fountain of incorruption, a gift of sanctification, a remission of sins, a healing of sicknesses, a destroyer of demons.

—Orthodox baptism liturgy

---

It started so small. My right thumb was shaking. Involuntarily. Repeatedly. Regularly. It didn't seem like a big deal. And there was a good explanation. It had been months since my last vacation, and my next one was only days away. Besides, I was spending a lot of time on the computer, working steadily—even evenings and weekends—to finish a book project. My posture was subpar. My workstation was overdue for an ergonomic adjustment. I was a little hunched over my laptop.

So I bought an ergonomically improved desk. I sent in my manuscript. I went on vacation. And my thumb still shook. My whole hand, once in a while. While kayaking, my leg shook too. That was strange.

Someone I love told me I should visit a doctor. It wasn't the first time she had suggested this. Or the second. But now I was curious enough to go. It was a late-afternoon appointment, and my regular doctor had left for the day, so I got a pinch hitter. An after-hours emergency drop-in specialist. After some doctor-patient banter, he reviewed my symptoms, listened to my self-diagnosis, and checked my reflexes. He took me into the hallway and asked me to walk a straight line. I teased him. Did he think I was drunk? Was he borrowing a line from the cops? No, he bantered back, the police borrowed that directive from us.

After studying my gait, he sat me down and asked, "What's the rest of your evening like?" I hoped he wanted to buy me a steak.

He continued, "I'd like you to go to the imaging clinic up the road tonight to get a CAT scan."

"A CAT scan?" I stammered with evaporating confidence. "Why a CAT scan—and why tonight?"

"I'm action-oriented," he said. "This way I can call you later tonight with an update."

He didn't call that night, which made me wonder. But who hasn't waited for a doctor's overdue call? Their schedules are notoriously overbooked. So midway through the next morning, I called him. To my surprise, he phoned right back.

"I don't like the CAT scan," he said. "Neither does a neurologist friend I sent it to. I'd like you to get an MRI of your brain. And I'd like you to go and see a neurologist."

Did I mention this was on Friday the thirteenth?

I'm not one to visit doctors quickly or easily. But when a doctor says he wants a detailed scan of your brain, I'm not one to argue. So I scheduled the MRI as soon as I could. I even drove an extra thirty miles to downtown Sacramento to get an earlier appointment. Brain scans are not for the faint of heart—or the claustrophobic. Why does the machine make so many unsettling banging and clanking noises?

Later I called his friend the neurologist. A hospitable office assistant said the doctor would indeed be very happy to see me at her first opening—eight months into the future. I called my after-hours doctor back and asked if he had any other neurologist friends or special access to this one's schedule. He found me a more readily available neurologist with an opening the following Thursday.

Almost every Thursday morning for the past eighteen years I've met with four fellow pastors. We talk about life, share problems over coffee poured on ice, and theorize about how best to make the world a better place. Mostly it involves people paying better attention to our genius ideas.

That Thursday, knowing my doctor visit was imminent, we ended the meeting in prayer. Out loud. Around an outdoor table at Peet's Coffee. I held back tears as they ended by praying for my wife, Gerry. As they prayed for her, a picture of her pushing me in a wheelchair flashed through my mind. I didn't want this mystery diagnosis to wreck her life. After they finished, one friend walked me to my car—or really, because we were parked side by side, back to his. I repeated that I had some sorrow about what this might mean for me, my kids, and especially my wife. When I got to my darkening thoughts about her future, imagining what might be ahead after the morning's prognosis, I could no longer hold back tears. "Hey," he said in his gentle and steady pastor's voice. "No future tripping."

Gerry and I drove to the neurologist with the profound and unspoken sense that this day was going to change the direction of our lives. Waiting together, we had the sinking feeling we were joining a group we very much did not want to join. This exam was almost identical to that of my new general practitioner friend: checking reflexes, watching me stand and walk a straight line. But this time the visit ended with a diagnosis: "You have Parkinson's disease. I don't want to tell people they have it, and I don't want to have to tell you, but there it is."

The cause? We don't know.

The cure? Unknown.

The treatment? One medication is widely effective for several years. Then treatments vary and increase in intensity.

He handed me an outdated trifold brochure titled "Tips for Further Understanding Parkinson's," encouraged us to Google the Parkinson's Foundation website, and ushered us out his office door.

That was it. One visit. And suddenly I was part of a club I never wanted to join, a fraternity for which I didn't pledge, a team for which I didn't try out, a membership for which I never filled out an application. It was a rite of passage I desperately wanted to avoid. We walked out of the flat medical office and into the bright California sunshine with dark storm clouds inside. Instinctively, we went to lunch, eating our high-calorie comfort food mostly in silence, holding hands across the table. The air was thick with a palpable sense of foreboding. This seemed the most likely diagnosis—but oh, to be wrong!

Later we discovered other members of this club: actors like Michael J. Fox and Ian Holm, comedians like Robin Williams and Billy Connolly, musicians like Linda Ronstadt and Ozzy Osbourne, athletes like Muhammad Ali, astronauts like Michael Richard Clifford, and so many clergy—Pope John Paul II, Jesse Jackson, Billy Graham, and my mentor, Haddon Robinson. Each wakes every day with a tremor, a reminder of what is and what will come.

I salute the people on this list. I admire their talents. I'd gladly join them for dinner. I'd be happy to offer each a prayer. I'd even write a large check to a foundation created to find a cure for them. But do I have to join them?

My daughter texted from her teaching gig in Spain. On hearing the news, she typed back a particularly European response: "Well that **** sucks." Exactly. Our son drove home from work and asked us in the driveway, "What did the doctor say?" We simply responded, "It's Parkinson's." Tears welled in his eyes as he whispered downheartedly, "That sucks." Later our oldest son added his own "That sucks" to the gloomy chorus, adding "I'm sorry."

Sleep that night was fitful. How do you stop thinking about the particular? After the first day's numbness, a gloom settled in. We drove to a mountain getaway. Talking as we drove, lost in conversation, we were apparently oblivious to our speed. An alert California Highway Patrol officer was not, and introduced himself with a question: "Do you know you were going 83 in a 65 maximum zone?"

I wanted to ask, "Are you really going to add to my misery?"

He followed up his first question with another, "When was last time you had a ticket? Never? In over forty years? You're due!"

My thoughts weren't especially Christian. I was tempted to share some of them with the officer. But I was afraid he'd make me walk a straight line. And with Parkinson's, I wasn't sure I could.

My cadre of pastor friends—the only people who knew of my condition besides immediate family—called to encourage me. Their support was gratifying. But each new day I woke awash in gloom. It felt like I had been handed an unjust, unwarranted, mean-spirited sentence by a capricious judge. My fate had flipped upside down. Reading Parkinson's websites only added details to the sobering sentence. Likely there would be a few tolerable years. Then the complications would intensify.

Three mornings after my diagnosis I was scheduled to preach. The night before, my right cheek started to flutter. I had embryonic plans about communicating this new reality to our church and to my wider family. But as my unstable cheek muscle reminded me, none of this was really in my hands. My face, its shape or steadiness, could communicate the disease against my wishes.

I rose early, unable to sleep. Usually I spend a couple of hours finalizing my sermon. That morning, alone in the house, I wept. I realized that what I had previously described as tears barely qualified. I wept bitterly. I blubbered. I bargained. I pleaded, "Lord, I don't want to do this." "Lord, don't make me do this." And "Lord, I'm too weak to do this." These were tears of lament. A pile of losses stared me down, and each seemed inevitably disastrous: walking my daughter down the wedding aisle, holding a grandchild without shaking him or her like a tossed salad, being an active and involved grandparent, taking interesting retirement trips and vacations, even simple things like walking around the park. My life was going to be stunted by Parkinson's.

At church I carried an inner emotional stew. Every song offered a line or phrase that got me choking. My emotions burbled near the surface, about to spill over. I was gladdened when our associate pastor, who knew my diagnosis, could "pass the peace of Christ" to me. Later his wife came up to a circle of conversation I was in and simply gave me a hug. Such deep understanding and grace in one hug.

My illness is no worse than many, and it's better than some. I had a friend who died thirty days after being diagnosed with pancreatic cancer. Another buried his young wife after a multi-year, fully engaged battle with cancer. My brother's grandson has leukemia—at two years old. Someone I know was diagnosed with Parkinson's and cancer on the same day.

I used to be able to complete medical forms in a moment. I'd simply check "no" to every disease listed on the two-page inventory. Now forms feel a lot more complicated. Isn't that how it is for all of us? At some point our lives become a lot more complicated, and our medical prognosis becomes an uncertain mess.

On hearing my diagnosis, a friend who has lived with the effects of polio since third grade phoned. "Welcome to the club," she began. "Welcome to the group of people with chronic [she could have added 'degenerative'] diseases." She made the statement without a shred of putdown or unkindness. Disease is the dark side of living on this beautiful, broken planet. And each of us will bear an ailment in a way custom-fit to us, or witness it in someone we love.

As we've seen repeatedly, the early church saw the life-giving grace of baptism at every turn. All through the Old and New Testaments they found baptismal life. Every water-infused story evoked the grace of baptism. When the children of Israel escaped from the Red Sea—baptism. When Moses struck the rock in the desert (Exod. 17) and water flowed out to meet the needs of God's thirsty people—that was baptismal water.[1] Part of baptism's life-giving grace, they believed, was healing. When Elisha instructed Naaman to wash in the Jordan River, he experienced the healing of baptism. When the angel stirred the pool of Bethesda (John 5) for healing—that was baptism. Even Jesus using spittle to heal a blind man's eyes (John 9)—baptism. Especially looking at these stories intertwining physical and spiritual healing, the church believed baptism's power to heal was almost limitless, if not always guaranteed.

Tertullian (AD 155–240) contrasts the regenerative healing of baptism with what he calls the empty "widow waters" of other religions, whose repeated washings and constant sprinklings are hollow. Devotees of pagan rites, he says, without mincing words, "flatter themselves with a belief in omens of purification." By contrast, baptismal waters "render that service through the authority of God, by whom all their nature has been constituted! If men

---

1. This story became a favorite symbol in Christian art (Everett Ferguson, *Baptism in the Early Church: History, Liturgy, and Theology in the First Five Centuries* [Grand Rapids: Eerdmans, 2009], 514).

think that water is endued with a medicinal virtue by religion, what religion is more effectual than that of the living God?" We see this, he makes clear, in Jesus's healing of the invalid at the pool of Bethesda (John 5).[2]

Ephraem the Syrian (306–373) describes one recipient of Jesus's healing (John 9) as "the blind man who washed in the 'baptism of Siloam.'" This now-sighted man was "enlightened by the water," and his baptism made him "clad in light."[3]

Gregory of Nazianzus (329–390), a much-loved pastor and archbishop of Constantinople, is considered the greatest theologian of his era. In cautioning people against the populist trend to delay baptism, he urged, "Why wait for a fever to bring you this blessing, and refuse it from God? . . . Heal yourself before your extremity; have pity upon yourself the only true healer of your disease; apply to yourself the really saving medicine."[4]

Stories of baptismal healing, though not routine or common, continue through the centuries. When Vladimir took the throne of Kiev in 980, he was a lusty and enthusiastic idolater who had accumulated a coterie of wives from assorted countries. Various leaders of nearby nations had tried to persuade him to follow their faith. But rather than take their biased word for it, he sent his own trusted envoys to learn which of the neighboring countries had the true religion. "Of the Muslim Bulgarians of the Volga," the envoys reported, "there is no joy among them; only sorrow and a great stench. In the gloomy churches of the Germans [we] saw no beauty; but at Hagia Sophia, where the full festival ritual of the Byzantine Church was set in motion to impress [us]," they found a winner: "We no longer knew whether we were in heaven or on earth, nor such beauty, and we know not how to tell of it."[5]

---

2. Tertullian, "Use Made of Water by the Heathen. Type of the Angel at the Pool of Bethsaida," in *On Baptism*, https://www.sacred-texts.com/chr/ecf/003/0030727.htm.

3. Ephraem of Syria, *Hymns on Faith* 83.2, in Ferguson, *Baptism in the Early Church*, 515.

4. Gregory of Nazianzus, *Oration* 40.12, 40.34, in Ferguson, *Baptism in the Early Church*, 601.

5. Graham E. Fuller, *A World without Islam* (New York: Little, Brown, 2010).

Enlightened "by the grace of God," Vladimir became a Christian. At his baptism he "came forth from the font not only healed of a blindness lately afflicting him, but also from being passionate and warlike; he became meek, peaceable, and exceedingly godly." In fact, he devotedly "spread Christianity throughout his realm like a new Constantine," commanding all his subjects to be baptized as well.[6]

Our congregation has also experienced the way baptism offers healing. Two delightful sisters attend our church. One came first. She loved the music and the people. As a professional percussionist, she found great delight when she soon was invited to participate. A Christian for much of her adult life, she had been praying her sister would join her. One day she did.

In her own words, this second sister had "tried everything." She explored Eastern religion and various churches, independent and organized, formal and loose, orthodox and experimental. Nothing "fit" until she joined her sister. She said, "By the end of that first service I knew I was home." But the third worship service changed her life.

Periodically, to remember our baptisms and to accent our new creation identity in Christ, we, like generations of Christians before us, dip a branch into a bowl of water and fling water into the congregation. I confess, as a pastor I was at first a bit anxious about this practice. Would folks think we'd lost our collective mind? Would it feel too showy? Would it detract from the words of confession and assurance that framed it rather than enhance and add to them? The first week my fears evaporated. Grade-schoolers reveled in the experience, some motioning enthusiastically for more water to come their way; adolescents delighted; some seniors closed their eyes as if gathering memories.

The second sister remembers it well because it healed her. The flung water didn't seem any more foreign to her than anything else; every part of worship was novel. She had no expectations. But she could not have anticipated what actually did happen. When the water hit her, she felt like she was new. "I've had all kinds of highs,

---

6. "Vladimir, Equal-to-the-Apostles of Kiev," July 15, in *Daily Readings*, App 1.6.7. Approved by the Greek Orthodox Archdiocese of America.

art and music and sex, LSD and marijuana," she said, "but this was a high of another scale. It was as if the love of God surrounded me and lifted me off my chair. As if right then, I was baptized by the Holy Spirit. Right then I became a Christian."

One of the new congregations our church helped to begin once had a healing baptism. Eighty-year-old Ted was determined to be baptized with all the significantly younger attendees. He had to be helped down the steep embankment of the American River, where they held their baptisms. Given his long-diagnosed degenerative arthritis, he could barely walk, and made it to the riverbank only with significant discomfort. During Ted's baptism the pastor felt a tingling anointing of the Spirit. It hadn't happened with the other baptisms that day. Ted felt it too. After his baptism he bounded back up the hill to greet people, much to the congregation's great surprise and delight.

Two friends recently lost their spouses, one after decades together. As you might imagine, after so many years of two-becoming-one, living solo often feels vacuous, lonely, and desolate. The other is a parent of two grade-schoolers. Looking ahead at decades of solo parenting would feel daunting to anyone. Both are people of deep and abiding faith. And both told me in different times and ways that when they participate in the liturgy, when they are in a worship service, they feel most whole. In their times of grief, the place of consolation is a worship service that rehearses the story of their belonging to Jesus, of their baptism into the name of the Father, Son, and Holy Spirit.[7]

These experiences remind me of what the Orthodox liturgist Alexander Schmemann wrote: the liturgy "actualizes" the church. In other words, when we enact the liturgy, we become our true self.[8] As we live our true story, we more deeply enter our identity. We are never more our true selves than when we live out

7. Adapted with permission from Kevin Adams, "Our True Selves," *Reformed Worship* (blog), accessed April 30, 2021, https://www.reformed worship.org/blog/our-true-selves.

8. Alexander Schmemann, *For the Life of the World* (Yonkers, NY: St. Vladimir's Seminary Press, 1973/2002).

the story—the call to worship, the confession, the assurance, the gospel proclamation, the Eucharist, and baptism.

Baptismal liturgies in the Orthodox tradition include blessing the water. Prayers ask God to restore water to its full creation goodness. During the baptismal service, an attending priest prays over the water: "Give to it the grace of redemption, the blessing of Jordan. Make it a fountain of incorruption, a gift of Sanctification, a remission of sins, a healing of sicknesses, a destroyer of demons."[9]

Later in the liturgy the blessing continues: "O Master of all, make this water, the water of redemption, the water of sanctification, a purification of flesh and spirit, a loosening of bonds, a forgiveness of transgressions, an illumination of the soul, a washing of regeneration, a renewal of spirit, a gift of adoption, a garment of incorruption, a fountain of life."[10]

Baptism redeems, sanctifies, purifies, loosens, forgives, illumines, renews, and *heals.*

My friend Chris is an Orthodox priest, and one of a group of pastor-friends who meet together Thursday mornings. His doctoral dissertation was on initiation rites in the early church. I asked him how holy (blessed) water works in his tradition. Unlike Christian traditions that bless themselves with holy water as they enter a sanctuary, Orthodox Christians "have holy water people can take home with them. Some use it for cooking, others drink a bit every day, maybe especially as they say their prayers. Some take sips of it when they are ill. Others sprinkle their homes." The rites for blessing holy water are based on baptism. The water is blessed for the parish to use during the coming months. Blessed water can then be used fully for its created purpose—as "an instrument of life."[11]

Abbot Tryphon, another Orthodox priest, explains that "Holy Water is so important to the Christian life that Saint Luke the Sur-

9. "The Mystery of Holy Baptism," Saint Anna's Greek Orthodox Church, Roseville, CA. Used with permission.
10. "The Mystery of Holy Baptism."
11. Author conversation with Dr. Christopher Flesoras, January 21, 2021.

geon, Archbishop of Simfe, recommended that we should 'Drink Holy Water, the more often, the better. It is the best and most effective medicine. I'm not saying this as a priest, I'm saying it as a doctor, from my medical experience.'"[12]

Chris is quick to say that these worship rites do not guarantee fully restored physical health for every participant. Baptism and holy water affect individuals personally. He knows this firsthand. He lost his young wife to cancer after a courageous fight. Holy baptismal water is not a magical incantation guaranteeing results to our specifications. Chris says we "take elements God created good and consecrate them so they do good," adding, "There is no downside. . . . We know this stuff works."[13]

Several years ago I spoke to a group of pastors at a conference aiming to raise our missional IQ. Their invitation suggested I offer the group "elder wisdom." A phone call with the group organizer offered clarification: "Yes, that does mean we think of you as an 'older pastor.' And we hope to learn from you."

I spoke that evening about baptismal identity. I suggested that the best gift a pastor (or anyone) can give his or her church or neighborhood is an identity deeply grounded in God's grace and symbolized in our baptism. To live our baptism is to live our truest, deepest, most life-giving selves. It is to push away temptations to do ministry (or life) as performance or show or theater. It is to live life as an unwarranted gift.

I concluded my talk by referencing the nightly ritual Benedictine monasteries have performed for 1,400 years. Each evening, the abbots sprinkle holy (baptismal) water on the monks as the concluding act of the day. As they enter the evening's grand silence, they remember again that they are the apple of God's eye (Ps. 17:8). They sleep with a fresh physical reminder that they live in the shadow of God's wings (Ps. 91:4). So at the conference, inspired by our monastic colleagues, in a group humming with a

12. Abbot Tryphon, "Holy Water," The Morning Offering, January 26, 2021, https://blogs.ancientfaith.com/morningoffering/2021/01/holy -water/.

13. Conversation with Flesoras, January 21, 2021.

restless desire to "do stuff" for Jesus, I sprinkled them with water from an aspergillum. Afterward several described the healing
grace of being struck with water. Apparently even being reminded
of baptism can be a kind of healing. No wonder Chris says that
"baptism brings healing and restores us to the original state of
Adam and Eve."[14]

How does baptismal healing work? "I don't know," answers
Chris. None of us does. The suffering of many continues. The
chronic conditions of many worsen. Each day doctors send people
to get damning CAT scans and MRIs. Every hour people learn they
have Parkinson's or cancer or multiple sclerosis. The irreverent
Scottish comedian Billy Connolly was diagnosed with Parkinson's
and remembered this conversation:

"I had a doctor in New York who said, 'You realize this is an
incurable disease?'

"And I said: 'You got to get a grip of yourself, stop calling it
an incurable disease, say we have yet to find the cure. Give the
guy a light in the tunnel. Incurable is such an awful thing to say
to somebody.'"[15]

Is "work" even the right word? What if baptism is really about
pointing us to God's surprising grace? What if it is the grace
that heals?

In his remarkable book *Of Water and the Spirit*, Schmemann
argues that to walk in "newness of life," the church needs to re-
discover and practice the restorative powers of baptism. Baptism
is a "permanent reality" illuminating a person's "whole life, an
ever-living source of joy and hope." Baptism is the sacrament of
"regeneration." It is a mystery "which fills with joy the angels and
the archangels and all the powers from above and earthly creatures."[16] The "ultimate goal of baptism [is] the restoration of true

---

14. Conversation with Flesoras, January 21, 2021.

15. Joe McAweaney, "Sir Billy Connolly: Stop Calling Parkinson's 'Incurable,'" *Parkinson's Life*, October 24, 2019, https://parkinsonslife.eu/sir
-billy-connolly-parkinsons-incurable/.

16. Alexander Schmemann, *Of Water and the Spirit: A Liturgical Study
of Baptism* (Crestwood, NY: St. Vladimir's Seminary Press, 1974), 8–11,
20, 26, 39.

life." Schmemann says, "The whole world is poisoned and sick, and the act of liberation [baptism] is not only 'spiritual' but also 'physical.'" Baptismal water "washes away stains, it recreates the pristine purity of the earth."[17]

Flannery O'Connor says the same thing in her own jarring, unpredictable storytelling way. She believed a violent literary shock was a necessary, often healing, medicine that brought both her characters and her modern secular audience to an awareness of the powerful reality of a mystery that transcends human ability. She wanted to display the miracle of grace in a world convinced it could survive on its own moral grading system, portraying her characters as they might be touched by divine grace.[18]

Her story "The River" describes the baptism of Harry Ashfield. Just five years old, Harry escapes a beating from older children, only to be ushered to a revival meeting. His babysitter, Mrs. Conlin, believes everyone needs healing, including this young boy in her charge and his neglectful parents.

When asked at the revival what he needs healing from, Harry answers, "Hunger." After being used as a prop, Harry is baptized by a faith healer named Bevel. Harry isn't sure what all this means. But the next morning, as he feeds himself raisin bread and peanut butter while his parents sleep off their latest hangover, he comes to the stark realization that he desperately wants what baptism offers: He wants to "count," as the preacher promised. He wants to be loved by his Father in heaven. He wants to be healed.

After secretly taking bus fare from his mother's purse, he traces the previous day's steps to the riverside, now minus the gawking crowds. There "he intended not to fool with preachers anymore but to Baptize himself and to keep on going this time until he found the Kingdom of Christ in the river." But while he repeatedly baptizes himself, he drowns. "For an instant he was overcome with surprise; then since he was moving quickly and knew that

17. Schmemann, *Of Water and the Spirit*, 26.

18. Kevin Adams, *The Book That Understands You* (Grand Rapids: Faith Alive Christian Resources, 2009).

he was getting somewhere, all his fury and his fear left him."[19] He wanted to be free from his sufferings. He wanted to meet Jesus. And now he did.

As promised, her story shocks. Some might even call it grotesque. But maybe what O'Connor is saying through Harry is what Schmemann says through his liturgical theology, something we already know, whether we have Parkinson's or polio or not: Baptism is too big for us to understand all at once. It offers a grace bigger than a lifetime of knowing.

Readers often try to untangle tensions in O'Connor's story—and in their own. How can one "document the sacrament of Baptism," she once wondered. It's a mystery beyond our knowing. No wonder she keeps pointing any who will listen to random moments of grace. Of "The River," she "once stated in an interview: 'He comes to a good end. He's saved from those nutty parents, a fate worse than death.'"[20] In that way Harry was healed, in a way he couldn't expect or maybe even desire. Monk and literary critic Gregory Schweers writes, "O'Connor reminds us that the only thing more valuable than life itself in this earthly kingdom is life eternal in the Kingdom to come."[21]

Maybe that's how most of us get healed as well.

19. Flannery O'Connor, "The River," in *A Good Man Is Hard to Find* (New York: Houghton Mifflin Harcourt, 1955), 49.

20. Gerard E. Sherry, "An Interview with Flannery O'Connor," in *Conversations with Flannery O'Connor*, ed. Rosemary M. Magee (Jackson: University Press of Mississippi, 1987), 58.

21. Gregory Schweers, "Flannery O'Connor and the Problem of Baptism: Sectarian Controversies in 'The River,'" *Way*, January 2015, 65–74.

# TWELVE

# One Baptism

## Uniting with the Global Church

---

We are one in the Spirit; we are one in the Lord.

—Peter Scholtes

Make every effort to keep the unity of the Spirit through the bond of peace. There is one body and one Spirit, just as you were called to one hope when you were called; one Lord, one faith, one baptism; one God and Father of all, who is over all and through all and in all.

—Ephesians 4:3–6

Baptism is not just a picture; it also *does* something. . . . It *makes* what it promises: a new person and a new people.

—James K. A. Smith

For we were all baptized by one Spirit so as to form one body—whether Jews or Gentiles, slave or free—and we were all given the one Spirit to drink.

—1 Corinthians 12:13

---

Brooke started attending church as a high school freshman. Her parents, raised as spiritual mutts, wanted their children to make spiritual decisions for themselves. Kind, thoughtful, and winsome people, they considered themselves simply "spiritual." Their philosophy was, "We'll let the kids decide when they get old enough." It's a standard California line. Together the family went to church on Easter, but they didn't do much else that was "spiritual."

Brooke battled cancer as a ten-year-old, a reality she says shaped her into the person she is. She spent hundreds of hours visiting pediatric medical specialists. For reasons that aren't clear even to her, she decided after one Easter service that she wanted to get more spiritually engaged. She was ready now to make a faith decision for herself. Her first thought was to ask a friend where she went to church. She determined, and her family joined in her plan, to visit Anne's church once and then shop around. But, Brooke said, "We knew right away this was 'home' for us."

Three years later, now a senior, she is in my office telling me why she wants to get baptized. "I was raised to have spiritual choices," she says, opening our conversation, "and this is mine."

"What does baptism mean to you?" I ask.

"It means," she says with that special seventeen-year-old confidence, "that I'm all in." I smile to myself. How perfect that a high school senior uses a poker term to describe her faith!

The day of her baptism, her friends and family grab seats in the front row: her boyfriend (a spiritual agnostic), her extended family (Mormons and Jehovah's Witnesses), her parents (only a few steps behind her in embracing the Christian faith), and her friends—a parliament of California spirituality. A few rows behind her supporters, children crane their necks to see. Brooke is a popular teacher in our children's ministry. The kids love her.

Before the service begins, she tells me she has been practicing her plunge into the water. Ever the overachieving honors student, Brooke tells me, "I'm all set to go. I've been practicing on my bed."

Why does someone so eagerly want to join this motley crew of people? Why join this congregation that represents in the most modest way the global church of all times and places? There are a hundred other activities for a high school senior to be involved in. She has a boyfriend, advanced placement classes, and group social gatherings. But she wants everyone to know she's "all in." It's not because church is teeming with other high school seniors; it isn't. Maybe her illness has given her a deep sense that she wants to belong to something bigger than herself.

By contrast, Andy took much longer to make up his mind about faith and about baptism. He first came to our church after his sister-in-law received our mass-mailing Easter invitation. She faithfully attends another congregation across town, where she is much-loved and respected. But after reading our mailing, she intuited that Andy would more readily find a spiritual home with us. Andy's a bright, articulate, Ivy League–trained engineer. He's gentle, wise, and reflective, and when he first attended, he was a skeptic. His sister-in-law knew he needed a place offering time and space to wonder.

He began attending in part to please his wife. For six years he brought his doubts and disbelief. During those years he volunteered, assisting first with his daughter's preschool class and later as a key part of our technical team. For six years we loved him, prayed for him, and accepted him as part of our community. During an extended family campout, he finally, in his words, "crossed the line" to claim faith as his own. His baptism was a grand all-church celebration. Andy was already part of the church family; now he was a believer.

In our prebaptismal conversations, Andy and I had a great time talking about the wide variety of baptism's meanings and practices. But sometimes its logistical details are assumed rather than

spoken. Andy had opted to be sprinkled rather than dunked. But I
forgot to ask Andy to kneel during his baptism. As I baptized him,
I could barely reach the top of his head. At six feet four, he was,
without a doubt, the tallest person I've ever baptized. His wife was
beaming! So was his sister-in-law, who made the first invitation.
So were we all.

Andy's story shows that our congregation, following the practice
of many, invites people into community *before* they believe. People
without any church experience often want to "try on" the faith, as
you might test-drive a new car or look at a new shirt in the dressing-
room mirror. Many folks in our neighborhood, even senior adults,
have no Christian memory. Christian virtues—generosity, chastity,
secret serving, giving—seem outlandish. It takes time—often a lot
of time—before people find themselves believing. So we let them
join our family as they test-drive the faith. We find that an experience of belonging, more than well-shaped arguments, helps the
gospel become real to our friends. Then they become ready to join
the church of all times and places—at any age.

One Sunday we baptized six siblings. Their mom and dad, first
converted in a believer's-baptism-only congregation, had recently
moved to our city. In finding their way into our congregation, they
also found their way into the historic covenant baptism we practice. According to the example given in the Acts of the Apostles,
when parents are baptized in our congregation, so is the rest of
their family—like Lydia and her household or the Philippian jailer
and his (Acts 16).

These young parents, people of outspoken conviction and obvious principles, confirmed their new belief in covenant baptism
soon after the birth of their sixth child. They realized they wanted
all of their children baptized. And seeing the trough we often used
for baptisms, they asked with a twinkle in their eyes if they could
all be immersed! So one unforgettable Sunday I baptized six siblings, from the oldest to the youngest, each symbolically dying and
rising with Christ. Each egging on their younger siblings. Each
dripping with baptismal joy.

The last baptism had special significance. Over the years I have
baptized children of all ages, including many infants. But I had yet

to immerse one. I confess that the logistics made me uneasy. What would happen if he squirmed at just the wrong time? Would he come out of the water sputtering for air? I didn't want to drop him in the tank in front of God and everyone.

I wish you could see a video of what happened. He was dunked like his siblings, plunged into and raised out of the water before he knew what was happening. He emerged with a look of utter surprise and astonishment. He scanned the room, checking for visual confirmation that he had, as he strongly suspected, been thoroughly mistreated. Instead, he saw smiling, elated faces everywhere and heard gasps of delight and spontaneous, enthusiastic applause. What could he do but enjoy the revelry?

I could relay all sorts of baptism stories. There was the day we baptized three generations—a grandpa, father, and son. Or the day we baptized an attorney who hadn't practiced falling into the water and banged his head (gently enough to not get hurt) on the edge of our baptismal trough. Each story connects a person to a group—the visibly and notably imperfect group called the church.

In a culture that highly prizes individualism and independence, one where everyone lives their own brand of free-roaming cowboy, what makes anyone join a congregation? What makes someone get baptized into the global church? Do they do so knowing how baptism makes us all *one*?

In a thoughtful sermon on baptism, Kathleen Norris says, "I suspect that to many Christians baptism seems a curious and antiquated custom. People want their children baptized but can't say much about why they want it, and what the rite is meant to signify." But baptism, she says, "is about celebrating the incomparable gift we receive as creatures beloved of God." It's about our "call to the community of the church." Its "import is so much larger than Christians generally acknowledge when they say, 'I was baptized a Catholic,' or an Episcopalian, or a Methodist. A Christian is baptized into the Christian faith, and not a particular denomination."[1]

1. Kathleen Norris, "Marked for a Purpose: Isaiah 42:1–9; Acts 10:34–

Certainly what is essential about baptism is not the amount of water used, or the age at which we are baptized, or even the setting. What really matters is this startling statement from Saint Paul: just as there is only one Lord and one faith, so there is only one baptism (Eph. 4:3–6). Baptism profoundly alters—or *should* profoundly alter—our racial, social, economic, and sexual barriers. In the waters of baptism, old, bitter enemies unite. We become a permanent part of a new global family. We become one.

In her soaring, Pulitzer Prize–winning novel *Gilead*, Marilynne Robinson tells the story of Rev. John Ames. Ames's grandfather was an abolitionist preacher who stirred people to leave Iowa and join the Union army during the Civil War. His father was a pacifist minister who fought against the hawkishly militant emphasis of his rearing. Ames's best friend is a Presbyterian minister across town who raised a full house of five children, a profound contrast to John's quiet decades since losing his first wife and their infant daughter in childbirth. Now in his seventies, this third-generation Congregationalist pastor pens a kind of love letter to his seven-year-old son, the grace and surprise of his old age. He wants his young child to know his father and what he cherishes. You can hear Ames's sense of the oneness of the wider church as he talks about baptism:

> When I was in seminary I used to go sometimes to watch the Baptists down at the river. It was something to see the preacher lifting the one who was being baptized up out of the water and the water pouring off the garments and the hair. It did look like a birth or a resurrection. For us the water just heightens the touch of the pastor's hand on the sweet bones of the head, sort of like making an electrical connection. I've always loved to baptize people, though I have sometimes wished there were more shimmer and splash involved in the way we go about it.[2]

---

43; Matthew 3:13–17," *Christian Century*, December 25, 2007, https://www .christiancentury.org/article/2007-12/marked-purpose.

2. Marilynne Robinson, *Gilead* (New York: Farrar, Straus & Giroux, 2004), 63.

Ames believes in baptism. Not because he has a faith beyond doubt. But because "it bestows blessing." As a young boy he baptized a family of kittens. The reality of that blessing stayed with him into his old age: to baptize is to bless. It is to enter into and participate in the mystery of life—"Not that you have to be a minister to confer blessing. You are simply much more likely to find yourself in that position. It's a thing people expect of you."[3]

Like Reverend Ames, I have good friends who are fellow pastors. One leads a thriving Assembly of God congregation that he and his wife began three decades ago in Orange County, California. Doug is friendly, gregarious, and generous in spirit. When he meets people, they often become friends for life.

We were swapping baptism stories one day as we walked along a Southern California beach. He couldn't wait to tell me his favorite from thirty years of ministry, the one folks urge him to repeat. It is about Sara.[4] A fairly new Christian, at the time of her baptism the church welcomed both Sara and her son, a keen lover of Jesus and a bass aficionado.

One summer night each year their congregation gathers for worship on the beach at Corona Del Mar. The highlight is after dinner, when they all migrate from the fire pits down to the water for their annual baptism service. Doug spends a few minutes explaining baptism—"everything that's going on, what we're going to do." People stand on shore taking in the lovely sights and smells and the majesty of the Pacific Ocean.

Then Doug and those about to be baptized wade out a good forty yards to where it gets deep enough to immerse people easily without hurting the pastor's late-middle-aged back. Neither those on shore nor those getting baptized can hear much. Waves are crashing, seagulls are arguing, and noncongregants amble about.

Still, the congregation on shore can see Doug and the baptizing. When people emerge from the water, the congregation claps and cheers enthusiastically, all while other beachgoers surf

3. Robinson, *Gilead*, 23.
4. Not her real name.

or boogie-board, fly kites or walk the beach. Passersby often stop and watch for a few moments. But then they mostly go back to whatever they're doing. As they notice what's happening, they do their best to move out of the way, out of the line of sight.

Corona Del Mar is known for its calm waters. Waves typically die over a series of jetties long before they get near shore. So it's especially safe for kids. But that day the waves were huge. Still, Doug and those baptized successfully navigated the extralarge breakers. One by one folks were baptized. Those immersed arose wet but assured, breathing easily. Then it was Sara's turn.

As he did for each person, Doug held Sara's arms and shoulders and repeated their congregation's simple baptismal formula: "Sara, because of your public proclamation of faith in Jesus Christ, I baptize you in the name of the Father, and the Son, and the Holy Spirit." There was an expectant pause as Doug got ready to immerse Sara. Everyone on shore felt the anticipation; some cheered.

During the previous baptisms, a particularly strong undertow had been developing. Doug remembers digging his feet into the sand to keep himself and those being baptized from being pulled out to sea. He was able to brace himself against the pull, but it felt more and more like the ocean was plotting to yank them farther out.

In the pause before baptizing Sara, the water around them got particularly shallow, and Doug saw a portentous wave approaching. He remembers thinking, "Sara is not a particularly frail person. There is no reason to dip her into the shallow end. Let's wait for a big one." As Sara faced the congregation on the shore, Doug positioned himself to see both the congregation and the wave. It was coming. It was big. And it would make an impact.

Doug has a flair for the dramatic. He loves to offer spiritual experiences; he wants people to *feel* their baptism. Here was a special moment, delivered. He timed the wave to match his words: "In the name of the Father . . ."—he sees it closing in—". . . and the Son . . ." Then he says, with perfect timing, ". . . and the Holy Spirit." The wave slammed into them, knocking them down and into the swirling surf. For a while both baptizer and baptizand were disoriented. Neither knew which direction was which. Doug lost his sunglasses. But he popped out of the water in time to hear Sara enthusiastically utter her first postbaptismal words: "Holy s\*\*t!!"

"That," Doug says, "is not the phrase you typically hear at the moment of baptism. But it totally shocked her. It caught her completely off guard."

Doug loves this story and tells it with glee as we walk together along that same beach. We stop to enjoy breakfast together and to catch up. Like Reverend Ames, Doug believes in blessing. He aims, to use his phrase, to "bless me" by being my host and tour guide to all things Orange County. He's even arranged for me to stay in a home near the beach.

Still, even in his desire to bless, he feels a need to inform me that he "can't call that sprinkling you do a baptism." It comes out like a confession, as if he thinks he owes me this truth. It causes a break in our casual storytelling between friends. Yes, as Bible readers we both believe in "one Lord, one faith, one baptism." But his convictions tell him that what we do in our congregation is not a baptism. To him, it's something else.

I admit that what often happens in our congregation is far less dramatic than immersion in the Pacific Ocean, epic wave or not. Following Paul's letter to the Romans and the model of the early church, we do immerse people—young or old—as often as we can. Still, after Doug's declaration, I was silent for a while. I know he's not alone in this conviction. And I know he loves me. I know he respects me as a fellow believer and as a pastor. But I also know (I knew it before he said anything that glorious California morning) that he doesn't think of our baptism as legitimate. In his mind, we do not share "one baptism."

How ironic that the global church splinters over the very sacrament designed to symbolize our unity in Christ. I do appreciate the value of spiritually memorable experiences. Baptism is worth remembering all our life. But I also believe none of us understands the meaning of our baptism as it happens. It's something we all must grow into, no matter what age we are baptized. So how do Doug and I—and all of us—live the Nicene Creed's words, "We believe in one holy catholic and apostolic church. We affirm one baptism for the forgiveness of sins"?[5]

What is so striking about the first Pentecost and every one since is the way baptism unites people from a stunning variety of nations and zip codes: those in Huntington Beach, California, and the fictional Gilead, Iowa; an Ethiopian eunuch and a Philippian small-business owner; legalized Roman citizens and immigrants on the margins of society. It even unites old enemies sworn to perpetual opposition: Jew and gentile, male and female, even slave and free. At least it's supposed to.

The timeless wisdom of the biblical text and the timeless teaching of the church are that all believers are one in baptism. But individual Christians and the church itself find it painfully difficult to live this oneness. Doug doesn't agree with me, but he honors me. That is not always the case. Through the centuries and still today, the church has often failed to live its baptismal oneness. We separate by doctrine, by race, by nationality, by geography, by language, by age, and by economics. Still, the glimpses of unity, the times we see boundaries crossed or ended, give us a vision of what should always be.

More than two decades ago my friends David and Susie Lindner moved to a new neighborhood to begin a church. It was an act not of power or coercion or paternalistic pride, but of love. Sociologists call their neighborhood a "corridor of neglect." Many retailers and home builders and city planners write it off, considering it not worth their time. The Lindners see it as a place of hope and beauty.

One summer Rachel served as an intern there. Reflecting on her stint with the Lindners and their neighbors, she described her last Sunday there. The church gathered for worship at the American River to baptize three new believers. Everyone brought food to share, which they set up on the riverbank, "placing our tables between several small clusters of homeless folks camping out in the woods."

5. Nicene Creed, Christian Reformed Church, https://www.crcna.org/welcome/beliefs/creeds/nicene-creed.

That location was purposeful. Homeless folks know about the church. They know their baptismal food was for sharing. What the congregation did not intend, however, was to set up their food tables at what was essentially the base of the homeless camp's "poop tree," a fact some of them later relayed to the unsuspecting church folks with great delight.

Curious bystanders gathered around as those about to be baptized—Babak, Gilbert, and Christina—gave witness to God's surprising grace. One homeless onlooker, a shirtless, redheaded "fellow with an attitude" called Guns, was so enthusiastic about participating that he jumped right in with those being baptized, responding to the vows. He heartily agreed with the first question, shouting, "I do! Praise the Lord!" But when Dave moved on to the next three questions, Guns wasn't so sure, and he revised his answers to "Naw. You're gettin' too complicated for me now with all this 'redemption' business."

When the river baptisms and baptism photos were complete, everyone gathered around the tables of food to enjoy the feast. Homeless folks drifted over, some waiting for an invitation, others making themselves immediately at home, plopping down and starting conversations.

Guns said to Dave, "You know, you folks should bring your picnic down here more often. Whatever you bring in food, we'll match in drugs. We'll throw us a *real* party."

Rachel remembers, "It was simultaneously heartwarming and heartbreaking to see the camaraderie that existed between the people we met: it was a camaraderie that they extended to us, but one that revolved largely around their shared brokenness, around drugs and a sense of displaced-ness. They were looking out for each other, but it was in the most basic sense of survival. Their strong bonds with each other and the laughter they shared with us didn't change the fact that they were living an existence limited and defined to a great extent by hardship, mental illness, and poverty."[6]

---

6. Thanks to Rachel for granting permission to share her reflections, and to the Calvin University staff who support and guide the summer Jubilee Fellows Program, of which she was a part.

It is profoundly moving and beautiful when the church lives Jesus's vision of oneness. To celebrate a milestone wedding anniversary, my wife and I spent a week in Rome. We toured the Colosseum, ate pasta at a quintessential Italian café, and tossed coins into the Trevi Fountain, hoping for a return visit. And, of course, we toured churches. Gerry indulged my fascination with all things church-related. So even on our anniversary trip, we visited many of Rome's most famous places of worship: the Pantheon, converted from worship of Roman gods; the Basilica di Santa Maria Maggiore, with mosaics from the fifth century; the San Lorenzo Fuori le Mura, with frescoes from the thirteenth century; and the San Giovanni in Laterano (St. John Lateran), the official seat of the bishop of Rome, with a baptistery built by Emperor Constantine in AD 315.

Of course, no trip to the Eternal City is complete without a visit to St. Peter's Basilica. We toured the dazzling art collection and stood in awe, staring at the Sistine Chapel. And we stayed for worship. Huddled with the growing masses, we stood at a considerable distance from those leading the service. But we were all helped by strategically placed projection screens. The gathering congregation, like the local Catholic church I occasionally attend, was a study in diversity, with people of every age and skin tone and economic class. And so many languages. But we were one.

We sang together. We confessed together. We received absolution together. We received a benediction together. We even took Eucharist together. And most unexpectedly for me, we danced in delight when the pope left his podium and gleefully wheeled through the congregation. As he motored about, waving from his popemobile, I was taken by the outpouring of love as people around us cried out to him in their native tongues. It wasn't the adulation of a rock star or movie icon; it was love for someone who had just blessed people bound in wheelchairs and those staggering forward on crutches.

I was raised in the Reformed family of churches. Our church youth groups had serious names like Calvinettes (for girls), the Calvinist Cadet Corps (for boys), and the Young Calvinist Federation (for high schoolers). We were taught to be loyal to our tribe and to mistrust all things "papish."

Our dearly loved Heidelberg Catechism, written in 1563, is beautiful in so many aspects. Its eloquent words on comfort and faith and the Lord's Prayer are worth memorizing. But it also offered an enthusiastic condemnation of the Roman Catholic Mass, the very thing I had participated in, calling it "a condemnable idolatry." In 2008, hundreds of years into our denomination's history (change often comes hard and slow in the church), we abandoned the statement. It's no longer part of our official confession. Still, suspicions linger. This is not just a characteristic of the denomination of my birth. No church is sure it can trust another's music or clergy or communion or baptism.

I don't share every doctrine held dear by the Roman Catholic Church, or any church. For example, I'm disturbed by the Catholic Church's torturously slow response to abuse. I'm put off, frankly, that as a Protestant I am not officially welcome to share in the Eucharist. I'm concerned its decision-making structure breeds exploitation. And I'm sure it has equally as many heartfelt objections to my denomination's formula of the faith.

Still, on that glorious spring day in the Eternal City, surrounded by a throng of worshipers from every land and language, from every ethnicity and income, I saw a vision of baptismal unity. That morning's preview only stirred my desire. I know it to be true. I wanted it to be so. I believe there is "one Lord, one faith, and one baptism." And I resolved to do what I can to live that deep baptismal truth, even while living on this fallen planet Earth, as practice for heaven.

# A Baptized Imagination

---

The sacrament or sign of baptism is quickly over, as we plainly see. But the thing it signifies, the spiritual baptism, the drowning of sin, lasts as long as we live, and is completed only in death. . . . Therefore this life is nothing else than a spiritual baptism which does not cease till death.

—Martin Luther

For it is by grace you have been saved, through faith— and this is not from yourselves, it is the gift of God— not by works, so that no one can boast. For we are God's handiwork, created in Christ Jesus to do good works, which God prepared in advance for us to do.

—Ephesians 2:8–10

---

It's time to return to the couple in my church office squabbling about work and food and sex, so lost in their bitter rivalry that they forget that I'm in the room or that anyone else is in the world. They carry a lifetime of hurts as they row: old wounds that scarred, new lesions and cuts, some self-inflicted, many done to them out of spite, or rage, or frenzy. They've lost themselves (and their souls) and lost sight of each other as they live out their default emotional settings: wounded and wounding, wrecked and wrecking, combatants in a lifetime of attacks.

Only occasionally do they visit someone like me. Only occasionally, in stretches that last a few weeks, do they walk into a church or consider their spiritual life. Only occasionally do they dust off thoughts about their long-ago baptisms, looking at them as devalued trophies, relics from a long-ago youth sports league. Leftovers of unknown value, too sentimental to toss away but too minor to have any real value. And yet, there it appears. An unexpected surprise in a riposte: "I am *baptized*!"

Baptismal identity is for them a pit stop they use to refuel only when the dashboard gauges of their lives are desperately low. But what if instead they were to let it shape every turn, every curve, every straightaway, every mile of the rest of their lives? What if their baptism guided them through the inevitable engine failures and tire blowouts each of us meets on this mysterious marathon we call life? Can we imagine them as people with their one-of-a-kind *imago Dei* (image of God) in full flower?

Imagine them ten years later, back in those same office chairs. Imagine they have received their baptisms not as just another episodic event but as the reality that shapes their identity and all their decision making. Imagine that baptism, including all its compelling images—of dying and rising, of spiritual washing, of anchoring faith, of being anointed, of putting on the clothing of a new creation, and of joining a universal family—has become the defining script of their lives. Imagine that it redefines their past suffering and current wounds, adding tangible grace to the trite and terrible things that have happened to them.

Imagine that instead of squabbling over daily sinful realities and hurtful words they are renouncing them. Maybe they are not able to detox from their past all at once. Maybe they are not able to quit cold turkey. But imagine if more and more they are recognizing these diminishing behaviors for the evils they are, vices that sabotage their own lives and those of all who know them. What if, following the ancient church, they are wearing their baptisms, daily "putting on" virtues like compassion, kindness, and long-suffering? What if for the past ten years they have tossed aside their self-centered bickering and are more and more living as people anointed as God's own emissaries? Perhaps they are key volunteers in a refugee resettlement program, or a grief-sharing ministry, or a neighborhood Alcoholics Anonymous meeting, and marked by their generosity.

Imagine that, instead of experiencing life through their default squabbling, they live with a healed and healing vision, seeing each other, their families, and even people of other nationalities or races or ethnicities or religions as the remarkable beings God has made. Imagine they are agents of remarkable hospitality. They see how their baptism profoundly unifies, joining together siblings from past marriages and people from various centuries and continents and languages, so with grace-laced hospitality they open up their tables and homes and lives to people astonishingly different from themselves, becoming people with an eye and heart and passion for justice. Imagine they not only love the congregation to which they belong but feel a marked unity with every congregation in their city, sensing there is one baptism we all share.

Is this vision of a life shaped by baptism overly idealized? Is the transformation outlined hopelessly optimistic? Is this a hallucination, the result of too much drinking from the baptismal font so that we have now become tipsy with a vision of grace?

The couple in my story attended worship for a couple more Sundays. Then they floated off. In the small wake of their leaving was a series of mild accusations: our church was not, according to the friend that originally recommended us, "biblical enough," and our worship wasn't "engaging enough."

This often happens. After more than thirty years as a pastor, I have a hundred stories like this, and so do my colleagues. But there are also stories of baptism-shaped transformation.

Linda came to our church the very first Sunday we met. Huddled together in our dilapidated warehouse, we were quite a sight. Worn green carpet covered the floors—and some of the walls. The sound system quarreled with our cement walls. A forbidding street sign outside read "No Exit." A young, slightly anxious, and inexperienced pastor spoke. Volunteers from a church ninety miles away led our children's ministry and staffed our nursery. Linda was there. And she came back. Every Sunday.

At first she participated in small ways. She joined a small group and volunteered for nursery. She helped with church cleanup days and serving refreshments. Week after week, then month after month and year after year, to our great delight and hers, she showed up. Slowly her commitment deepened. She took a turn leading a group. And once, to my great surprise, she stopped by my office and showed me her pay stub so I would know she was being as generous as she possibly could be.

After a dozen years or so, people started calling her "Grandma Linda." It wasn't because of her age; she was barely retired. It was because of her love. She would first hug and then shake hands with young persons about to go to college, and they'd find a $100 bill in their hand. She helped people through AA and Al-Anon. She guided our fledgling grief-sharing program. She loved her family through thorny situations. She could have tough but loving conversations. Occasionally and spontaneously she would start singing (and dancing) to Elvis songs. Eventually we declared her to be what she already was: an elder. Once, when we surveyed the staff about their favorite things about our congregation, one responded thoughtfully, "Linda's lilting laugh."

A self-described army brat, Linda as a child had followed her father every three years in a series of moves throughout the United States and overseas. When asked on a government form to state her religion, she checked the box that said "Protestant." Linda was not baptized at our church; this had happened years before. But before our very eyes she was transformed into someone who every day and in every way *lived* her baptism.

She's not alone. After Mia[1] had been coming to our church for a few months, she shared her story. She became a Christian mentored by several of her school friends but was hesitant to share this new reality with her family, and with good reason. Her dad was a shaman healer well known in the Hmong community. Her baptism, many felt, would be interpreted to mean she had turned her back on her culture and upbringing and family. As a healer's child, her community believed, she had an obligation to carry on the age-old traditions of her father. Her baptism, they said, could only be interpreted as an insult deliberately aimed to wound him. How could the community trust its spiritual health to someone who can't even control his own daughter?

What no one knew, or took time to hear, was that Mia had struggled with baptism for almost two years. She knew well—too well—what her Hmong community would say about her father and his abilities as a father, a leader, and a healer. For his part, he never said anything. But she thinks he knew.

She believed in Jesus. She was following Jesus. She was committed to Jesus. But she didn't get baptized. Her nonbaptism years were still a way to live her baptism identity, to do her youthful best to honor her father and mother, to engage in that dance of the faithful who renounce and heal in the best combinations, to live baptism as the script of her life before it actually happened, to honor both her earthly father and her heavenly Father in the best way she knew how.

1. Not her real name.

In a profound understatement, she said, "When I was baptized, I did not have a lot of supporters in my family." Two years after her conversion, no one in her family was really speaking to her. She received very few invitations to family gatherings but attended as many family functions as she was allowed. This would continue until she had children of her own. For the most part, in the eyes of her family of origin, she simply did not exist. But, like the two sitting in my office, and like Grandma Linda, she was baptized.

Ralph C. Wood, now a theology professor at Baylor University, tells of a remarkable baptism he witnessed in a minimum-security prison.[2] The convict had committed a horrible crime against his family, one by any human standards loathsome and unforgiveable. On the way to the facility, Wood says, "My suspicions were instant and numerous. Was this a convenient jailhouse conversion that might lead to a quicker parole?"

But one of his former students, now the part-time prison chaplain, assured him it was not. Recently "the man's wife and daughter had visited the prison in order to forgive him." In the astonishing light of their forgiveness, the prisoner "got on his knees and begged for the mercy of both God and his family."

The witness list was unremarkable: Wood, the chaplain, and the convict, all three watched carefully by a nearby armed guard. Together they "sang a croaky version of 'Amazing Grace'" and "did not balk," Wood said, "at declaring ourselves wretches." Then,

after a pastoral prayer, the barefoot prisoner stepped into a wooden box that had been lined with a plastic sheet and filled with water. It looked like a large coffin, and rightly so. . . . Pronouncing the trinitarian formula, the pastor lowered the new Christian down into the liquid grave to be buried with Christ and then raised him up to life eternal. Though the water was cold, the man was not eager to get out. Instead, he stood there weeping for joy. When at last he left the baptismal box,

2. Ralph C. Wood, "Baptism in a Coffin," *Christianity Today*, January 1, 1993, https://www.christianitytoday.com/pastors/1993/winter/93l2096.html.

I thought he would hurry away to change into something dry. I was mistaken. "I want to wear these clothes as long as I can," he said. "In fact, I wish I never had to take a shower again."

Wood reflects, "It was as close to a New Testament experience as perhaps I shall ever have."

After the baptism, the three-person congregation "sat quietly in the Carolina sun." The prisoner glowed. "I'm now a free man," he declared. The long-term Christians cautioned that this new baptismal life would be more difficult than he guessed. The chaplain quoted "Martin Luther's confession that, even in baptism, the old Adam remains a frightfully good swimmer."

Undaunted, the man declared his postprison plan to return home, "find work as a carpenter, and to become a faithful father and husband." He pledged "to join a local church and to live out his new life in Christ as a public witness to the transforming power of God's grace."

Will he, Wood wondered, make good on his prison pledges? Will he become new in Christ? Will he, like Linda and Mia, become an agent of healing in his family and community, living the countercultural reality of baptism? Will he, as he intended that day still dripping in the sun, be shaped by the grace of a lifetime of living his baptism? Will we?

# Bibliography

Adams, Joanna. "God Believes in You." *Day1*, January 10, 2010. https://day1.org/weekly-broadcast/5d9b820ef71918cdf200 28d6/god_believes_in_you.

Adams, Kevin. *The Book That Understands You.* Grand Rapids: Faith Alive Christian Resources, 2009.

———. "Our True Selves." *Reformed Worship* (blog). Accessed April 30, 2021. https://www.reformedworship.org/blog/our -true-selves.

———. "Scythian Worship? Nations and Cultures at Worship." *Reformed Worship* (blog). Accessed April 30, 2021. https://www .reformedworship.org/blog/scythian-worship-nations-and -cultures-worship.

Anderson, Paul Thomas. *There Will Be Blood.* Directed by Paul Thomas Anderson. 2007.

Anonymous. "I'm Getting Forced to Get Baptized, HELP PLEASE!??" *Yahoo!answers*, Pregnancy & Parenting Board, 2011. https://an swers.yahoo.com/question/index?qid=20080819232200AAs KHzF&guccounter=1.

Bailey, David. "Sincere Faith and Steadfast Hope: The Life and Witness of Frederick Douglass." *Arrabon Weekly* (email digest), February 27, 2021.

Bailey, Sarah Pulliam. "Megachurch Pastor Steven Furtick's 'Spontaneous Baptisms' Not So Spontaneous." Religion News Service, February 24, 2014. https://religionnews.com/2014/02/24 /megachurch-pastor-steven-furticks-spontaneous-baptisms -spontaneous/.

Baldoni, John. "Knuckle Down: Leadership Lessons from R. A. Dickey." CBS News, *MoneyWatch*, April 16, 2012. http://www.cbsnews.com/news/knuckle-down-leadership-lessons-from-ra-dickey/.

"Baptism." OrthodoxWiki. Last updated August 13, 2018. https://orthodoxwiki.org/Baptism.

"Baptism of Fire." The Godfather Wiki. Accessed April 30, 2021. https://godfather.fandom.com/wiki/Baptism_of_Fire.

Barnes, M. Craig. "After Adoption." *Christian Century*, July 13, 2012. https://www.christiancentury.org/archive/74902/201207.

Bass, Diana Butler. *A People's History of Christianity: The Other Side of the Story*. New York: HarperCollins, 2009.

Bauckham, Richard. *Bible and Mission: Christian Witness in a Postmodern World*. Grand Rapids: Baker, 2005.

Beal, Rose M. "Priest, Prophet and King: Jesus Christ, the Church and the Christian Person." In *John Calvin's Ecclesiology*, edited by Gerard Mannion and Eduardus Van der Borght. New York: T&T Clark, 2011.

Beardsley, Eleanor. "Off the Record: A Quest for De-Baptism in France." NPR, *Weekend Edition Sunday*, January 29, 2012. https://www.npr.org/2012/01/29/146046428/on-the-record-a-quest-for-de-baptism-in-france.

Bellah, Robert N. "Civil Religion in America." *Daedalus* 96, no. 1 (Winter 1967): 1–21. http://www.robertbellah.com/articles_5.htm.

———. "Heritage and Choice in American Religion." *Sociologica* 4, no. 3 (2010).

"Billy Graham (1918–2018)." Regular Baptist Ministries, February 21, 2018. https://www.garbc.org/ministry-highlights/billy-graham-1918-2018/.

Bonhoeffer, Dietrich. *The Cost of Discipleship*. London: Touchstone, 1995.

Borreson, Glenn. "Bonhoeffer on Baptism: Discipline for the Sake of the Gospel." *Word & World* 1, no. 1 (1981). http://wordandworld.luthersem.edu/content/pdfs/1-1_Evangelism/1-1_Borreson.pdf.

*Brittanica Concise Encyclopedia*. London: Encyclopaedia Brittanica, 2006.

Brown, Michael. "Does Baptism Matter?" *Day1*, January 13, 2013. http://day1.org/4406-does_baptism_matter.

Brueggemann, Walter. "Counterscript: Living with the Elusive God." *Christian Century*, November 29, 2005.

Bruner, Frederick Dale. *Matthew: A Commentary*. Vol. 1, *The Christbook, Matthew 1–12*. Grand Rapids: Eerdmans, 2004.

Calvin, John. *Calvin's New Testament Commentaries: Harmonies of the Gospels Matthew, Mark, and Luke*. Translated by A. W. Morrison. Grand Rapids: Eerdmans, 1972.

———. *Institutes of the Christian Religion*. Book 4. Chapter 15, "Of Baptism." Accessed April 30, 2021. https://www.ccel.org/ccel/calvin/institutes.vi.xvi.html.

Camacho, Daniel José. "Common Grace and Race." *Reformed Journal* (blog), January 10, 2015. https://reformedjournal.com/common-grace-and-race/.

Cavendish, Richard. "The Battle of the Milvian Bridge." *History Today* 62, no. 10 (October 2012). https://www.historytoday.com/archive/battle-milvian-bridge.

———. "John Calvin Dies in Geneva." *History Today* 64, no. 5 (May 2014). https://www.historytoday.com/archive/john-calvin-dies-geneva.

Clement, Olivier. *The Roots of Christian Mysticism: Texts from the Patristic Era with Commentary*. New York: New City Press, 1993.

Colwill, Sarah A. "Dying and Rising with Christ." Sermon, Church on the Mall, January 11, 2015. https://static1.squarespace.com/static/582a3a6020099eab9d4d6647/t/58aa56811e5b6ce697e60804/1487558273737/Sermon+1_11_15.pdf.

"Constantine: First Christian Emperor." *Christianity Today*. Accessed April 30, 2021. https://www.christianitytoday.com/history/people/rulers/constantine.html.

Copenhaver, Martin B. "Starting Over: Genesis 9:8–17; 1 Peter 3:18–22; Mark 1:9–15." *Christian Century*, February 21, 2006. https://www.christiancentury.org/article/2006-02/starting-over.

Criswell, W. A. "Simony in the Sanctuary." W. A. Criswell Sermon Library, August 14, 1977. https://wacriswell.com/sermons/1977/simony-in-the-sanctuary/.

Davies, Dave. "'Winding Up' as the Mets' Knuckleball Pitcher." NPR,

*Fresh Air*, April 10, 2012. http://www.npr.org/2012/04/10/150
283169/winding-up-as-the-mets-knuckleball-pitcher.

Doody, John, Kevin L. Hughes, and Kim Paffenroth, eds. *Augustine
and Politics*. Lanham, MD: Lexington Books, 2005.

Dow, Joseph A. *Ancient Coins through the Bible*. Mustang, OK: Tate,
2011.

Drilling, Peter. "The Priest, Prophet and King Trilogy: Elements of
Its Meaning in *Lumen Gentium* and for Today." *Eglise et Theologie* 19 (1988).

Edwards, Lee. "Catholic Maverick: A Profile of William F. Buckley,
Jr." *Crisis*, February 1, 1995. http://www.crisismagazine.com
/1995/catholic-maverick-a-profile-of-william-f-buckley-jr.

Eisenhower, Dwight D. "Address at the Freedoms Foundation,
Waldorf-Astoria, New York City, New York." December 22, 1952.

Emmons, Mark. "New York Mets Ace R. A. Dickey Says Oakland A's
Reliever Grant Balfour Kept Him from Drowning in 2007." *San
Jose Mercury News*, July 29, 2012. http://www.mercurynews
.com/ci_21188127/new-york-mets-ace-r-dickey-says-oakland.

Ferguson, Everett. *Baptism in the Early Church: History, Liturgy,
and Theology in the First Five Centuries*. Grand Rapids: Eerdmans, 2009.

Finn, Thomas Macy. *Quodvultdeus of Carthage: The Creedal Homilies*.
Ancient Christian Writers 60. New York: Newman, 2004.

Fitzmyer, Joseph. *The Acts of the Apostles: A New Translation with
Introduction and Commentary*. New Haven: Yale University
Press, 1998.

Flint-Hamilton, Kimberly. "Gregory of Nyssa and the Culture of
Oppression." *Christian Reflection: Racism* (2010). Center for
Christian Ethics at Baylor University, 2010. https://www.bay
lor.edu/content/services/document.php/110976.pdf.

Fox, Kara. "They Baptized Their Children for School Places. Now
Regret Is Setting In." CNN, August 25, 2018. https://www.cnn
.com/2018/08/25/europe/ireland-baptism-barrier-education
-intl/index.html.

Fuller, Graham E. *A World without Islam*. New York: Little, Brown,
2010.

"God in the White House." PBS, *American Experience*. Accessed April

30, 2021. https://www.pbs.org/wgbh/americanexperience/
features/godinamerica-white-house/.

Gorman, Amanda. "The Hill We Climb: The Amanda Gorman Poem
That Stole the Inauguration Show." *Guardian*, January 20, 2021.
https://www.theguardian.com/us-news/2021/jan/20/amanda
-gorman-poem-biden-inauguration-transcript.

Greidanus, Morris N. "The Making and Shaping of *Our World Belongs to God: A Contemporary Testimony*." *Inside Story* (blog),
Christian Reformed Church in North America. Accessed
April 30, 2021. https://www.crcna.org/welcome/beliefs/con
temporary-testimony/our-world-belongs-god/inside-story.

Gross, Terry. "Price's 'Letter to a Godchild.'" NPR, *Fresh Air*, June 19,
2006. https://freshairarchive.org/index.php/segments/prices
-letter-godchild.

Grundy, Trevor. "Church of England Kicks the Devil out of Baptism
Rite." Religion News Service, July 15, 2014. https://religion
news.com/2014/07/15/church-england-kicks-devil-baptism
-rite/.

Harris, Dan, Eric Johnson, and Mary Flynn. "Atheists Break Out
New Ritual Tool: The Blow-Dryer." ABC News, July 10, 2010.
https://abcnews.go.com/Nightline/atheists-conduct-de
-baptisms/story?id=11109379.

Hayes, Carlton. *Essays on Nationalism*. New York: Macmillan, 1960.

Hess, Jared, and Jerusha Hess. *Nacho Libre*. Directed by Jared Hess.
2006.

Hitchcock, William I. "How Dwight Eisenhower Found God in the
White House." History Channel, updated August 22, 2018.
https://www.history.com/news/eisenhower-billy-graham
-religion-in-god-we-trust.

Hoezee, Scott. "Mark 1:4–11." *Sermon Starters*, January 5, 2015. Center
for Excellence in Preaching. https://cep.calvinseminary.edu
/sermon-starters/epiphany-1b/?type=the_lectionary_gospel.

Honerkamp, Nick. "What Are You Holding Out of the Water?" *Nick
Honerkamp* (blog), March 6, 2017. http://nickhonerkamp.com
/what-are-you-holding-out-of-the-water/.

"How Elevation Church, Pastor Furtick Produce 'Spontaneous' Baptisms." WCNC, February 20, 2014. https://www.wcnc.com/ar-

ticle/news/investigations/i-team/how-elevation-church-past
or-furtick-produce-spontaneous-baptisms/275-292975851.

Hunter, George G., III. *The Celtic Way of Evangelism: How Christianity Can Reach the West . . . Again.* Nashville: Abingdon, 2000.

Jennings, Willie James. "Being Baptized: Race." In *The Blackwell
Companion to Christian Ethics,* edited by Stanley Hauerwas and
Samuel Wells. 2nd ed. Hoboken, NJ: Blackwell, 2011.

Jensen, Robin M. *Baptismal Imagery in Early Christianity: Ritual, Visual, and Theological Dimensions.* Grand Rapids: Baker, 2012.

Mannion, Gerard, and Eduardus Van der Borght, eds. *John Calvin's Ecclesiology: Ecumenical Perspectives.* New York: T&T
Clark, 2011.

Kennedy, John F. "Inaugural Address of John F. Kennedy." Avalon
Project, Yale Law School, January 20, 1961. https://avalon.law
.yale.edu/20th_century/kennedy.asp.

Khabeb, Angela T. "Troubled Waters: Our Baptismal Identity." *Café,*
August 6, 2018. https://www.boldcafe.org/troubled-waters
-baptismal-identity/.

King, Martin Luther, Jr. "Address at the Detroit Council of Churches
Noon Lenten Services, March 1961." In *The Papers of Martin
Luther King, Jr.,* vol. 6. Berkeley: University of California
Press, 2007.

Kirkland, Patrick. "Know Your Ending: There Will Be Blood." *The-
ScriptLab,* April 6, 2011. https://thescriptlab.com/features
/screenwriting-101/script-tips-applied/1010-know-your
-ending-there-will-be-blood/.

Koyzis, David T. *Political Visions & Illusions: A Survey & Christian
Critique of Contemporary Ideologies.* Downers Grove, IL: InterVarsity Press, 2003; 2nd ed. 2019.

Kuehn, Regina. *A Place for Baptism.* Chicago: Liturgy Training Publications, 2007.

Kuyper, Abraham. "Calvinism as a Life System." In *Lectures on Calvinism.* Peabody, MA: Hendrickson, 2008.

Lewis, C. S. *Mere Christianity.* New York: Macmillan, 1960.

Long, Roy. *Martin Luther and His Legacy: A Perspective on 500 Years
of Reformation.* Morrisville, NC: Lulu.com, 2017.

Long, Thomas G. "Called by Name." *Day1*, January 11, 2004. https://day1.org/weekly-broadcast/5d9b820ef71918cdf2002429/view.

Luther, Martin. *Sermons of Martin Luther: The House Postils*. Edited by Eugene F. A. Klug. Grand Rapids: Baker, 1996.

Martens, John W. "Simon Magus Tries to Buy the Holy Spirit." *America*, August 28, 2015. https://www.americamagazine.org/content/good-word/acts-apostles-online-commentary-24.

McAweaney, Joe. "Sir Billy Connolly: Stop Calling Parkinson's 'Incurable.'" *Parkinson's Life*, October 24, 2019. https://parkinsonslife.eu/sir-billy-connolly-parkinsons-incurable/.

Merton, Thomas. *The Seven Storey Mountain*. Boston: HMH Books, 1998.

Meštrović, Stjepan. *The Road from Paradise: Prospects for Democracy in Eastern Europe*. Lexington: University Press of Kentucky, 1993.

Michener, James A. Introduction to *Years of Infamy: The Untold Story of America's Concentration Camps*, by Michi Weglyn. New York: Morrow, 1976.

Molina, Alejandra. "At Amanda Gorman's Black Catholic LA Parish, 'It's like Everybody Here Is a Freedom Fighter.'" Religion News Service, January 28, 2021. https://religionnews.com/2021/01/28/at-amanda-gormans-black-catholic-l-a-parish-its-like-everybody-here-is-a-freedom-fighter/.

Mouw, Richard J. "The Danger of Alien Loyalties: Civic Symbols Present a Real Challenge to the Faithfulness of the Church's Worship." *Reformed Worship* 15 (March 1990). https://www.reformedworship.org/article/march-1990/danger-alien-loyalties-civic-symbols-present-real-challenge-faithfulness-churchs.

———. *Political Evangelism*. Grand Rapids: Eerdmans, 1973.

———. "Richard J. Mouw: It's Time for America to Embrace a Patriotism of Compassion." *Dallas Morning News*, October 4, 2020. https://www.dallasnews.com/opinion/commentary/2020/10/04/americans-need-a-patriotism-inspired-by-compassion/.

"The Mystery of Holy Baptism." Saint Anna's Greek Orthodox Church, Roseville, CA. Used with permission.

Nicene Creed. Christian Reformed Church. https://www.crcna.org
    /welcome/beliefs/creeds/nicene-creed.

Norris, Kathleen. "Marked for a Purpose: Isaiah 42:1–9; Acts 10:34–
    43; Matthew 3:13–17." *Christian Century*, December 25, 2007.
    https://www.christiancentury.org/article/2007-12/marked
    -purpose.

Nouwen, Henri J. M. *Life of the Beloved: Spiritual Living in a Secular
    World*. New York: Crossroad, 1992.

O'Connor, Flannery. "Writing Short Stories." In *Mystery and Man-
    ners*, edited by Sally Fitzgerald and Robert Fitzgerald. New
    York: Farrar, Straus & Giroux, 1957, 1969.

———. "The River." In *A Good Man Is Hard to Find*. New York:
    Houghton Mifflin Harcourt, 1955.

Old, Hughes Oliphant. *The Shaping of the Reformed Baptismal Rite in
    the Sixteenth Century*. Grand Rapids: Eerdmans, 1992.

*Origen: Homilies on Luke, Fragments on Luke*. Fathers of the Church.
    Translated by Joseph T. Lienhard. Washington, DC: Catholic
    University of America Press, 1996.

O'Toole, G. J. A. *Spanish War: An American Epic, 1898*. New York:
    Norton, 1984.

*Our World Belongs to God*. Grand Rapids: Christian Reformed
    Church, 2008. https://www.crcna.org/welcome/beliefs/con
    temporary-testimony/our-world-belongs-god.

Parsons, Mikeal C. "All the Families of the Earth Shall Be Blessed."
    *Christian Reflection: Racism* (2010). Center for Christian Eth-
    ics at Baylor University, 4. https://www.baylor.edu/content
    /services/document.php/110994.pdf.

Price, Reynolds. *Letter to a Man in the Fire: Does God Exist and Does
    He Care?* New York: Scribner, 2000.

Quasten, Johannes, and Walter J. Burghardt, eds. *Ancient Christian
    Writers: The Works of the Fathers in Translation*. Translated by
    Paul W. Harkins. Vol. 31. New York: Newman, 1963.

Reston, James, Jr. *The Last Apocalypse: Europe at the Year 1000 A.D.*
    New York: Doubleday, 1998.

———. "Norway Part 1: 'Be Christian or Die.'" *Christian History* 63
    (1999). https://www.christianhistoryinstitute.org/magazine
    /article/norway-part-1-be-christian-or-die/.

Riley, Hugh M. *Christian Initiation: A Comparative Study of the Inter-pretation of the Baptismal Liturgy in the Mystagogical Writings of Cyril of Jerusalem, John Chrysostom, Theodore of Mopsuestia, and Ambrose of Milan.* Washington, DC: Catholic University of America Press, 1974.

Roberts, Alexander, and James Donaldson, eds. *Ante-Nicene Christian Writings: The Writings of Tertullian.* Vol. 1. Edinburgh: T&T Clark, 1872.

Roberts, Alexander, James Donaldson, and A. Cleveland Coxe, eds. *Ante-Nicene Fathers.* Vol. 2. Buffalo: Christian Literature Publishing Co., 1885.

Robinson, Marilynne. *Gilead.* New York: Farrar, Straus & Giroux, 2004.

Rushdie, Salman. Introduction to *Best American Short Stories, 2008*, edited by Heidi Pitlor and Salman Rushdie. Boston: Houghton Mifflin, 2008.

"Sailors and Marines Baptized in Jordan River during Israel Visit." *Breaking Christian News*, March 20, 2014. https://breaking christiannews.com/articles/display_art_pf.html?ID=13543.

Sanneh, Lamin. *Whose Religion Is Christianity? The Gospel beyond the West.* Grand Rapids: Eerdmans, 2003.

Schaff, Philip. "The Conversion of the Saxons. Charlemagne and Alcuin. The Heliand, and the Gospel-Harmony." In *History of the Christian Church*, vol. 4, *Mediaeval Christianity, A.D. 590–1073.* Oak Harbor, WA: Logos Research Systems, 1997. http://www .ccel.org/ccel/schaff/hcc4.i.ii.xxii.html.

Schmemann, Alexander. *For the Life of the World.* Yonkers, NY: St. Vladimir's Seminary Press, 1973/2002.

———. *Of Water and the Spirit: A Liturgical Study of Baptism.* Crestwood, NY: St. Vladimir's Seminary Press, 1974.

Scholtes, Peter. "They'll Know We Are Christians." Brentwood, TN: FEL, 1966, assigned to The Lorenz Corp., 1991.

Schweers, Gregory. "Flannery O'Connor and the Problem of Baptism: Sectarian Controversies in 'The River.'" *Way*, January 2015.

Scott, Sophfronia. "I Want to Talk to Thomas Merton about Race." *Christian Century*, March 11, 2021. https://www.christiancen

tury.org/article/first-person/i-want-talk-thomas-merton
-about-race.

Severance, Diane. "Hudson Taylor's Heart for China's Millions."
*Christianity.com*, May 3, 2010. https://www.christianity.com
/church/church-history/timeline/1801-1900/hudson-taylors
-heart-for-chinas-millions-11630493.html.

Sherry, Gerard E. "An Interview with Flannery O'Connor." In *Conversations with Flannery O'Connor*, edited by Rosemary M.
Magee. Jackson: University Press of Mississippi, 1987.

Silvieus, Leah. "Confronting Whiteness in Theological Education:
Q&A with Prof. Willie Jennings." Yale Divinity School, October 8, 2020. https://divinity.yale.edu/news/confronting-white
ness-theological-education-qa-prof-willie-jennings.

*The Simpsons.* Season 7, episode 6, "Home Sweet Homediddly-Dum-
Doodily." Directed by Susie Dietter. Written by Jon Vitti. Aired
October 1, 1995, on Fox.

Smith, James K. A. *Desiring the Kingdom: Worship, Worldview, and
Cultural Formation*. Grand Rapids: Baker, 2009.

Smith, Warren Cole. "Lonnie Frisbee: The Sad Story of a Hippie
Preacher." *BreakPoint*, March 10, 2017. https://www.break
point.org/lonnie-frisbee-sad-story-hippie-preacher/.

Specia, Megan. "'The Power of Life and Death Is in the Tongue,'
Senate Chaplain Says in a Powerful Prayer Calling for Unity."
*New York Times*, January 7, 2021. https://www.nytimes
.com/2021/01/07/us/politics/senate-chaplain-prayer-capitol
.html.

Stauffer, S. Anita. *On Baptismal Fonts: Ancient and Modern*. London:
Grove, 1994.

Stott, John R. W. *The Message of Acts: The Spirit, the Church, and the
World*. Downers Grove, IL: InterVarsity Press, 1990.

Stowe, David W. *No Sympathy for the Devil: Christian Pop Music and
the Transformation of American Evangelicalism*. Chapel Hill:
University of North Carolina Press, 2011.

Stringfellow, William. *Dissenter in a Great Society: A Christian View of
America in Crisis*. New York: Holt, Rinehart & Winston, 1967.

Swarns, Rachel L. "Nonprofits Provide Jobless Men with a Fitting for
a Second Chance." *New York Times*, August 3, 2014. https://

www.nytimes.com/2014/08/04/nyregion/a-fitting-for-a-sec
ond-chance.html.

Taylor, Barbara Brown. *Home by Another Way*. Lanham, MD: Rowman & Littlefield, 1999.

———. "Matthew 11:2–11." Sermon. Washington National Cathedral,
December 13, 1998. https://cathedral.org/sermons/sermon
-1998-12-13-000000.

———. *The Preaching Life*. Lanham, MD: Rowman & Littlefield, 1993.

ThoughtCo. "The Daily Prayer of Mother Teresa." *Learn Religions*,
updated August 28, 2018. http://catholicism.about.com/od
/dailyprayers/qt/Daily-Prayer-Of-Mother-Teresa.htm.

Timmer, John. "Owning Up to Baptism." In *A Chorus of Witnesses:
Model Sermons for Today's Preacher*, edited by Thomas G. Long
and Cornelius Plantinga Jr. Grand Rapids: Eerdmans, 1994.

Tisby, Jemar. *The Color of Compromise: The Truth about the American
Church's Complicity in Racism*. Grand Rapids: Zondervan, 2019.

Tomkins, Stephen. *A Short History of Christianity*. Oxford: Lion Hudson, 2005.

Torvend, Samuel. *Flowing Water, Uncommon Birth: Christian Baptism in a Post-Christian Culture*. Minneapolis: Augsburg Fortress, 2011.

Trueman, C. N. "Church Abuses." History Learning Site, March 16,
2015. https://www.historylearningsite.co.uk/tudor-england
/church-abuses/.

Tryphon, Abbot. "Holy Water." The Morning Offering, January 26,
2021. https://blogs.ancientfaith.com/morningoffering/2021
/01/holy-water/.

Twigg, Julia. "Clothing, Identity, and the Embodiment of Age." In
*Aging and Identity: A Dialogue with Postmodernism*, edited
by Jason Powell and Tony Gilbert. New York: Nova Science
Publishers, 2009. https://www.researchgate.net/publication
/326254641_Clothing_identity_and_the_embodiment_of_age.

Warren, Earl. *The Memoirs of Earl Warren*. Garden City, NY: Doubleday, 1977.

Wells, Samuel. "Remade: Matthew 22:1–14." *Christian Century*, October 7, 2008. https://www.christiancentury.org/article/2008
-10/remade.

Westminster Longer Catechism. http://thewestminsterstandards
.com.

Wilkins, Steve. "Baptism as Exorcism." Theopolis, March 24, 2015.
https://theopolisinstitute.com/baptism-as-exorcism/.

Williams, Rowan. *Being Christian: Baptism, Bible, Eucharist, Prayer.*
Grand Rapids: Eerdmans, 2014.

Willimon, William H. *Remember Who You Are: Baptism, a Model for
Christian Life.* Nashville: The Upper Room, 1980.

Wills, Garry. *Font of Life: Ambrose, Augustine, and the Mystery of Baptism.* New York: Oxford University Press, 2012.

Witvliet, John. *Worship Seeking Understanding: Windows into Christian Practice.* Grand Rapids: Baker Academic, 2003.

Wood, Ralph C. "Baptism in a Coffin." *Christianity Today,* January 1,
1993. https://www.christianitytoday.com/pastors/1993/winter
/93l2096.html.

Wright, N. T. "Space, Time, and Sacraments." Lecture at Calvin
College, January 6, 2007. In "N. T. Wright on Word and Sacraments: Baptism (Part 2 of 3)," *Reformed Worship* 90 (December 2008). https://www.reformedworship.org/issue/de
cember-2008.

Wright, Robert C. "Martin Luther King Jr's 90th Birthday." Sermon
at Christ Church Grosse Pointe Episcopal Church, January 20,
2019. https://www.christchurchgp.org/worship-music/ser
mons/martin-luther-king-jrs-90th-birthday.

Wymer, Andrew, and Chris Baker. "Drowning in Dirty Water:
A Baptismal Theology of Whiteness." *Worship* 90 (July 2016).
https://www.academia.edu/29630768/Drowning_in_Dirty
_Water_A_Baptismal_Theology_of_Whiteness.

# Index of Subjects

Ambrose (bishop), 40, 42–43, 111–12, 141, 177
Anabaptists, 151–52
Aphrahat, 102–3
Augustine, Saint, 40, 111, 130, 135, 141

Bailey, David, 77–78
Bañuelas, Arturo J., 75–76
baptism: as adoption, 28; as anointing, 88–95, 109, 182–83, 185, 225; annulment of, or "un-baptism," 164–65, 167–68; clothes for, 91, 100, 102–4, 109–11, 113–14, 186, 229; as declaration of faith or identity, 33–34, 45, 79, 87, 121–22, 130, 153, 167; fonts and pools for, 38–39, 40–43, 52–56, 58; identity of (baptism as alternate way of life or "counterscript"), 18, 23–25, 27–28, 35–38, 43, 45, 54–55, 87, 102–4, 108–10, 113–14, 120–21, 125, 128, 130–31, 136, 153, 176, 183, 204, 224–27; of Jesus, 82–89, 158; liturgies for (formula, rites), 16, 40, 69–71, 90–91, 109, 156–57, 159, 178–79, 202–3; as membership in a community/kingdom citizenry, 25, 59, 121, 130, 134–36, 211–14, 217–18, 220–21, 225; in the Navajo Nation, 112, 160–61; and race or racism, 172–78, 180–86; as regeneration, rebirth, or healing, 27, 33–35, 38–39, 44, 89, 120, 135, 167, 185–86, 199–206, 214, 225; as repentance and renunciation of "Satan's pomps," 22, 44, 68–80, 84, 91, 109, 178–82, 225; in Scripture, 19, 70; as suffering, dying, and rising with Christ, 25, 33, 35, 40–42, 44, 49–52, 55, 57, 59–60, 62, 127, 177, 214, 225, 228; and training and examination, 73–74, 109, 111–12, 135, 168–69; unwanted, involuntary, or empty, 141–52, 156–58, 160–66, 170, 199; as washing, 27, 35, 42–44, 54, 83–84, 86, 110, 203, 225
Barnes, Craig, 27–28

243

# Index of Biblical Texts

## Titles Published in the Series

*A Primer on Christian Worship:*
*Where We've Been, Where We Are, Where We Can Go*
    William A. Dyrness

*Christian Worship Worldwide:*
*Expanding Horizons, Deepening Practices*
    Charles E. Farhadian, editor

*Gather into One: Praying and Singing Globally*
    C. Michael Hawn

*The Touch of the Sacred:*
*The Practice, Theology, and Tradition of Christian Worship*
    F. Gerrit Immink

*The Substance of Things Seen:*
*Art, Faith, and the Christian Community*
    Robin M. Jensen

*Our Worship*
    Abraham Kuyper, edited by Harry Boonstra

*The Whole Church Sings:*
*Congregational Singing in Luther's Wittenberg*
    Robin A. Leaver

*Becoming What We Sing:*
*Formation through Contemporary Worship Music*
    David Lemley

*Missional Worship, Worshipful Mission:*
*Gathering as God's People, Going Out in God's Name*
    Ruth A. Meyers

*Wonderful Words of Life:*
*Hymns in American Protestant History and Theology*
    Richard J. Mouw and Mark A. Noll, editors

*Discerning the Spirits:*
*A Guide to Thinking about Christian Worship Today*
    Cornelius Plantinga Jr. and Sue A. Rozeboom

*Evangelical versus Liturgical? Defying a Dichotomy*
    Melanie C. Ross

*Voicing God's Psalms*
    Calvin Seerveld